WHAT PEOPLE ARE SAYING ABOUT

Why progressives need God

xtraordinarily wide-ranging study, Jonathan Clatworthy s the case that ethics, taken seriously, requires monotheism as its foundation. He surveys various kinds of theism and atheism, and shows that monotheism makes more sense of the world than any variety of secularism. A challenging and important book, accessible to anyone interested in ultimate questions.
John Barton, Oriel & Laing Professor of the Interpretation of Holy Scripture (Emeritus), University of Oxford.

At a time when economic, social and environmental crises loom large, and authoritarian Right-wing leaders appear to be in the ascendancy, the future looks particularly bleak. But Jonathan offers hope not just that a better society is possible, but that by working together progressives can achieve it.
Jonathan Bartley, Co-leader, Green Party of England and Wales

In a long and distinguished ministry, Jonathan has interpreted the Christian faith sensitively and wisely to those with liberal and progressive views. This book distils his thinking and teaching in ways that will help any sincere and open-minded seeker after truth. It is the fruit of a lifetime's discipleship, of a lifetime's rigorous honesty and of a lifetime's prayer. I commend it warmly.
Paul Bayes, Bishop of Liverpool

The 21st century is not working out so well and this provides the justification for an essay in natural theology. In this remarkable book—sharp but never polemical—Jonathan Clatworthy

addresses theism's cultured despisers and offers a defence of the public force of theism and the moral 'necessity' of God. This book will annoy some and intrigue others—but should be read by all.
Peter Scott, Samuel Ferguson Professor of Applied Theology, University of Manchester

Jonathan Clatworthy argues that belief in God can provide a better foundation for ethics than a wholly secular approach can. The argument is developed through careful historical study of how such beliefs have evolved and presupposes the importance of a liberal and non dogmatic understanding of religious beliefs.
Paul Badham, Emeritus Professor of Theology, University of Wales, Lampeter

In this thought-provoking and timely book, Jonathan Clatworthy makes the case for a reasoned and reasonable faith in a world that is both troubled and fascinated by religion.
Elaine Graham, Grosvenor Research Professor of Practical Theology, University of Chester

With characteristic scholarship, clarity and humanity, Jonathan Clatworthy holds together the rational and the religious and seeks a synthesis. A thoughtful, accessible and hopeful book for our times
Guy Elsmore, Archdeacon of Buckingham

A clear and thoughtful defence of Christianity, liberalism and progress – at a time when all are under threat.
Linda Woodhead, Professor of Politics, Philosophy and Religion, Lancaster University

Why Progressives Need God

The Ethical Defence of Monotheism

Why Progressives Need God

The Ethical Defence of Monotheism

Jonathan Clatworthy

CHRISTIAN
ALTERNATIVE

Winchester, UK
Washington, USA

First published by Christian Alternative Books, 2017
Christian Alternative Books is an imprint of John Hunt Publishing Ltd.,
Laurel House, Station Approach,
Alresford, Hants, SO24 9JH, UK
office1@jhpbooks.net
www.johnhuntpublishing.com
www.christian-alternative.com

For distributor details and how to order please visit the 'Ordering' section on our website.

ISBN: 978 1 78099 774 2
978 1 78099 780 3 (ebook)
Library of Congress Control Number: 2016959096

A CIP catalogue record for this book is available from the British Library.

Design: Stuart Davies

Printed and bound by CPI Group (UK) Ltd, Croydon, CR0 4YY, UK

CONTENTS

Preface

Home, for my childhood, was a large Victorian vicarage. Church was where most of the interesting social events took place. When Mother sent me to fetch Father for lunch, I often found him in church, praying. It was what adults did. Later, discovering people who treated God as non-existent and churches as pointless, I had to think it through.

In a sense the seeds of this book were sown then. Which pictures of reality best account for life as we experience it? Today many people are repelled both by the emptiness of atheist life and by the dogmas of traditional religions. Two opposed traditions have both worn thin. This book describes the understanding of the divine which seems to me most credible, relevant and helpful. I hope it will be to you too.

In the process I draw attention to the many weaknesses and contradictions in secular discourse about current affairs. I have drawn on a wide range of scholarly disciplines. Nobody is an expert on all of them, least of all me. I have therefore depended heavily on secondary and introductory literature. In each case I have tried to ensure that I am being fair to the current scholarly consensus, though specialists will no doubt disagree with some of my generalisations. I plead in mitigation that, while we benefit from the detailed work of a great many specialists, we also need people who will join up the dots and provide an overview of what is worth doing and why.

Many people have helped me produce this book, and although I cannot mention them all they include the following. People who have helped me think through the issues over the years include members of Modern Church at our various theological discussions; the congregation at St Brides, Liverpool; and the Philosophy in Pubs group at Lark Lane, Liverpool. Scholars who have contributed information and helpful advice on sections of the text are John Barton, Chris Allen, Paul Badham and Chris Southgate. Dave Bradley and Kieran Turner have read through the entire text making suggestions. Rosalind Lund proofread it. My ability to write it at all has depended heavily on my wife Marguerite providing for my needs. I am deeply grateful to them all.

Questions of detail relate to the divine. On the capitalisation of divine names I decided that for the sake of clarity custom should give way to consistency. I therefore submit God to the same rules as everybody else. I capitalise 'God' when using the word as a proper name like 'Peter'. Otherwise I use lower case. The same applies to Satan. Heaven and Hell, whether or not conceived of as places, are capitalised on the same basis as Manchester and Tuesday.

I use gendered pronouns when referring to a deity conceived of as male or female. This includes the Hebrew Yahweh. Otherwise I avoid attributing gender to God because in Jewish and Christian thought God is usually thought of as beyond gender. Logically I suppose I should be equally gender neutral about the devil, but nobody seems so bothered about this. Here I have used male pronouns. My excuse is that in 447 the Council of Toledo described the devil as 'A tall, black creature, horned and clawed, with asses' ears, glittering eyes and gnashing teeth, endowed with a large male member and giving off a sulphurous smell'. Definitely male then.

For dates, I use the increasingly common BCE (Before Common Era) and CE (Common Era) rather than BC and AD.

As I was finishing the writing, a Congolese relative in his early sixties, living in the south of England, was unexpectedly diagnosed with cancer and died a month later. Relatives responded in true Congolese fashion, coming to the house to sit with the dying man, expecting that the widow-to-be should not be left on her own at any time, day or night, until after the funeral. For a few weeks the house was full of families coming to take their turn at staying with the dying man, and then with the body. British friends and neighbours found it harder. They would have to go to work the following morning. They could not drop everything in the same way. The British are too busy. Yet—what is our busyness achieving, if we cannot spare the time to be with someone at the end of his life? What kind of lifestyle do we believe in? Where do we get our priorities from? I hope this book will help explore these questions.

If you would like to explore them with me you can follow me on www.clatworthy.org or email me on jonathan@clatworthy.org.

Chapter 1. Introduction

Climate change, poverty, war. The biggest problems facing the modern secular world are getting bigger all the time. Mountains of literature detail what needs to be done but it remains undone. The governments of our modern democracies fail to achieve it, and perhaps do not intend to.

This book breaks the most sacred taboo of secular society by arguing that the problem lies with secularism itself. This is the principle that religious belief can be permitted in private but must be excluded from public debate about what society should be like and how governments should govern. There were good reasons why it came about, but the long-term effect is disastrous. By denying any moral authority higher than humanity, at least on public matters, it leaves the ruling classes as the decision-makers not only on what we do but on what we ought to do. What they want becomes right by definition. Being humans, just as flawed and selfish as the rest of us, they view the world's problems through the lenses of their own vested interests. Until we admit—publicly, not just behind church doors—that there are better ways of doing things, we shall continue to destroy ourselves and our children's future.

Being different from each other, we want different things. If a society believes there are no answers except the ones we think up for ourselves, there is no reason for supposing we shall ever agree on what should be done. We are trapped in endless conflict. If, on the other hand, a society believes there are right answers that transcend the desires of any one group of people, it has reason to believe that consensus on the right answers is worth looking for. In the process a consensus may develop about some of the wrong answers: torture, or slavery, or genocide. Progress becomes possible.

The biggest problems we face are well known. The most

urgent is environmental destruction. Scientists have been drawing attention to the damage done by human activities since the nineteenth century, and their concerns reached popular awareness in the 1960s. Species are now being driven to extinction at the fastest rate for 65 million years. Soil is being lost as deforestation and over-farming turns topsoil into dust that gets blown away by the wind. Non-renewable energy resources like oil are being used up at an increasing rate. The widespread use of pesticides in agriculture poisons the soil. Industrial processes pump poisons into air and water. All these are major threats to human well-being and our future. Yet scientific observers of environmental change have been telling us that they are overshadowed by the greatest threat of all, climate change, as greenhouse gases are released into the atmosphere in ever-greater quantities.[1]

Vested interests in the old ways work hard to prevent change. Transnational corporations award lavish grants to scientists willing to deny that climate change is caused by human activities. The continuing focus on economic growth leads to the impression that the main environmental problem is access to energy supplies.[2] What governments tell us is possible is nowhere near what environmental scientists tell us is necessary.

Much the same can be said of poverty. At the end of the Second World War many governments set out to ensure basic provision for their populations. The British Welfare State was designed to provide everyone with good housing, food, health care and a guaranteed minimum income. To achieve it high taxes were imposed on the rich. In response to opposition, however, high taxation was gradually supplemented, and then replaced, by economic growth. Governments came to see it as their task not to create jobs and provide incomes, but to manage the economy so as to achieve these aims indirectly. Economic growth has become the dominant aim of governments. Because governments focus on the size of the economy, not its distribution, even the most extreme destitution is consistent with growth.[3] There is much evidence that the quality of life is best in more equal societies, not in the richest ones,[4] but it is the economy that governments measure, not the quality of life.

Militarisation continues apace, despite all attempts to restrain it. After 'the war to end all wars'[5] Europeans, horrified at the destruction of the First World War, produced a generation of pacifists determined to turn their backs on military conflict. It was not to last. The League of Nations proved a failure as governments jockeyed to secure advantages against each other, with blatantly unfair results. After the Second World War a successor organisation was established, the United Nations. Again the populations on both sides longed for peace, but again governments jockeyed for advantages against each other. The Cold War began. Both sides piled up so many nuclear weapons that the entire population of the world could have been obliterated many times over. Some couples felt it would be irresponsible to bring children into the world since an early death by radiation sickness would be their inevitable fate. When the Cold War ended, around 1991 when the USSR was disbanded, there were over 65,000 nuclear warheads in the world. Since then the stockpile has decreased but still stands at 17,000.[6] An alien from outer space might have asked whether it would have been better to learn how to live together in peace before we learned how to split the atom.

It seemed that the West had won and the USA was the only remaining superpower. However this did not bring in an era of peace. The flight of refugees is now greater than ever since the Second World War. With a few honourable exceptions most governments are determined to keep them out, even if it means sending them back to a certain death. It is one thing to believe, like John Pilger in his speech of March 2016, that 'a world war has begun',[7] another to recognise that despite all the self-congratulation about modern progress with its science and technology, we have not learned to live in peace. Losers often learn lessons:

winners rarely do. Steven Pinker has argued[8] that over the millennia violence is gradually decreasing. The last few decades have not provided evidence for his thesis.

So we live at a time of competing crises. Countless publications tell us the things we need to do, but we do not do them. The most determined attempts to solve one only make another worse. Naomi Klein describes our present situation:

> Our economic system and our planetary system are now at war. Or, more accurately, our economy is at war with many forms of life on earth, including human life. What the climate needs to avoid collapse is a contraction in humanity's use of resources; what our economic model demands to avoid collapse is unfettered expansion.[9]

There must be something underlying them all that stops us, some reason why we studiously fail to make improvements. The reason, I believe, is secularism itself. By abolishing all moral standards higher than humanity, it exalts society's leading spokespeople to the rank of supreme judge of everything. As G K Chesterton said, 'Once abolish the God, and government becomes the God'.[10]

To do better we need to believe that there are right answers that transcend every government. There must be moral truths competent to pass judgement on the ruling classes, higher standards to which others can appeal *against* governments.

People often do. We often claim that an action by a powerful person is unjust, or contravenes human rights. Usually, though, we stop there. We do not ask ourselves what this authority we are appealing to really is. It is part of our secular inheritance that we stop thinking at this point. This leaves us unable to explain our values. Moral truths are pretty meaningless if they just happen to exist, like invisible rule books floating around the sky. They only become something to appeal to when we have good reason to obey them, reason to treat them as a source of higher wisdom. It is difficult to imagine how this might be the case unless these moral authorities *know* more than we do. They must know how we can live well, and know it better than we know it. So most societies have thought of their moral authorities as personalities with minds and intentions. Gods.

Secularism applies its own moral systems to public debate, but separates them from all references to the divine. As long as we keep them separate we are unable to engage well enough with the questions that underlie our problems. What does human well-being consist of? Is there a healthy and constructive way of life we should aspire to, or is it up to each of us to decide how to live? Do societies depend on shared moral norms, or is it up to each individual to decide their own morality? What makes us think we can, or cannot, make the world a better place? How do we decide what counts as progress?

Secularism cannot answer these questions on its own. It has inherited Christian concepts. Among them are the unity of humanity, the harmony of human well-being with the natural environment, the possibility of progress, moral truths and moral responsibility. All these concepts were developed within a commitment to a particular kind of god. When this god is removed from the picture, over time people notice that they can no longer be justified. They cease to convince.

Before the seventeenth century, all over the world as far as we know, there was no separation between beliefs about gods and explanations of the physical world. Societies had a more unified understanding of reality, relating the physical questions to the ethical ones. What are the forces that created the world and us? What, if anything, do they intend? In the light of their intentions, how can we make the most of life? From the nature of the world they speculated about the purposes behind it, and vice versa. They were right to do so. We need to reconnect our sense of spirituality with our understanding of the physical universe.

We need, therefore, to recognise a moral authority higher than any human. I shall refer to it as God. The word has disadvantages, as images of God vary widely, but it would be too artificial to invent some other word. As the book proceeds I shall describe the kind of god we need to believe in. My intention is to mean no more than my descriptions state, not to smuggle in additional features. I shall not argue for God's existence; I have done this elsewhere[11] and many others have done it too. Suffice it to say that there are other reasons for believing in God apart from the pragmatic claim, offered here, that belief in this higher moral authority is essential for public ethics.

It matters what kind of god this is. Secularism arose for good reason. In seventeenth century Europe it was the best available alternative to a Christianity so pessimistic and oppressive that an alternative was desperately needed. As far as historians know this is the only time any society has decided to exclude all transcendent authorities from its public decision-making. With western dominance it has spread all over the world, and for many today it seems normal and obvious; but its origins are unusual. It comes from that distinctive reaction against pessimistic Christianity and its wars.

The kind of transcendent authority which is adequate to the task is the god of monotheism. Theological discourse has usually associated monotheism with Judaism, Christianity and Islam, and described its god as all-powerful, all-knowing and completely good. What enables this god to offer a convincing vision of how we can solve our problems is that it knows how we can solve them—it wants the best for us and has designed the universe accordingly.

This is the account of God I shall affirm. These days it is often attacked. As Gore Vidal put it,

> The great unmentionable evil at the center of our culture is monotheism. From a barbaric Bronze Age text known as the

> Old Testament, three antihuman religions have evolved—Judaism, Christianity, and Islam. These are sky-god religions. They are, literally, patriarchal—God is the omnipotent father—hence the loathing of women for 2,000 years in those countries afflicted by the sky-god and his earthly male delegates. The sky-god is a jealous god, of course. He requires total obedience from everyone on earth, as he is in place not just for one tribe but for all creation. Those who would reject him must be converted or killed for their own good. Ultimately, totalitarianism is the only sort of politics that can truly serve the sky-god's purpose. Any movement of a liberal nature endangers his authority and that of his delegates on earth. One God, one King, one Pope, one master in the factory, one father-leader in the family at home.[12]

Vidal's critique summarised a generation of campaigners against the Cold War, especially Americans. Many commentators, including theologians from Christian and Jewish backgrounds, reacted strongly against their own government's threat of nuclear annihilation in the name of defending western values against Communism. To the feminist Carter Heyward,

> This cold deity is the legitimating construct of the patriarchal desire to dominate and control the world. He is the eternal King, the Chairman of the board, the President of the institution, the Guru of the youth, the Husband of the wife, the General of the army, the Judge of the court, the Master of the universe, the Father of the church. He resides above us all. He is our superior, never our friend. He is a rapist, never a lover, of women and of anyone else beneath Him. He is the first and final *icon of evil* in history.[13]

To Sharon Welch a god like this encourages governments to seek absolute power, by enabling the powerful to 'regard themselves as merely the agents of a higher power'.[14]

In the USA those values were so tightly wrapped up in the rhetoric of Christianity that it was easy to connect the bullying attitudes of trigger-happy governments with belief in a supreme god who tolerates no opposition. This was an exceptionally strong instance of a pattern that has been observed all through history. Emperors have often claimed that there is one supreme god ruling the whole world, so there should be one supreme king. The idea is then used to justify imperial conquests and intolerance of dissent. Genghis Khan is reputed to have said: 'In heaven there is no-one but the one God alone; on earth no-one but the one ruler Genghis Khan'.[15]

The idea of a single god of the world suited emperors for two reasons. One was that the god would bless the empire with prosperity in return for due obedience—to the god and therefore to the emperor. Otherwise offence might be taken and the nation might face divine punishment. The other was that a large empire was easier to manage if the population had a sense of loyalty to it. This became easier with an empire-wide cult.[16]

Critics of monotheism argue that it justifies imperialism and is intolerant of other beliefs. I shall argue, to the contrary, that imperialist religions like this, while claiming to be monotheistic, are not and cannot be. When emperors and governments justify their rule by appealing to a single, all-controlling god of the whole world, they do so not because they have complete control but because they *lack* it and want it. This is what makes them intolerant. It would be foolish to take imperialist and wartime propaganda at face value as truth claims about the nature of God, for all that opponents of monotheism have often done just that. The monotheism I shall be defending is very different.

Roughly speaking the book is in three parts. The first summarises the historical development of polytheism and monotheism. One reason for beginning here is that we usually find it easier to describe foreign cultures than our own. We think of our own as normal, obvious. We notice the characteristics of others. Familiarising ourselves with very different cultures should help us perceive the distinctive features of our own.

Chapter 2 describes how nearly all societies have in the past believed in some transcendent beings. Believing in them enables people to reflect on how the universe works, why it was made, why humanity was made and how to go about making the most of life. Chapter 3 describes the distinctive story of the development of monotheism in the Hebrew scriptures. I define it as *divine harmony*, not divine singleness, because what makes monotheism ethically distinctive is unity of will, not unity of personality. Christians often debate monotheism within the context of the Trinity or the divinity of Jesus, but this book will leave these aside. Instead I shall contrast the monotheism of divine harmony with the divine conflict of many polytheistic traditions. Chapter 4 then analyses the distinctive ethical implications of monotheism when compared with polytheism.

The next two chapters provide background material in preparation for the second, and largest, part of the book. Chapter 5 describes the polytheistic features which undermined Christianity's monotheism and eventually made it so pessimistic that it provoked the secular and atheist reactions against it. These reactions are described in Chapter 6. My hope is that describing how secularism and atheism arose will make it easier to see why, and how, they still bear the scars of their origin.

Chapters 7, 8 and 9 describe different ways secular thinkers have responded to the absence of divine authority by proposing alternative imperatives for society: control of the physical environment, social engineering and liberal individualism. Each began within some kind of Christian agenda. As it lost its Christian roots it replaced them with other justifications, generally weaker ones. Over time it became clear that if there is no transcendent moral authority to tell us what to do, we do not have to do anything. The collapse of moral authority is described in Chapter 10 and the implications for our values in Chapter 11. Concluding this middle section, Chapter 12 offers a parallel to Chapter 4, comparing the ethical implications of secularism with monotheism.

There remains the challenge of defending monotheism against the most common criticism: that it cannot account for the world's suffering and evil. No defence of monotheism would be adequate without addressing this question. Chapter 13 argues that, contrary to popular belief and much of the literature, the problem of evil is no harder in the case of monotheism than in the cases of polytheism and atheism. Chapter 14 describes my own defence of monotheism in the light of evil. Chapter 15 then builds on it to develop my positive account of what God is doing with us.

I write as a liberal Christian. My theological liberalism has only a little in common with liberal politics and nothing in common with liberal economics. One way to summarise liberal theology is to say that it is non-dogmatic. Since the nineteenth century many church leaders have accepted a restricted role for rational analysis on religious matters, instead giving priority to dogmas deemed to have been 'revealed' in a manner that by-passes human reason. This notion of non-rational divine revelation has a long tradition but hinders open, honest enquiry about the nature of reality.

As this book searches for an ethic coherent enough to help us solve our problems it will be critical of many religious claims, characteristically those that have developed a protective dogmatic shell defending them from critical scrutiny. The theological liberalism I am appealing to expects to co-operate with unbelievers in seeking solutions to the issues of our day, while adding that our moral claims are better justified when we believe in a particular kind of transcendent moral authority.

All human societies reflect on the meaning and purpose of life. Why are we here? What is the point of life? Who made us, and why? In the light of these, how should we live? Monotheism answers these questions in characteristic ways. It accepts the dominant scientific accounts of how the universe works and enables human life to flourish, but it adds that these forces have agency and purpose. To this extent we can think of them as personal and reflect on how we can relate to them. Since we are so dependent on them there is an obvious implication that the best way to live is in keeping with these divine purposes. The advice to 'follow the maker's instructions' seems inevitable. Compared with making them up as we go along, or leaving it to the ruling classes to make them up, we have better reason to trust them.

Chapter 2. Who invented gods?

You are stranded alone on a small desert island, just like in the cartoons. Sand, a few rocks, palm tree in the middle. No sign of other humans. Nothing to eat or drink, no way of escape. Night comes and you go to sleep. In the morning you wake up hungry. On a rock nearby you are surprised to see a plate with a fried egg, bacon, sausage and baked beans, and next to it a glass of fruit juice and a mug of coffee. There is absolutely no sign of how your breakfast got there: no footprints, no sound of a helicopter, no ships on the horizon. You scoff the lot. The next morning exactly the same thing happens. And the morning after. Day after day this food keeps appearing and there is no sign of how it gets there.

After a few weeks you will probably start taking this food for granted. You will assume that tomorrow's food will arrive in the normal manner. The fact that you take it for granted does not, of course, mean you understand how it gets there. You would not be so silly as to mistake the *regularity* of the food's appearance for the *cause* of its appearance.

It is this mistake that modern secular culture makes. Scientists and non-scientists alike are used to thinking of the regularities of nature as though they were causes. The regularities are described as laws of nature and each law is defined, usually as an equation. Equations do not make anything happen. They only describe. What makes them happen is another question altogether, but anti-religious rhetoric has persuaded many of us that the laws of nature are what makes things happen.

Our distant ancestors were wiser. However regular the appearances of the sun and stars were, however reliable the annual cycle of growth, harvest and decay, the regularities did not explain why these things happened. As far back in time as we can discover every society seems to have believed in some kinds of intentional divine forces to account for the ways of nature. There is evidence of a few ancient individuals who may not have believed in any, but even that is uncertain.

In this chapter I offer an overview of how different ideas of gods developed. Many of the details are still debated but for present purposes the general picture should suffice. This will set the context for the next chapter which concentrates on monotheism.

The beliefs of our distant ancestors were first studied systematically by nineteenth century anthropologists and sociologists. Most of them were atheists. They were puzzled: hunter-gatherers had never seen any gods and had no evidence that there were any, but all over the world they believed in them. Why, they asked, did so many independent communities make the same mistake?

Later the reason became clear. People believe in things they have not seen when it helps them explain the things they have seen. Scientists do this all the time. They gather information and develop theories to explain it. When the best theory posits the existence of something unknown, perhaps they have discovered something new. Gods, rejected by nineteenth century atheists because they could not be perceived with the senses, have now been joined by countless other unobservables. Terms like 'black holes' and 'dark matter' are just memorable terms for unobservables which scientists propose to make sense of what they have discovered so far. It is not so surprising that our ancestors did the same. The difference is not whether to believe in unobservables—we all do that—but whether some of them are agents with minds and intentions.

To study the beliefs of societies which did not write things down anthropologists depend on archaeological findings like funeral remains. They also study societies that still have traditional, archaic lifestyles comparatively unaffected by modern society, and this can often help them understand the lifestyles and beliefs of our distant ancestors. With the immense amount of data now available it is possible to recognise that some features of human living and believing are universal. One is that before modern times all societies believed in divine agents.

The gods of hunter-gatherers

For most of our history humans have been hunter-gatherers living in small communities. They interacted closely with the forces of nature surrounding them—sun and rain, heat and cold, health and illness, the need to eat and the danger of being eaten. We too are surrounded by natural forces and depend on them, but we think of them differently.

They experienced the forces of nature as imbued with *value*. These forces made life possible, but sometimes took it away. They gave good health, but sometimes gave illness. They provided sunshine and rain, but sometimes too much or not enough. They gave babies, but sometimes dead ones. In other words the forces of nature were mainly good but sometimes hostile.

Thus value was built into the way things were. We do not know, for example, of any society where mothers do not long for their children to flourish. They understood their senses of value, purpose and meaning not as their own inventions but as part of the value, purpose and meaning of their community, their environment and reality as a whole.

They interpreted natural resources as *gifts*. Rather than taking them for granted they had reason to respond with gratitude. This meant developing *relationships* with the providers.

They could not forget their *dependence* on these forces. We today, especially city-dwellers, are more aware of how we depend on the work of other people. Many of us live in places which are too hot or cold, too wet or dry, or too high up, to be habitable without constant human intervention. For our ancestors the human community was an integral part of the natural environmental community with its diverse range of rocks, plants, animals, fishes and birds each behaving in their own distinctive ways to produce the richness of life. Human life was, to them, quite obviously dependent on this order.

They had to accept their *lack of control*. Modern western society has inherited the idea that a combination of science and technology should enable us to control nature. Our ancestors knew they could not. They had to live within whatever nature provided. The environment had to be accepted as it was.

From the perspective of modern control we prefer it if nature has absolutely no agenda of its own, so that we can establish our own agenda. We relate to nature as children relate to the toys scattered around their playpen, assuming that it is up to us to do what we like with it. From the perspective of our ancestors, for nature to have no agenda would be the worst possible prospect; it would have left them with no hope of relating to the forces they depended on.

The difference between the two is a bit like the two agendas in a military invasion. When invaders occupy a new country they face the task of finding out how things work there in order to control it. They seek knowledge for the purpose of control. Those occupied on the other hand face a different task: as they lose their freedom they need to work out how to cope. Learning to cope with powerlessness is more a matter of how to evaluate the situation, how to make sense of life in view of their new circumstances, how to maintain hope. At its most practical the agenda will be to explore what kinds of relationships to establish with the invaders: how to plead with them, how to spot their weaknesses, how to make them feel generous.

These characteristics gave our ancestors a worldview very different from ours. As long as they understood their sense of value as part of the value of reality as a whole, it was a natural next step to think that reality as a whole valued them. As long as they interpreted life as a gift it was natural to seek a relationship with the giver. As long as they understood that they were dependent on their natural environment they would have sought to protect it and acknowledge the deeper value within it. As long as they knew they lacked control they would have aimed to live within its limitations and make the most of the opportunities it offered them.

Mircea Eliade[1] has described some characteristic features of hunter-gatherer spirituality. The sun, rising and setting in the same way each day, represents order. The moon, with its regular pattern of dying and rising, represents measurement, death and new life. Water represents fertility. Often a society would focus on whichever natural force was at issue at the time; in times of drought they would long for rain, in times of epidemic for healing. They could therefore think of each natural force having a personality of its own, in a good mood one day and a bad mood the next. The different personalities seemed sometimes to work together but sometimes to conflict with each other or destroy life. As Robert Gnuse puts it,

> Polytheism is natural. People who live surrounded by the diverse forces of nature could be expected to affirm polytheism. It expresses the natural diversity of reality quite well, and enables people to cope with the individual numinous expressions of nature by making each one a god.[2]

They related to their gods with different activities. Early anthropologists classified them as rituals and often dismissed them as pointless, but their successors today describe their functions more sympathetically. One is celebration. Another is the preservation of cultural information. We remember things better if, in addition to hearing and seeing them, we perform a related action. For societies which did not read and write, the way to retain the memories of their past and affirm their shared values was by repeated actions.

One type of ritual which seems strange to us is sacrifices. They are found all over the world. A practical reason was that, before the days of refrigeration, if a large animal was to be killed and eaten it made sense for the whole community to gather and eat it together. Such occasions would naturally constitute celebrations. We today tend to separate out our social activities, so that birthday parties do not mention God and events which do mention God are classified as religious. The ancients did not divide up their actions like this. When they celebrated or cooked meat they would do so with reference to the relevant god. The celebrations were not *just* about the gods, but were performed in their company.

There is evidence that animal sacrifices characteristically began as expressions of regret for taking an animal's life, though anthropologists have not found societies where that was their only meaning.[3] By the time writing developed, they had become offerings to the gods. Societies which did not have money had systems of gift exchange. One person would give something to another and the community would expect the recipient to give something in return. Sacrifices to the gods will have been offered on this basis, either as thanksgiving or in the hope of reciprocation.[4] A common practice, in many parts of the world, was to cut off a finger as an offering to a god, to plead for something one wanted.[5]

Many people have puzzled over the fact that ancient societies offered regular food to their statue-gods despite the fact that the statues cannot possibly have eaten any. Sometimes they thought the gods consumed the smoke and perhaps also the bones.[6] In some cases the gods ate in solitude, in their own room in a temple. One priest presented the food and another cleared away the 'leftovers'.[7] The desire to give to one's god is characteristically independent of what ultimately happens to the gift. People who give money to a church today do not usually enquire about the end use of it: from their perspective the gift expresses a relationship. Similarly, in Christian Communion services the priest may say over bread, wine and money, 'All things come from you and of your own do we give you'. Nobody thinks God literally uses them. The action expresses a relationship in which God gives to us generously and we come as close as we can to giving something in return.

Activities like these often survive long after their original purposes have been forgotten. When people have been brought up to perform particular holy actions and treat them as meaningful, they often continue to find them meaningful quite independently of the original purpose behind them. The same must have been true of our ancestors. Sacrifices to gods continued for thousands of years, relatively unchanged, but many of the people taking part in them would not have been good at explaining the point of them.

There were many forces of nature so there were many gods. There was also scope for conceiving of an underlying harmony, often associated with sky gods. Looking up at the sky on a clear day can easily provoke a sense of wonder. We today have been taught to distinguish this sense of wonder as completely different from any religious beliefs we may have. They did not. According to Eliade,

> There is no need to look into the teachings of myth to see that the sky itself directly reveals a transcendence, a power and a holiness. Merely contemplating the vault of heaven produces a religious experience in the primitive mind... The phrase "contemplating the vault of heaven" really means something when it is applied to primitive man, receptive to the miracles of every day to an extent we find it hard to imagine.[8]

We may interpret this as a religious experience, God being revealed through contemplation of the sky. However this is a modern interpretation as it separates the divine revelation from the sense of wonder at the sky itself. To the archaic mind, Eliade tells us that the contemplation 'is the same as a revelation. The sky shows itself as it really is: infinite, transcendent.' So

> The vault of heaven is, more than anything else, "something quite apart" from the tiny thing that is man and his span of life. The symbolism of its transcendence derives from the simple realization of its infinite height. "Most High" becomes quite naturally an attribute of the divinity.[9]

The sky stays put, just there. Sky gods tend to be supreme gods, but without playing a leading role. They tend to have neither a cult nor a place in the calendar of seasonal rites. It seems that, being supreme and passive, the sky does not require a cult in the way that, say, fertility and health do.[10]

Most of the time, then, the focus of attention for hunter-gatherers would have been their immediate needs. This meant engaging with the various gods who provided each one—pleading with them, offering them sacrifices. In addition they often conceived of an underlying unity of the created order, symbolised by the sky. The sky did not need to be offered any sacrifices and therefore could easily get forgotten.

The gods of ancient literature

With the development of agriculture societies changed. Populations increased. With them came cities, empires, professional armies, hierarchies, social classes, trade, taxes and writing.

Writing developed first in Mesopotamia around 3,000 BCE. Over the last two centuries many ancient Mesopotamian and Egyptian texts have been discovered which help build up a picture of what the people who wrote them believed. This enables us to compare the Bible with nearby texts from the same era. With Greek literature we have much more information, both because more has survived and because the Greeks had a wider vocabulary. This helps us to better understand the changes in the way people understood the gods.

In ancient city life it became less important to know about the physical environment, more important to know how one fitted into the social structure and related to other people. Over the centuries the gods changed accordingly. While retaining their connection to natural phenomena they came to be known for their personality types and their relationships to each other. Pantheons developed, like the Greek gods of Mount Olympus. 'For the high civilizations of the ancient world', Walter Burkert writes, there was

> ...a plurality of personal beings who are understood by analogy with man and imagined in human form; the notion of the 'gods', anthropomorphism and polytheism are found everywhere as a matter of course.[11]

Gods continued to live, invisibly, in the physical universe. Some lived in temples, some in the sky and some below the earth. Humans, gods and nature were formed from the same substance. Myths described how some degraded gods became mortal while some outstanding humans became immortal. Gods and goddesses could have sexual intercourse with humans and produce demigods.[12]

Over time it became possible to think of the personality independently of the natural phenomena. As long as the same word was used for both it could be used with either meaning or both together. People might have used them without making the distinction in their own minds, a bit like Christians today who speak of consecrated bread being the body of Christ, or the Bible being the word of God, while leaving unclear the relationship between the two. Often enough believers today are unclear, and happy to remain so, even when their religious authorities declare exactly what they ought to believe. No doubt many of our distant ancestors lived with the same uncertainties.

In addition to chief gods and ruling pantheons the ancients believed they were also surrounded by many lesser deities, or demons. Demons were usually held responsible for illness. Typically, healing would consist of driving it out. The usual components of exorcisms were ritual actions, eating foods and herbs, and words spoken to the demon. Some of the foods and herbs would indeed have been beneficial. As for the speaking, some demons needed to be cajoled, others threatened. A threat to appeal to a superior god was often considered effective since demons had limited knowledge and could often be tricked. Some people gained reputations for being good exorcists with a personal charismatic power to confront demons. Another view was that success depended on knowing exactly which words to say and which actions to perform. Many records from ancient Mesopotamia have survived, listing illnesses, which demon caused each and how to exorcise it, though physical causes are mentioned as well. The information will have been produced by trial and error, observing which exorcisms 'worked' and which did not.[13]

The Axial changes

Modern scholars have given the term 'the Axial Age' to an important development that took place between around 800 and 300 BCE, seemingly independently, in China, India, Judea and Greece. This was the age of Confucius, Taoism, the Buddha, Jainism, the Upanishads, the Bhagavad Gita, the prophets of Israel, Pythagoras, Socrates, Plato, Aristotle and probably Zoroaster.

Pre-Axial theology was conservative. The focus of concern was on preserving the community as it was. Varro, a Roman writing in the first century BCE, offered an account of the gods in his time which modern scholars still consider a fair account of pre-Axial theology. It had three aspects. The first was 'natural theology', corresponding to the cosmic dimension. The gods co-operated in creating and maintaining the world, and were revealed in nature—sun and moon, life and death, war and peace, and so on. To this extent he thought it was impossible to deny their existence. The second was cult and political organisation. The important gods were gods of towns, located in their temples. People related to them through public cults in much the same way as ordinary citizens in Roman society would pay their respects to lords and ladies. The third was myth. The main concern of the gods was with their relations with each other. Generally, within pre-Axial culture the emphasis was on preserving society. Change meant danger. There was an emphasis on the unity of the community, so the task of the individual was to be loyal.

In hierarchical city life, however, what oppressed most people was their powerful rulers. Group loyalty declined. In time enough of the scribal classes were dissatisfied to leave us records of changing attitudes. One change was *individualism*. It became possible for individuals to reject the values of their own society, offer an alternative and gain a following. A second was *universalism*. Their messages often referred to humanity as a whole rather than to life in a particular society. A third was *redemption*. They considered human life unsatisfactory and sought something better. Some taught inner peace and reconciliation, others a better afterlife or divine rewards and punishments in the next life. Others again put their hopes in history as a means of progress towards a better future.[14] These ideas were new to the Axial Age and developed only gradually. They characterise all the major world faiths today, though pre-Axial beliefs and practices still have some influence.

We can see some of the tensions producing it in the literature of classical Athens. Once the gods had come to be seen as personalities, primarily engaged in their own interrelationships, stories about them could develop—a bit like our soap operas. This was very much the case in Homer's *Iliad* and *Odyssey*. This literature, especially the *Iliad,* described a heroic age full of battles and quarrels where gods fought each other just as humans did. If natural disasters were caused by gods who were either angry or uncaring, knowing what each god was like provided detail. However, the more we think we know what a god is like, the more puzzled we get when our expectations are not fulfilled. The overall conditions of life were still controlled by divine forces, but this role was often allocated to the Fates, more shadowy characters.

The Athens of the fifth century BCE was a much more sophisticated and educated society. However it had inherited Homer's epic poems as the most highly venerated scriptures of Greek culture, their nearest equivalent to our Bible. Their tragedies explored the nature of human life in the context of Homer's gods. In Aeschylus' *Agamemnon,* for example, Zeus sanctions the expedition against Troy but Artemis insists that first Agamemnon must sacrifice his own daughter Iphigenia—thus setting the scene for him to be murdered by Iphigenia's mother on his return home. Apollo both inspires and destroys Cassandra. Meanwhile the Furies make sure that every murder is avenged by another murder.[15] It is characteristic of these tragedies that one disaster leads to the next, either because the Fates predestine it or because of divine action.

In these tragedies the overall picture of human life is utterly pessimistic. At the same time as they were written and first performed, pre-Socratic philosophers were speculating about the nature of the world and sophists were developing ethical and social theories. Hardly surprisingly, they had little time for the Homeric gods. Some seem to have gone further. As the gods were known primarily for their personality and their role as natural forces had faded into the background, it became possible to doubt whether they existed at all. Scholars continue to debate how much we can deduce from the texts questioning the existence of these gods, but a need had clearly arisen to provide a better account of how to relate to the forces governing the world. Soon afterwards Plato would produce one.

With developments of this kind the Axial Age changes—with their affirmation of the individual, their universalism, and some kind of hope for a better future—established new theologies and laid the foundations for most of the faith traditions that flourish today.

Unifying gods

The literature witnesses to a long-term trend to unifying the gods. The number of gods seems to have been huge at first; one second millennium BCE Babylonian text listed nearly two thousand. At this stage people would have been thinking in terms of one god per natural process. Over time the number declined and attempts were made to systematise them.[16]

As we have seen from the earliest times there is evidence of belief in an ultimate god underlying all the other gods. The idea that the gods were all part of a unified divine system took different forms. Akhenaten, Pharaoh of Egypt in the fourteenth century BCE, seems to have been exceptional in that he worshipped only a single god, the sun. After his death the cult was suppressed. Scholars debate whether it produced a long-term trend towards monotheism.[17] More common seems to have been the idea of unity in multiplicity. The Leiden hymn comes from a little after Akhenaten:

> All gods are three:
> Amun, Re, Ptah, they have no equal.
> His name is hidden as Amun;
> he is Re in the face,
> his body is Ptah.

Here three gods are named, and then referred to with a singular pronoun. Scholars think this is designed to indicate that deity was both multiple and singular.[18] We might compare it with Catholics today who can address Our Lady as one person while still distinguishing between Our Lady of Lourdes and Our Lady of Medjugorje. One way to explain it would be to say that the same divinity is revealed in different ways.

Gods were often combined. Amun-Re is common in Egyptian texts: just as gods can inhabit temples or animals, one god can inhabit another.[19] Mesopotamian texts make similar connections. The Babylonian and Assyrian word *ilu* usually referred to divine persons who could eat, marry and travel, but because they were associated with forces of nature and human powers, the name of a god could also refer to that power. One inscription describes the god Enlil as '*ilu* Enlil, supremely great lord' but then five lines later describes another god, Marduk, as 'principal heir, *ilu* Enlil of the gods' and two lines later again describes Nergal as a god 'who overwhelms enemies, *ilu* Enlil of the wide underworld'. Here Enlil was the supreme ruler, so other gods who were supreme rulers in their sphere could be described as Enlil to that extent.[20]

There was a similar trend in Greek literature. The presocratic philosopher Xenophanes made a word play similar to the Leiden Hymn:

> One god among gods and men, the greatest.
> Neither in form nor in thought resembling mortal beings.[21]

Scholars debate the extent to which ancient Greeks would have thought of their gods as a unity. Some think they were conceived as an ordered hierarchy, others that the relationships were more chaotic.[22] There were different kinds of gods. For example, Versnel cites the practice of treating Hellenistic kings and Roman emperors as gods:

> As long as he was god—for instance during restricted periods in which his divinity was ritually staged or politically deployed—the display of human frailties was frowned upon: no sneezing for the deified emperor during his *adventus*. However... he was *not* a god like the other 'real' gods. The few megalomaniacs who did fail to observe the boundaries were considered insane.[23]

Anyway there was much inconsistency. Herodotus, the Greek historian of the fifth century BCE, is a good example. He refers to the gods and god, or the divine, in contrasting ways. The oracles usually turn out to have been right. Events may be predestined, or the work of the Fates or chance or universal laws or 'the will of the gods' or one particular god. Herodotus juxtaposes these explanations without any suggestion that they are alternatives, let alone that there is any contradiction between them.[24]

From the fourth century BCE onwards texts increasingly referred to a particular god as 'the one god' or 'the only god' while not denying the existence of others. Scholars usually refer to it as 'henotheism', and distinguish it from 'monolatry' which refers to a long-term commitment to worshipping only one god while accepting the existence of others—a bit like the way some people today believe they relate to their own guardian angel. There was a practical reason for these developments. The more gods there were, the harder it was to work out which one to appeal to at any one time.[25]

A rather different process of unifying gods was imperial theology. We saw in the Introduction that one of the most common criticisms of monotheism is that it is imperialistic. Imperial theology is often presented as monotheistic for reasons of propaganda. In ancient Egypt and Mesopotamia kings would claim to have been appointed by the supreme god to maintain order. Other gods were subordinated to this supreme god. This subordination provided a model for kingly rule: just as they believed their supreme god had defeated divine enemies to establish order and peace, the king's role was to establish order and peace by defeating human enemies. They thus interpreted their rule as a divinely established natural order; if the political order collapsed the order of nature would collapse too.[26] This is especially emphasised in Assyrian texts. Sargon II described how he united different nations in his empire 'to teach them how to fear God and the king'. In Babylon and Assyria the main word to characterise gods was *puluhtu*, fear.[27]

> The king, as representative of the god Assur, represented order. Wherever he was in control, there was peace, tranquility, and justice, and where he did not rule there was chaos. The king's duty to bring order to the entire world was the justification for military expansion. This idea pervaded royal rhetoric. All that was foreign was hostile, and all foreigners were like non-human creatures. Images of swamp-rats or bats, lonely, confused, and cowardly, were commonly applied to those outside the king's control.[28]

Some scholars have argued that this indicates the beginning of monotheism. As with military dictatorships today, when ancient Mesopotamians were given a command by a person in authority the identity of the person giving it was unimportant; all they needed to know was that it came 'from on high'—that the ultimate authority was the king. In the same way they could think of the world being governed by 'the gods' acting as one. Other gods would be representatives of the supreme god.[29] Simo Parpola, defining monotheism as belief in 'unity in multiplicity', has argued that monotheism was not just incipient but fundamental from early times. Assur was the maker and sovereign lord of the whole universe and thus transcendent, distant from ordinary people. The connection with humans was established through the other gods, who were emanations of Assur. The other gods, therefore, were 'aspects or powers of a single universal God', a bit like the archangels of Jewish and Christian thought. Other scholars, though, disagree: the gods whom Parpola describes as aspects of one god were also worshipped as individual gods.[30]

Since Parpola's evidence depends heavily on imperial propaganda, we can see his account of Assyrian theology as exactly the kind of imperialistic theology which has recently been so heavily condemned. However, there is a contradiction at its heart. It builds a monotheistic veneer on top of a thoroughly polytheistic substance. The veneer is that there is one god of the whole world so there should be one king of the whole world. Anyone who resists the king's rule, whether inside or outside the empire, is resisting the supreme god and should be punished. This is the broadcast claim: the king is supreme, everybody else must obey. The polytheistic substance is the justification for conquest: the national god established supremacy by defeating other gods in battle, so the king should establish supremacy by defeating other kings. Without those enemy gods the theological model would have been a peaceful one. Assyrian invaders sometimes made a point of destroying the images of foreign gods, believing that thereby they were depriving their enemies of divine protection—which of course implies that those enemy gods were real enough.[31]

Hence the contradiction. Internally it suited Assyrian kings to present other gods as totally subservient to Assur, just as they expected their human subjects to be subservient to them. On the other hand, for the purposes of warfare there were enemy gods. In this worldview war represented the natural order sanctioned by the gods. An ideal reign would be victorious rather than peaceful. Each king's role was to establish supreme power by defeating his enemies. Other Mesopotamian nations felt the same about *their* god, and the inevitable result was war upon war. No doubt the powerless and terrorised longed for peace, but their views have rarely been recorded; peace was not the aim of the ruling classes or their national god.

The development of this theology seems to have been something like this. A society would acknowledge a divine creator and sustainer of the world. This god was also the sustainer of society, and was thus identified with the world they knew and the society they knew. To the extent that they thought of this god as located in a place, the place was likely to be their capital city and temple. When horizons expanded they discovered other societies who also believed in a divine creator and sustainer, but one with a different name and living in a different city. Later, Romans would 'translate' gods by, for example, identifying Zeus with Jupiter on the basis that the same god was known under different names. For domestic purposes Babylonians, Israelites and Assyrians might have thought in these terms. In wartime however their respective gods were fighting against each other; at the most only one of them could be the rightful governor of the world. It is the attempt to identify the national fighter with the world ruler which provides the theological justification for conquest, and this is the point at which the contradiction arises. Polytheism is dressed up as monotheism. By contrast, if there really is only one god of the whole world, there is no divine model for fighting. It then does not follow that the king should fight to become the ruler of the world, or indeed that anyone should fight anyone.

What we have in these texts is of course imperialist propaganda, not serious theology. It presents itself as monotheistic in order to claim the status of supreme authority, while depending on a polytheistic worldview to justify conquest. Even in ancient times, some Greek and Roman sceptics thought those cults must have been established simply for the purpose of justifying the regimes.[32] Since then, throughout history governments have sought to shore up their power with propaganda designed to convince their populations that they have benevolent intentions for universal peace and prosperity, while in fact seeking to benefit themselves at the expense of others. The Cold War governments of countries like the USA which, as noted in the Introduction, did so much to discredit Christianity and monotheism by presenting them as justifications for threatening nuclear war, were in fact continuing this tradition, claiming the authority of a universal truth while really just engaging in one more power struggle.

Power-crazy emperors and presidents may be attracted to the idea of being a unique representative of the one universal god, and interpret it as a vocation to conquer the world. Their subjects may find it in their interests to agree, and their hagiographers may reinforce it; but if there is any logical connection between the existence of a single supreme god and the need for a single world emperor, it is yet to be shown. Of course governments claim to act in accordance with God's will whenever they think their populations will believe it. For the same reason they often make false claims to have improved the economy, but this does not lead us to reject all economic theories. Such a deduction would clearly be a logical error. Yet this is the error made when monotheism is blamed for the way governments use it in their propaganda.

Scholars therefore distinguish between 'monotheism from above' and 'monotheism from below'. 'Monotheism from below' represents the interests of the oppressed as they appeal to a divine authority higher than the ruling powers. We shall examine it in the next chapter. 'Monotheism from above' is this imperialistic kind, really just self-interest dressed up as monotheism to give it a veneer of divine authority.[33]

Summary

To summarise, as far back as we can go humans have always speculated about their condition: who made them, for what purpose and how therefore should they live? Our hunter-gatherer ancestors lived in small groups, in constant engagement with the processes of nature which together made up their environment. Between them they provided the good things of life, but sometimes pain and tragedy. People looked for ways to relate to them. They therefore thought of them as personalities with intentions, sometimes helpful and sometimes harmful. These intentions took on new dimensions as cities developed and the motives of gods were conceived along the lines of human hierarchies. Ancient literature depicts a world controlled by a variety of gods, often doing different things, often in conflict with each other, with limited interest in humanity, and generally unpredictable. By explaining human suffering and tragedy as results of divine activity they made it seem inevitable. Behind these divine forces, perhaps providing some kind of underlying unity, they often also had the sense of a supreme deity responsible for reality as a whole. At first this deity was comparatively remote and less in need of a cult, so could easily be forgotten. Over time, however, there was a trend towards conceiving of the gods as a unity with many different expressions.

To the modern mind it seems strange that they carried on believing in these gods for so long. We can distinguish between two different functions they performed. One is the specific concerns: when ill, they wanted to offset the cause of illness, when flooded they appealed to the cause of the flood. These were the many gods, and historians can see how over the centuries people came to believe the causes were not different divine personalities each doing their own thing, but a more integrated system, albeit complex. Eventually ancient comedians laughed at how the gods received none of the good meat at sacrifices, only smoke.[34] The trend towards unifying the gods brought their understandings of the world closer to our own. To contrast the extremes, if the natural environment is maintained by independent self-willed gods, each deciding for themselves what to do, the future is unpredictable. If on the other hand it is a consistent integrated system, the possibility of understanding it and making predictions opens up.

While their responses to their specific concerns changed over time, they still experienced life as a gift with accompanying dangers. Its ups and downs were still meaningful. When life is good it is natural to feel thankful, so there must be someone to thank. When things go wrong it is natural to ask why, so there must be someone to ask—perhaps for an authoritative answer, or maybe just for a transcendent hug, some kind of reassurance that in the grand scheme of things everything is alright.

Today we can look on all these ideas from the outside as a system for understanding reality and call it 'polytheism'. The word was used in the first century CE by the Jewish philosopher Philo to distinguish non-Jewish cults from Judaism.[35] It first appeared in English at the end of the seventeenth century.

Ancients who did not know of any alternatives to polytheism would not have thought of it as a system at all. What was more obvious was the *variety* of different gods, different accounts of how the world was made and different ways humans could and should relate to them. We, looking at these traditions from outside, can see that they share certain features which characterise polytheism and distinguish it from both monotheism and atheism. Monotheism and atheism also offer theories of who made us, for what purpose, and how we should live; but as we shall see, their answers are very different.

Chapter 3. Divine harmony

Monotheism is usually understood as the distinguishing feature of the 'Abrahamic faiths': Judaism, Christianity and Islam. Each of them traces its roots back to the Hebrew scriptures, known to Christians as the Old Testament. Here, the story goes, we get the real thing.

Except that Hebrew scholars are not so sure. Is monotheism central to these documents, or does it only appear in the later ones, or was it long after they were written that they were interpreted as monotheistic? Anyway, how should we define it?

In the last chapter I described some trends towards monotheism within ancient societies that were characteristically polytheistic. From early days there were believers in a god underlying all the gods, a symbol of unity. Various ancient texts found ways to describe the many different gods as unified. To the extent that they were still associated with forces of nature, unifying them depicts the physical environment as more ordered, more akin to modern science. In addition there is the imperialist 'monotheism from above' and the anti-imperialist 'monotheism from below'.

In this chapter I aim to describe this 'monotheism from below', drawing on its classic instance—the Hebrew scriptures. My aim is to follow the consensus of mainstream biblical scholars.[1] Unfortunately, the picture is complicated by their disagreements about when monotheistic beliefs arose and how to interpret relevant texts. However, my main concern is theological rather than historical: to draw out its distinctive features and ethical implications.

Early Israel

The histories in the Bible state that Israelites were committed monotheists from the time of Moses who led them out of slavery in Egypt under the guidance of the one god Yahweh to their promised land where they were surrounded by neighbours with very different beliefs. Later some of the kings abandoned monotheism for the worship of foreign gods. Disgusted with their infidelity, Yahweh sent them into exile in Babylon, allowing them to return home fifty years later when Cyrus the Persian conquered Babylon. It is a thoroughly racist narrative: Yahweh was the god of the Israelites and looked after them at the expense of other nations. By way of establishing who was who, 1 Chronicles records extensive genealogies linking post-exilic Jews with descendants of Jacob.

As long as people had precious little other information it was possible to treat this story as historically accurate. Today scholars draw on other sources of information, like archaeological remains. It turns out that the biblical account gives a false impression of Israel's history. This may trouble those committed to the reliability of the texts, but for purpose of understanding the development of monotheism and its ethical implications it makes the histories far more revealing. The authors were not simply trying to get the historical record straight. They had an agenda which was both political and theological.

The fact that biblical scholars can now draw on a wider range of resources does not stop them being influenced by the ideas of their age. Nineteenth century scholars thought in terms of gradual progress and evolution over time, and were often too quick to find them in biblical texts. In the early twentieth century the 'Biblical Theology Movement' reversed the trend and argued that Israelite religion had been radically different from that of its neighbours from an early age. They described Israel's god as a god of history acting through events like the Exodus and the conquest of Canaan, as opposed to the gods of Canaan who related to creation and fertility. Since then the evidence has pointed back towards an evolutionary development, though generated by historical events rather than the tidy gradualism of nineteenth century theories.[2]

The current consensus is that the development of monotheism contained less conflict than the biblical histories describe and more peaceful assimilation, less out-of-the-blue divine revelation and more insights provoked by circumstances.[3] Israel seems to have begun as a disparate collection of destitute people: refugees from debt and homelessness, bandits and escaped slaves. It may have included some immigrant groups, and some of these groups may have brought with them the story of escape from Egypt and the worship of Yahweh, but the archaeological evidence indicates that most Israelites were Canaanites.[4] The reasons for the migration from the lowlands to the highlands could have been social, military, climatic or a mixture of all three. Once in the highlands these Canaanites gradually evolved into Israelites. There was probably some conflict as populations moved, but the military conquests described in the book of Joshua now seem most unlikely.[5]

It was at first a co-operative, non-hierarchical society. After moving from the lowland cities to the less fertile highlands, clans and families needed to co-operate and diversify to minimise the danger of famine. Perhaps some were attracted by the egalitarianism of simple village life rather than the hierarchical life of the lowland cities, like people today who drop out of affluent society to live more simply. Without a supreme king Israel had neither a competitive agenda nor enthusiasm for wars.[6] Their co-operative society would have been a natural home for a universalist view of humanity, a bit like modern international socialism or environmentalism.

Success produced a rising population. As the Canaanite economy declined the highlanders expanded into the lowlands. Expansion led in turn to the rise of a state and the breakdown of the co-operative society, especially under Solomon.[7] Archaeological evidence shows that during the monarchy Israelites, like Canaanites, worshipped a supreme god El. In the north they also worshipped Baal, the god of fertility, while in the south it was more common to worship Yahweh. Variations like this were quite normal. Yahweh had a wife, Asherah, worshipped alongside him. The hostility between Israel and Canaan seems to have been invented by later writers.

Scholars once believed that monotheism first developed in the desert after the Exodus from Egypt. They now think it would not have arisen so early, but there may be a connection. Settled communities had statues of their gods. Statues were manufactured at the behest of the rich and maintained by priests. This gave power to the rich and the priests. While on the move the liberated Hebrew slaves would not have been able to carry a statue around. Instead they may have thought of Yahweh, who liberated them from Egypt, as a lone god who did not need an image. Centuries later the memory of this stage in their history would have provided opponents of the monarchy with an alternative account of how their national god should be worshipped and obeyed.[8]

During the monarchy the official worship at the temple in Jerusalem would have been similar to those in Mesopotamia and Egypt. The god of the nation would have been the chief focus of worship, but other gods will also have been worshipped. In these states, we saw in Chapter 2 how the chief god of the nation characteristically had two conflicting roles. On the one hand he was closely tied up with political, economic and military policy and took part in the nation's wars. The propaganda of the winners would rubbish the gods of the losers, describing them as weaklings or non-existent. On the other hand, in the context of internal law, morality and custom the chief national god was also considered the creator of the world and thus identified with the supreme god and moral authority. If we focus on this side of the picture, it has monotheistic features. A good example is the eighth century prophet Isaiah of Jerusalem. A number of his prophecies describe God as ruling the world through a divine plan, even using foreign powers to punish Israel.[9] John Barton writes that Isaiah

> ...begins with a picture of the world in which God is the creator and preserver of all things and occupies by right the supreme position over all that he has made. The essence of morality is co-operation in maintaining the ordered structure which prevails, under God's guidance, in the natural constitution of things, and the keynote of the whole system is order, a proper submission to one's assigned place in the scheme of things and the avoidance of any action that would challenge the supremacy of God or seek to subvert the orders he has established. Such is the basic premise from which all Isaiah's thinking about ethical obligation begins.

Those who ignore this moral order lose moral and practical insight. They overestimate their own importance and take pleasure in their own prestige, wealth and status. They fail to put their trust in God and instead rely on other sources of strength. Thus Isaiah's overall approach

> ...begins with a hierarchically ordered universe whose moral pattern ought to be apparent to all whose reason is not hopelessly clouded, and one which derives all particular moral offences from the one great sin, a disregard for natural law.[10]

Another likely precursor of monotheism was the common practice of concentrating worship on a single god at a time of crisis. Normally when kings made alliances with other nations they would establish a cult to the ally's chief gods. However when the population was under threat of annihilation there was little point; all the focus had to be on the god who could save the nation. Political disagreement about foreign policy would therefore lead to disagreement on which gods to worship.[11] Thus arose what Morton Smith called the 'Yahweh-alone party'.[12] The royal court at Jerusalem may have popularised the worship of Yahweh,[13] but it would have been normal to worship other gods as well. The eighth century prophets opposed the worship of other gods, but this was a normal part of political debate. When kings were faced with decisions they had to take into account the god's wishes, and this might mean deciding which prophet to believe. The Hebrew scriptures record the prophecies of the Yahweh-alone party. Usually the views of opposing prophets have not survived, but they too would have been claiming divine guidance. Religious spokespeople did this all over the world; in Britain the practice remained common until the end of the seventeenth century.

Exilic Israel

With the Exile the situation changed dramatically. After two punitive attacks in 597 and 587 BCE, Jerusalem was sacked. The temple was destroyed. The leading classes were exiled to Babylon.

Living in a foreign land, one has to adapt. Some will have been fully assimilated and have been lost to history. Others clung to some aspect of their homeland culture. If we ask what was distinctive about Judean culture, it was not the monarchy: Babylon's king was far richer and more powerful than any king in Jerusalem had ever been. Instead they looked back to the days before they had had a king, when—according to folk memory—Yahweh had been a lone god rescuing his people from slavery in Egypt, giving them a promised land, a co-operative, kingless society and a cult with no need for statues. This earlier version of Yahweh could be presented as an alternative to the dominant culture of their day. Thus the political opposition to the Israelite monarchy, now proved right by political events, offered the exiles a set of values which helped them retain their own identity in a foreign country.[14]

So arose what scholars call the Deuteronomic movement. Its histories, the biblical books of Joshua, Judges, Samuel and Kings, describe how Yahweh had given Moses instructions for the promised land and the people had conquered it, thus proving Yahweh's military superiority. Israel had then been governed by a succession of judges until eventually the people had clamoured for a king so that they could be like the other nations with the trappings of wealth and glory. Samuel had warned them that this was a big mistake but at this point we hear both sides of the story: presumably it was impossible to suppress the popularity of their greatest king, David. Thereafter a succession of kings had ignored the covenant with Yahweh, with the honourable exceptions of Hezekiah and Josiah. Eventually Yahweh had had enough and had allowed the Babylonians to defeat them.

By offering this account the Deuteronomists were doing what politicians do today: they redescribed the history of their nation in a selective way designed to justify their own agenda. From their perspective a good king was one who promoted the worship of Yahweh, forbade the worship of other gods and centralised worship in Jerusalem. Like the people who a few years ago described AIDS as God's judgement on homosexuality, these historians interpreted the biggest events of their day as divine judgement on misgovernment.

How they thought the kings should have governed is described in the book of Deuteronomy. Kings are permitted, but they must be chosen from among the people, must not acquire great military power, must not have a large number of wives, must not acquire a lot of gold and silver, must govern in accordance with the laws and must not raise themselves above the people. The tithe, the ten percent tax imposed by the monarchy, was to be used to support the poor and finance an annual celebration and feast. Every seventh year all debts were to be cancelled and all slaves freed. The big national celebrations were to be available to the poor and weak. Lending money at interest was forbidden. When farmers harvested their fields they were to leave some of the produce for the hungry. These laws borrowed heavily from the earlier laws in Exodus, written perhaps a century earlier. Both sets of laws were put into the mouth of Moses.[15]

The laws matched the history. Yahweh had given the land for a purpose: to provide for everybody's needs. Here we have a combination of views which was more explicit in the ancient world than it is today: to worship a particular god was to affirm that god's values. By the time Deuteronomy was written, the values it attributed to Yahweh were a throwback to the more co-operative and egalitarian society it attributed to the days before the monarchy. Big palaces, temples and wealthy kings were on the agenda of most national gods, but not Yahweh. Deuteronomy was no doubt written with an eye to apportioning blame for the military defeat; but it could also be read as an expression of hope, a manifesto for a free and egalitarian nation which might one day become possible.[16] Many scholars believe this egalitarian policy was central to Jesus' later teaching about the Kingdom of God.[17]

Not worshipping other gods while accepting that they exist is one thing; denying that they exist at all is another. The text usually considered the first to make this claim is Chapters 40-55 of the book of Isaiah. We do not know who wrote it, so scholars call the author (or authors) 'Deutero-Isaiah' or 'Second Isaiah'. Here, some believe, is the point at which monotheism becomes overt.[18]

The context was the Persian invasion of Babylon. Fifty years earlier Jerusalem had been sacked by the Babylonians. Now Babylon was in turn being defeated. In ancient near eastern culture defeated gods would lose worshippers and eventually be forgotten. The Persian policy, however, was to permit conquered nations to maintain their own allegiances. Second Isaiah described their victory as Yahweh's doing. Yahweh is the sole creator and governor of the whole world:

> It is he who sits above the circle of the earth,
> and its inhabitants are like grasshoppers:
> who stretches out the heavens like a curtain,
> and spreads them like a tent to live in;
> who brings princes to naught,
> and makes the rulers of the earth as nothing.[19]

Other gods are rubbished as non-existent and their statues are ridiculed.[20]

Many scholars have argued that the breakthrough to monotheism took place at this point, in the urban setting of Babylon where both motivation and leisure were sufficient to generate intense intellectual struggle.[21] If so, Second Isaiah is a 'monotheism from below', representing the interests of the oppressed as they appeal to a higher authority than the ruling powers.[22] Before the Persian victory the emperor of Babylon was Nabonidus. Second Isaiah was appealing to the higher authority of Yahweh, who was sending the Persian king Cyrus to defeat him. Albertz writes:

> Given the later campaigns of conquest under Christian auspices which were justified by the absolutist claim of monotheism, it is all the more important to point to the sociological fact that Israel made the breakthrough to monotheism in a situation of absolute political helplessness.[23]

Others have argued that there is little evidence for any breakthrough at all. In all the Hebrew scriptures only Second Isaiah insists that other gods do not exist, and even there the main force of the claim is rhetorical: the author is rubbishing other gods. To this extent Second Isaiah's claims can be compared with Hebrew texts saying of other gods that they have died or been demoted, that they are mere idols, that they are not divine or that they are subordinate divinities.[24] Mark Smith describes Second Isaiah's assertions as 'a kind of inner community discourse' stressing Yahweh's exceptional status in order to persuade people to continue worshipping him.[25]

If, in this way, we treat the denials of the existence of other gods as nothing more than rhetorical exaggeration, Second Isaiah's claims are similar to non-Hebrew texts of the same time. The defeated Babylonian king, Nabonidus, had previously replaced the cult of Marduk with the cult of a different god, Sin. Cyrus claimed to have been called by Marduk to re-establish his cult. According to the Cyrus Cylinder, Marduk's priests welcomed Cyrus as a liberator in much the same way as Second Isaiah did.[26] Yet Marduk's priests were not monotheists. Realistically, Second Isaiah's hopes were still being pinned on the man with the biggest army.

Some scholars therefore deny that monotheism is an appropriate term at all for Second Isaiah, or even the whole Bible.[27] In Jan Assmann's view, monotheism 'probably did not emerge in its pure form until late antiquity in the struggles for contradistinctive self-definition involving Judaism, Christianity, and Gnosticism'.[28] This would date it to the second century CE. Nevertheless, whatever the author's intentions, later generations have seen in Second Isaiah a model for 'monotheism from below'—treating the supreme god as a moral authority passing judgement on powerful rulers.

These poems reflect the racism characteristic of the age, presenting Israel as God's chosen race:

> 'I will give you as a light to the nations,
> that my salvation may reach to the end of the earth.'
> Thus says the Lord,
> the Redeemer of Israel and his Holy One,

to one deeply despised, abhorred by the nations,
the slave of rulers,
'Kings shall see and stand up,
princes, and they shall prostrate themselves,
because of the Lord, who is faithful,
the Holy One of Israel, who has chosen you.'[29]

Critics of monotheism often argue that it encourages people to believe their nation is God's favoured nation, with a mission to dominate others.[30] On this point Second Isaiah has been immensely influential. When describing humanity's role as God's worshippers, Israel is given a unique place. Others who acknowledged Yahweh might join Israel,[31] but at the same time Yahweh's destruction of Israel's enemies was celebrated: 'the Chaldeans will be turned to lamentation... they lie down, they cannot rise, they are extinguished, quenched like a wick'.[32]

There is a contradiction here. A single, universal and transcendent god who can 'judge between the nations',[33] as Second Isaiah claimed, is consistent with monotheism since all humanity—including the Chaldeans—must have been created by the same god. The idea of a supreme god having a chosen race, on the other hand, has its natural home in nationalist polytheism. In ancient Mesopotamia, as we have seen, rulers justified their warmaking on the basis that their nation had been chosen by the supreme god and given the task of conquering other nations. The contradiction is never resolved in the Hebrew scriptures. They retain older stories of Yahweh defeating Israel's enemies in wars. For the disciples of Second Isaiah, recalling Yahweh's past victories no doubt seemed a good way to stress that Israel's god was far superior to other national gods. Looking back on these stories from our perspective, however, it does the opposite. To this extent Second Isaiah failed to draw out the universalist implications of monotheism.

Nevertheless these texts took a major step in this direction.

What distinguished Second Isaiah's claim for Israel was not its chosenness—every nation made that claim—but the absence of any military dimension to it. There was no interest in a restoration of the state with its king in Jerusalem. Yahweh had chosen Israel not to conquer, but to serve.[34]

The growth of monotheism

How, then, did monotheism develop? The debate continues. We can distinguish two different questions: its historical growth, and how to define it. Taking the historical question first, most of the history of Judea from 539 BCE when Cyrus conquered Babylon to the time of the Maccabees in the 160s BCE remains unrecorded. The most important exception, for our purposes, was the intervention of Nehemiah.

Nehemiah was an upper class Judean sent by the Persian government to rebuild Jerusalem in 445-444 BCE, probably due to a military threat. He restored the city walls, abolished interest on loans, cancelled debts and redistributed land and property. These actions could be justified by appealing to Deuteronomy.[35] Sometime later he gathered the Levites into the city and financed them with a 10% tax on agricultural produce. Before then they may have been the poorest people in the land. Giving them a role something like a police force for the city and the temple, he established a counterbalance to the power of the temple priests and a social class committed to preserving his reforms.[36] Having thus made himself popular and established a power base, he then turned to the most unpopular of his reforms. Judah was a tiny community nested within a vast empire. If its egalitarianism was to survive it would have to be insulated from foreign influence. Foreign husbands and wives would inevitably have brought in foreign gods and their very different values. He therefore banned marriages to foreigners.[37] As far as we know only Sparta had a similar law. To us it seems bizarre and offensive, but in the circumstances it would have been essential to maintaining the other reforms. Morton Smith writes:

> With that support and with those reforms the separation from the neighbouring peoples was now a *fait accompli*. The Judaeans had been made a peculiar people; the Yahweh-alone party had acquired a separate administrative district in the empire. Most of the people of that district were now marked off from those of neighbouring districts by exclusive devotion to Yahweh, limitation of their sacrifices to Jerusalem, peculiar customs (the observance of Sabbath), an attitude of hostility and a tradition of self-segregation.[38]

Without a king of their own, success ceased to be about military victory and prosperity ceased to be about emperors flaunting their wealth. Paradoxically, Judah's internationalist theology was preserved by separating the people from those who did not share it.[39] By the time the Persian empire ended Judah had been under Persian rule for two centuries. It was this period that established the distinctiveness of the people we now call Jews.

After Alexander's conquests the ancient near east became more cosmopolitan, with Greek culture pervading everywhere much as American culture does today. Nevertheless the sense of Jewish distinctiveness survived, and was revived from the time of the Maccabees (the 160s BCE) onwards. In Jesus' day Jews were known throughout the eastern Mediterranean and the near east for their distinctive beliefs and practices: one god; synagogue worship where they would hear the law read and expounded; refusal to marry foreigners; strict food laws; circumcision of baby boys; and refusal to work on the Sabbath.[40]

Was this monotheism? Two points are worth noting. One is that, as Matthew Lynch notes, authors do not always reveal their theological presuppositions, or even hold them consistently. Many biblical texts allow for varying interpretations. Some

> ...can function within, and contribute to, a henotheistic *or* monotheistic system, no matter what their originating purpose or context. Some such texts have the *potential* to be read as monotheistic, but might also "fit" within non-monotheistic contexts. Nevertheless, such texts can form the literary building blocks for the production of what, in the end, later Jewish communities deemed a monotheistic Bible.[41]

So Second Isaiah could for rhetorical effect ridicule the idea that other gods exist, a bit like an Everton supporter saying that Manchester United do not have a single player capable of kicking a ball, and later Jews would accept Second Isaiah's claim as literally true.

Secondly, while it is true that only Second Isaiah denies the existence of other gods, it does not follow that there were no other monotheists. When we hold distinctive beliefs today we do not declare them, let alone write them down, unless we have reason to respond to people who disagree. Similarly, some biblical texts do not deny the existence of other gods but fail to mention them, thus giving the impression—at least to some scholars—that they do not believe in them. Examples are the Priestly writings and Job.

The most significant text in this category is the first chapter of Genesis. On the age of the earth and the method of God's creation, issues which troubled nineteenth century scholars in the light of evolution theory, the authors of Genesis mostly followed the consensus of their day. It is the differences which reveal what they were positively asserting: the one god, with a good purpose, whose plan was fulfilled as intended. Even so some Hebrew scholars challenge the monotheism of the text. It refers to God in a plural form, the significance of which is much debated—perhaps the use of the plural is making a similar point to the Leiden Hymn.[42] Other gods are not even mentioned, let alone denied. Functionally, the text is monotheist as it describes creation according to a single and successful plan. Ancient near eastern conflict narratives are used but with the conflict omitted; even the sea monsters, previously described as hostile gods, are created good.[43] Mark Smith also argues that the blessings make this narrative distinctive: 'Blessing is clearly an important role for the author of Genesis 1; it appears not once but three times in this account, yet appears in no other creation narrative.'[44] It is often considered *the* classic text endorsing monotheism.

The theology of Hebrew monotheism

What, then, is the monotheism of the Hebrew scriptures? How should we define it?

The word 'monotheism' only dates from the seventeenth century CE, when the theology of Judaism, Christianity and Islam could be more easily distinguished from ancient paganism and dualist theologies like Catharism. The ancient world conceived of many different *kinds* of gods—for example, as we saw in the last chapter, deified Roman emperors were not equated with 'real' gods—so the question arises as to where to draw the line.

Most of the Hebrew scriptures were written after the Exile and before the Maccabean period. In most cases we do not know when the text reached its final form, but the overall picture is along these lines. Texts originating before the Exile were later edited to remove references to opposing gods; in some cases scholars can still recognise traces of earlier polytheist versions. Some gods, like Rahab and Leviathan, had previously been divine opponents but were demoted. Later texts, while not mentioning opposing gods, increased the number of heavenly figures subordinate to the one god.[45] There are no real divine threats to Yahweh.

Christians familiar with the New Testament's devil often expect it to appear in their Old Testament, but it does not. The closest we get is the word 'satan'. This word has often been interpreted as the name of a divine opponent of God, but it acquired this meaning later. In Hebrew a 'satan' is an adversary. Peggy Day's study lists five texts where the word applies to a human[46] and four where it applies to a heavenly being. In Numbers 22 an unnamed satan is sent by God to block Balaam's journey. In Job a member of the heavenly council adopts the role of a satan to persuade God to make Job suffer. Day's view[47] is that Job is presenting the heavenly scene as an unrealistic 'what if?' scenario, and is not expecting the reader to take the satan's existence seriously. The other texts are Zechariah 3:1-7 where a heavenly satan unsuccessfully tries to dissuade God from letting Joshua become High Priest in Jerusalem,[48] and 1 Chronicles 21 where a satan incites King David to conduct a census.[49] The earliest texts clearly using 'Satan' as the name of a divine being date from the 160s BCE.[50] Scholars attribute this innovation to the influence of the Persian religion Zoroastrianism, which seems to have believed that the world had been made by two gods, a good one and an evil one. Jews influenced by this belief gave the name 'Satan' to the evil one and Christians inherited it.[51]

Most remarkable of all is the lack of evil spirits in the Hebrew scriptures. The ancients thought they were ubiquitous in their environment and were the chief causes of illnesses and misfortunes, yet the Hebrew scriptures hardly ever mention them. When they do they are under God's control, not independent agents.[52] There is not a single exorcism in the Hebrew scriptures and only one in the Apocrypha.[53]

The Hebrew scriptures do, however, refer to other heavenly beings who are obedient to God. There are references to a heavenly 'council' which met to make decisions, much like the Mesopotamian equivalents except that nobody disagreed with God. In later texts Heaven is sometimes populated by famous figures from Israel's past, like Moses. This may have been a way to identify the god of the whole world with the Jewish religious heritage. Angels also became more numerous; Leonard Hurtado believes that this may have been intended to emphasise God's power as controller of a large retinue. James McGrath notes that wealthy people often sent agents to deal with their business affairs on their behalf, and it would have been natural to think of God doing the same. It seems that biblical authors disagreed with each other about whether attributing subordinates to God exalted, or detracted from, God's uniqueness.[54] There are also texts treating attributes of God as personal beings in their own right. The main ones are Wisdom and Logos (Word). Scholars disagree about whether Jews took them literally as independent beings separate from God or simply saw them as metaphorical ways of describing what God does.[55]

Putting together all the uncertainties, the history of the rise of Hebrew monotheism is a cloudy one. When we ask exactly who disbelieved in other gods, and which texts express the disbelief, there is much scope for debate. Nevertheless this messy tradition has proved productive. The 'Abrahamic' faiths Judaism, Christianity and Islam have found in the Hebrew scriptures a distinctive understanding of the divine.

Like most political and economic theories today, most theological theories in ancient times functioned as defences of the ruling classes. During the monarchy Israel's god was much the same as the gods of neighbouring kingdoms: the national god who was both the creator of the world and a warrior fighting with them against enemy nations and enemy gods. Success meant victory, wealthy kings and big palaces. The poor paid with their labour, fighters with their lives. In the case of the Hebrew scriptures the perspectives of the losers survived. Opponents of the monarchy preserved and exaggerated memories of the days before their kings: the lone god who led their ancestors out of Egypt, a co-operative and egalitarian society eking out a living on the hill-tops, laws ensuring that everybody had enough to eat. The Exile was their opportunity: Yahweh, it seemed, had had enough of the disobedient ways of the kings. The Persian victory could be interpreted, at least by Second Isaiah, as corroboration of this view. The subsequent Persian settlement, granting the community self-government and its own god but no army, enabled the ideas to develop into the distinctive features of Judaism. The runaway slaves, the debt refugees and bandits settling down to farm the least fertile land, the opponents of the monarchy, the eighth century prophets, Deuteronomy and the exilic prophets, Nehemiah and the Maccabees did not all believe the same things, but the surviving texts about them express values very different from the values of imperialist rulers. They describe a god who has created humanity as a blessing and provided for our needs, a god with a positive concern for the poor, the destitute, widows, orphans and refugees. A god who cares about the welfare of these people is very different from a god who exults in military victory and the bling of royal palaces.

Putting together the lone god Yahweh with the opposition to extremes of wealth and poverty made theological sense. As long as the world seemed to be maintained by gods with conflicting agendas, tragedies like defeat and starvation could be treated as the inevitable result of quarrelling gods. If, on the other hand, the world and all its people had been created according to a single plan by a god who designed everyone for well-being, it no longer made sense to treat these tragedies as inevitable. It made more sense to believe that co-operation in peace was possible.

What was distinctive about Hebrew monotheism, therefore, was not that there was only one *inhabitant* of the divine world, but that there was only one divine *will*. Biblical scholars have often argued that there is no theologically significant difference between monotheism and polytheism,[56] and it is possible to defend this position as long as monotheism is defined as accepting only one divine personality or agent. This, however, is to miss the immense practical difference it makes to conceive of the world as the product of divine harmony rather than divine conflict. This is the point where the practical significance lies. The ancient Hebrew ideas of a divine court and angels, and the Christian ideas of the divinity of Jesus and the Trinity, are consistent with divine harmony provided that there is no conflict between the different divine characters. I suspect that this is the best the human mind can do, as the nature of the divine is beyond our comprehension.

I am not suggesting that the Hebrews were the only people to have had these insights. Of course others have done so too, but history is usually written by the winners. The voices of the losers are usually suppressed. When monotheistic ideas appear they are usually mixed up with polytheistic ideas, with the result that the distinctiveness of divine harmony is obscured. What makes the Hebrew scriptures different is that the literature that got preserved expresses the perspective of the losers well enough to offer a radically different account of the divine. From this different account of the divine come different values and priorities for human life.

Although the authors of the Bible did not think in terms of the modern distinction between monotheism and polytheism, they were aware of the practical significance of different beliefs about gods. Those of us who live in secular societies today can afford to think of religious beliefs as inessentials. To the ancients, understanding the divine was an essential part of understanding their own lives and the world around them. The Hebrew texts, in all their untidiness, depict a harmony of divine will. It is this divine harmony which makes the all-important contrast with the divine conflict characteristic of many other traditions. It provides a radically different account of who made us, for what purpose, and how therefore we should live. John Barton describes the difference:

> Israelite ethics rests on an optimistic anthropology in which the human race is created as something good and is seen as

> capable of living in fellowship with God, whereas in Mesopotamia the creation of humans is an aspect of the chaotic in the world... This has implications for how the state is understood: in Mesopotamia, as a necessary evil, the only bulwark against disaster and the resurgence of chaos...; but in Israel, as an aspect of the co-operation between people, and between people and God, which was part of the divine intention from the first. This inevitably leads to a different way of thinking about society and about moral norms, and leads to that stress on human solidarity which is inimical to the idea of domination by one person over others and was bound to lead to a cautious attitude to the institution of absolute monarchy.[57]

A god who neither defeats nor is defeated, either in heaven or on earth, becomes a very different model for human behaviour. Societies acknowledging a god like this have reason to adopt more peaceful values. The new logic does not impress itself immediately; in retrospect we know it takes millennia. Nevertheless an essential foundation was laid in the Hebrew scriptures.

Chapter 4. Polytheist and monotheist ethics

Despite all the achievements of modern science, our lives are maintained by forces which far exceed our understanding. Most societies have attributed divine agency and purpose to these forces. In the last chapter I proposed to distinguish monotheism as divine harmony rather than conflict. This chapter explores why it matters. What is at stake?

To refer to this divine harmony I use the traditional word 'God'. One of the issues surrounding this word is whether God is conceived as *personal*. Many people today believe in some kind of sacred or spiritual presence permeating the universe but deny that it is personal. The kind of divine presence I seek to defend is personal in one sense but not in another: personal in the sense of being capable of relating to us, but not in the sense of being one being over against others. Fundamentally I mean that the forces that created and maintain the universe are not impersonal processes that just happen to be there. They include agency and intention. Because they are well beyond human understanding and language, the closest we can get to describing them is by analogical language, along the lines of Aquinas' account: that God's intending and loving are *something like* human intending and loving.

Monotheists have traditionally described God as omnipotent, omniscient and benevolent. All three are implications of divine harmony. Because there are no agents in a position to challenge God, God has complete power. This does not mean God can do anything the human mind can imagine: the point is the lack of external constraints. Contrary to Plato's cosmology, for example, God's creative work is not limited by the constraints of matter. Although it is not in the Bible, monotheists came to believe that God created the world out of nothing. This seems to follow from the absence of external limitations.

Omniscience follows too. The supreme deity should be able to access all knowledge. It is possible to imagine a relatively powerful god being ignorant; the idea was explored in great detail by Gnostics and Manicheans, as a way of explaining why the world was flawed and tragic. However it proved difficult to account for the most powerful god being ignorant; they ended up producing complex polytheisms attributing power to some gods and knowledge to others. In monotheism God is not constrained by lack of knowledge.

In the same way it has proved difficult to imagine a supremely powerful god who is not benevolent. A god who needs nothing yet creates this universe must surely feel positively about it. Hostile gods need to have their hostility explained.

Monotheism therefore naturally leads to the idea that God is omnipotent, omniscient and benevolent. The Bible does not say this, but it does provide the ingredients from which later monotheists drew out the implications. We might compare the process with the way Marxists today believe Marx produced significant insights but do not attribute to him all the beliefs of present day Marxists. Thus we can recognise the Hebrew scriptures not as a complete account of monotheism but as a source from which new insights about it have emerged.

Divine harmony and the world

When we believe the universe has been created by a god like this, we have reason to expect it to contain two characteristics which contrast with polytheistic accounts.

One is systemic unity. Polytheists could believe that each nation had been created by its own god. In this case it was possible to wonder what, if anything, one had in common with foreigners. Were they equally human? Similarly, perhaps the climate of foreign lands was different because a different god had created them.

The idea of humanity as a whole occurs in classical Greek literature, but most Greeks lived in self-governing city states and identified with their city. After Alexander's conquests the situation changed. People lived in vast empires bounded by military outcomes rather than cultural identity. Stoics developed the idea of humanity as a unity. Seneca spoke of 'the fatherhood of God and brotherhood of man' and Marcus Aurelius believed that 'we are all fellow citizens and members of one body politic, that is to say, the Universe is a species of state'.[1] Christianity inherited the idea and gave it greater substance, claiming that everybody in the world is created and loved by the same god. The nation's enemies are no longer God's enemies. Whatever purposes God has for the lives of our own community, there must be correlative purposes for the lives of foreigners. What is most significant about foreigners, therefore, is what they have in common with ourselves, not what makes them different.

The other characteristic is linear time. Ancient polytheists rarely conceived of time in this way. Instead they conceived of it in a variety of different ways. One is a distinction between primeval time and all subsequent time. Anthropologists have found it in many parts of the world. On this account the way things are was established during primeval time. From then on, nothing significant changes. What gives meaning to present time is the way it expresses or re-enacts the events of primeval time. Medieval Christianity had its own version, in which the significant events were the Creation, Fall and Redemption. In their own day the sacrifice of the Mass re-enacted the Last Supper and Christ's sacrifice.

Another view of history was that it goes round in circles, so that everything happening now happened thousands of years ago and will happen again in the future. This view tends to be deterministic, as it expects what we do to repeat whatever happened before.

In other cases the rule was chaos. When the relationships

between the gods were subject to change with unforeseeable effects on earth, anything could happen. Even the Babylonian creation epic, which asserted that Marduk was in complete control, has limitations compared with monotheism. It describes the creation of humanity as a decision by Marduk. Marduk was only contingently the chief god, as a result of winning battles with other gods. In principle that could change in the light of future divine battles. His decision to create humanity was also contingent, designed to meet specific needs of the gods. That too could change. In principle, therefore, these versions of polytheism presented the future as unpredictable.[2]

Compared with these accounts, monotheism expects a single divine purpose to be maintained throughout time without interruption. Linear time, a gradual and uninterrupted movement from past to future, is taken for granted today but is a product of monotheism.

These two characteristics, systemic unity and linear time, make modern science possible. They tell us that the processes we have observed are consistent with the processes we have not observed and that the future will be similar to the past. There may be diversity, potential for innovation and even freedom for created beings to oppose the divine plan, but the fundamental system will continue. Whatever God is doing, God is going to carry on doing. As W G Lambert noted,

> A universe controlled by one god who created it is susceptible of more purposeful direction than a universe housing a whole pantheon of deities, male and female, each with an individual will.[3]

Thus modern science inherited from monotheism one of its essential presuppositions: that the universe is ordered. Polytheism can describe the world as chaotic, dependent on the changing moods or fortunes of different gods. Monotheism, with its one god reliably in control, makes it seem worthwhile to interpret natural processes as regularities and expect them to continue in the future.

The other essential presupposition of science is that the human mind can understand the universe's order. We normally assume that, when we are not dreaming or hallucinating, our minds represent reality reasonably well. Everybody makes mistakes and nobody knows everything, but between us we can correct each other. So we need some account of the human mind which explains not only why we can normally trust it, but also why we make mistakes. This also is a product of monotheism. In early Christianity there was a debate between the Catholics, who affirmed the mind as God's good gift, and some Gnostics who argued that our minds had been created by evil or ignorant gods to systematically deceive us. The Catholics triumphed: faith in a monotheistic god became the reason for confidence in the reliability of our minds. Thereafter, for over a thousand years, the dominant Christian view was that our minds are designed to understand as much as a benevolent god has created us to understand, with as much certainty as we need. As Augustine put it, 'Do not seek to understand in order that you may believe, but believe in order that you may understand'.[4]

The principle was elaborated by the thirteenth-century philosopher Thomas Aquinas. Aquinas described the physical things we can see as part of a much greater reality, richer than we can understand. What we know can offer glimpses of what we do not know. By reflecting on what we already know we may expand our knowledge, but we neither expect nor need to know everything.[5] The natural sense of wonder or gratitude that we feel in the presence of great beauty or complexity can be taken as an honest guide, alerting us to the greater glory of the whole. In this sense our mental abilities are to be trusted as God's provision. This means that in God's dispensation the universe is ordered *enough*, and our minds competent *enough*, for legitimate human purposes.

As far as we can conceive, a god without constraints must have no needs. What, then, is God's purpose in creating this universe? Polytheistic myths offer answers. Typically the gods were concerned with their own interests.

Theologians often contrast the Babylonian creation narrative, the *Enuma Elish,* which would have been recited at the New Year festival at the time of the Exile, with the first chapter of Genesis.

In the *Enuma Elish,* after many battles between the gods Marduk emerges as supreme. To please the other gods he reduced their workload by creating humans to burn sacrifices and maintain temples. This kind of understanding seems to have been typical of the ancient near east. Eckhart Otto summarises:

> In Mesopotamian tradition man was created from the blood of a god who represents chaos and guilt, and thus bears within himself elements of a life bound to failure. This negative anthropology is linked to a pessimistic idea of the aim of human life, whose purpose is to relieve gods who have become guilty of the burden of work. Work as the object of human life is seen as a punishment for the guilt of the gods.

Otto contrasts this with the first chapter of Genesis, which 'is quite deliberate in providing a contrast: the one God had created humans to be partners and collaborators'.[6] Gerald Janzen describes Genesis 1 as

> ...a political statement sharply at odds with *Enuma elish,* which would have been the cosmological mandate for Babylonian power at the time Genesis 1 was emerging in its final form. The Israelite and Babylonian creation stories represent not merely two different divine claimants for world rule, Yahweh and Marduk, but, by their differing accounts of the way the divine creator has brought the cosmos into

> existence, represent two different conceptions of life-giving and community-building power.[7]

In monotheism, God is neither constrained by external circumstances nor in need of anything. Creating us and the universe was a free act. Since God has freely chosen to create us, the purpose must be something like our own well-being. God *blesses* us. We have been created to flourish. Genesis 1 describes the creation of the world as a succession of free decisions by God. In each case God commands, the command is carried out and God declares the result to be good. God blesses fish, birds, animals and humans, telling them to 'be fruitful and multiply'.[8] We might imagine God as a bit like a couple wanting to have a baby, with a kind of love for a person who does not yet exist. We have been created for our own good. Similarly Walter Brueggemann, commenting on creation texts in some psalms, observes that 'Yahweh characteristically intends not only to have a world, but to have a certain kind of world, one that generously and gladly attends to the goodness and extravagance of life.'[9] It is a point often made by philosophers of religion; thus Clayton and Knapp state of 'ultimate reality' that

> ...if it chooses to bring about the existence of beings other than itself... the infinite being must be doing so out of what, resorting to admittedly anthropomorphic terms, we can only regard as sheer generosity: sheer love for the finite others for whose sake it chooses to limit its own infinite power.[10]

Given a god like this with a purpose like this, we are bound to expect that realising the purpose is a real possibility. We are therefore right to see health and happiness as morally normative. Today we usually do; when we are ill we ask a doctor to put the situation right. We have largely forgotten that we inherited the belief from monotheism. The polytheism of divine conflict could only tell us that good and bad health, happiness and unhappiness, are equally normal.

Divine harmony and ethics

The powerful god of monotheism gives us security, but at first sight it comes at a price. God is in total control; nothing can possibly happen that is outside God's intentions. At least initially, everything is determined by God. We are puppets on a string.

There have been many determinists, both ancient Neoplatonists and modern materialists. They have usually seen determinism as a fundamental feature of the universe. In monotheism, however, the created order has been established by God's free choosing as an act of love. There is nothing to stop God choosing to selectively withdraw from complete control, so as to give us freedom while retaining an element of security. In Chapter 15 I shall argue that this is what God does.

This withdrawal by God from complete control can be seen as part of the divine blessing. It is a gift of freedom located between two extremes. At one extreme is the God of Aristotle who creates us, gives us the ability to do a range of things, and then takes no further interest in us. We are like children sent out onto the street to occupy ourselves in whatever way we can find. Anything could happen; there are no guarantees of security. At the other extreme is the god of some religious sects, who lays down exactly what we should do on every occasion. The divine blessing of monotheism is between these extremes. We are created for our own good and invited to choose between a wide range of options. The limits to our freedom are determined by God, but within these limits we are free. We shall examine the logic of freedom in more detail later; at this point we should note that divine blessing liberates us from having our every action micromanaged by God. We can make choices. Some of the options, if chosen, hinder the blessing. This gives us freedom to choose between good and evil.

Freedom brings responsibility. When polytheistic systems describe the forces of nature as personalities in conflict with each other they can explain sunshine and rain, drought and flood, as battles between gods; but by so explaining they tell us we are at the mercy of an unpredictable future. Unable to do anything about divine quarrels, we become fatalistic. If, on the other hand, the divine will is unified and consistent, we can understand more about how the world works. We can foresee results of our actions. To the extent that we are free, we are responsible. Barton illustrates how the Hebrew scriptures affirm this responsibility:

> The fact that David committed adultery with Bathsheba and then murdered her husband does not constrain the actions of his children: Amnon's rape of Tamar is an act for which he is entirely to blame, not one that is David's fault.[11]

Here we are worlds away from the Greek tragedies, where human actions are fated and tragedy is unavoidable. There is no Oedipus destined to unwittingly kill his father and marry his mother, no Agamemnon destined to be murdered by his wife. Because life is not inevitably tragic, to be free is to be responsible. We can make a difference, for good or ill.

We saw in Chapter 2 how a theology of divine conflict makes human conflict morally normative. In a similar way a theology of divine harmony makes human harmony morally normative. Lenn Goodman describes the difference:

> Pagan piety models the divine on human strengths, but also on the passions—whatever seems overwhelming. So there are gods of fever, and mischief. And when the gods are sharply delineated, not just as principles (wheat or wine personified) but as personalities, they will quarrel, and need a Zeus or Odin to adjudicate among them. Rival ideals of womanhood,

> facets projected from their human archetypes onto divine simulacra—Aphrodite, Hera, Athena—reflect back a sharp, if tinny gleam onto humanity, sparking the conflicts celebrated in the epic, drawing the tragedian's eye for drama, feeding the Sophists' illusion that values are ultimately irreconcilable, and elevating that illusion into a theory of the tragic sense of life. Monotheists take a different tack: we see one cosmos, and seek one law, a law of nature and of life, for individuals and their communities. Values, we think, can be reconciled. Persons can live at peace with one another and themselves.[12]

Thus monotheism produces a distinctive ethical agenda. There is a transcendent moral law, an authoritative truth about how to live well. This truth is not something we balance against conflicting truths, let alone create for ourselves. It is to be perceived through reflecting on experience in the context of a positive relationship with the divine. It is true not simply because God says so but because it is built into the way we and the universe have been designed. It is guidance designed for our own well-being. Characteristically, obeying it serves the common good.

There is thus a different role for legal systems. This also is expressed in the Hebrew scriptures. In ancient Mesopotamia the chief lawgivers were kings and the force of each law was relative to the king's power. Post-exilic Judah, lacking a king, filled the gap with written laws. The laws were attributed not to previous kings but to God: the first five books of the Bible were edited to claim that they were instructions given by God to Moses. If the one god has designed the universe to function in particular ways, to obey God's laws is more than a matter of pleasing God or the king; it is to act in accordance with the way the universe as a whole has been designed.

Thus monotheism establishes a different relationship between the order of creation, ethics and law. Since ethics expresses the purposes for which we have been created, law should express ethics. In the first century CE the Jewish philosopher Philo, assuming that Moses had written the first five books of the Bible, argued that

> ...in relating the history of early times, and going for its beginning right to the creation of the universe, he wished to shew two most essential things: first that the Father and Maker of the world was in the truest sense also its Lawgiver, secondly that he who would observe the laws will accept gladly the duty of following nature and live in accordance with the ordering of the universe, so that his deeds are attuned to harmony with his words and his words with his deeds.[13]

We should of course acknowledge that this account of law created a practical problem for ancient Jews. Most of the laws in the Bible are contingent, appropriate to particular times and places. By the time of Jesus many of them were so out of date as to be an embarrassment. Thus arose a tension: some insisted on maintaining the laws because they came from God, while others argued that they were no longer appropriate. The tension continues today; for example, Christians debate whether homosexuality should be permitted in the light of some biblical texts forbidding it. The problem arises because when a text is deemed to have come from God it would seem ungodly to modify it. The error is to imagine that the texts are nothing but divine revelation. By the time they are written down, of course, they have been interpreted by particular people in particular situations. The fact that detailed laws become inappropriate in different contexts should not beguile us into ignoring the more general monotheist principle: that our changing rules and laws should always be designed to facilitate the blessing and fulfilment for which God has made us.

Scholars have often noted the connection between monotheism and egalitarianism. In a polytheistic society where humanity has been created to serve the gods, it is only to be expected that humans will survive well enough to perform their tasks but no better. There is no justification for the idea that everybody matters, or that there should be enough food to go round. Self-centred gods with needs become models for self-centred humans competing for resources. By contrast, if the world has been designed for the well-being of creation, including all humans, then leaving anybody homeless or starving is contrary to the way we have been designed to live.

Political debate today continues to express the contrast between these two visions: is the nation's success to be judged according to a communal goal like victory over enemies or national prosperity, or according to an inclusive goal like providing for everybody's needs? In one case individuals are expendable, in the other they are not. In the thought of the Hebrew scriptures, contrary to the views dominant in Mesopotamia, humans had been created for their own good so the welfare of every human became a primary objective. It is not the means to anything else. Just as there is no longer a tribal favouritism, so also there is no longer an economic favouritism. Gnuse writes:

> All three high religions [Judaism, Christianity and Islam]... proclaim rhetoric which affirms human equality. Cultures touched by those religious traditions have provided democratic expressions in theory and practice. One cannot deny monotheism its connection to theoretic egalitarianism.[14]

This is not the egalitarianism of modern socialist theory, with its much more developed economic analyses. It is, however, a mandate for ensuring basic provision for all, in accordance with the principle that the world's resources are provided for this purpose. If each of us is a child of God, created for our own well-being, and just as important as anyone else, then to be deprived of the necessities of life must be contrary to God's intentions.

Thus the powerful and powerless alike have reason to believe in a supreme divine moral authority, but for opposite reasons. Rulers claim to represent this authority. What empowers the poor and oppressed, on the other hand, is a vision of a better society. To give moral legitimacy to their vision, they need to appeal to an authority that transcends the ruling classes—an authority competent to tell the ruling classes that their values are in error. These contrasting values are still debated in political and military discourse today.

Progress

Divine purpose, systemic unity and linear time between them make it possible to hope for long-term progress.

The idea of gradual improvement over time is common enough: individuals and communities can reflect on their past, observe a gradual process of improvement and hope for further improvements in the future. On an individual, local or national level this can be a zero sum game: progress for some may mean regress for others. Continuous progress for *humanity as a whole,* on the other hand, is difficult enough to establish for past history, let alone to predict for the future. Yet faith in future universal progress has been a dominant feature of modern western culture. Here I shall describe how it is a product of monotheism; later we shall see what happens to it in secular culture.

It is instructive to compare the histories of the idea of progress by John Bagnell Bury and Robert Nisbet. They agree that the ancient pagan Greeks and Romans showed no anticipation of future progress though they did sometimes note past progress in technology, the arts and civilisation.[15] Both treated Augustine's *City of God* and the idea of Providence as major influences, but in opposite directions. For Bury, Providence meant divine intervention in an otherwise ordered universe, thus denying the possibility of progress;[16] for Nisbet it meant an 'author and executor of a design within which all human cultures however widely separated in space and time fit smoothly'.[17] Bury lamented that, according to the early Christians and especially Augustine,

> ...the whole movement of history has the purpose of securing the happiness of a small portion of the human race in another world; it does not postulate a further development of human history on earth[18]

and added that the doctrine of Original Sin prevented the idea of moral improvement. He did though add that Christianity

> ...constructed a synthesis which for the first time attempted to give a definite meaning to the whole course of human events, a synthesis which represents the past as leading up to a definite and desirable goal in the future.[19]

Nisbet repeatedly referred to Augustine with approval, quoting his argument that God deliberately designed the whole human race to come from one person so that we would be bound to each other by family affection:[20]

> It is Christianity that most systematically and consecratedly set forth the idea of humanity and, more important, the unity of humanity.

Acknowledging the ancient Greek awareness of humanity and its development he adds:

> But neither this nor an awareness of a great multiplicity of peoples and cultures on earth is the same thing as a rooted

> conception of humanity or mankind existing in its own right, unified and also possessed of a capacity to develop and to progress over a long period of time. This conception is peculiar to Western civilization, and is not to be found prior to about 200 AD. It was then that Christian theologians, eager to promote the theme of the Church's universality and its availability to all human beings irrespective of family, local, ethnic, or cultural origin, and to advance the idea of God's suzereignty over all the peoples on earth, found themselves going increasingly beyond Roman civilization in their writings, going to - mankind![21]

For the early Christians, the unity of humanity was not just a useful way of looking at the world: it was *God's* way of looking at it, and therefore gave a *correct* view of it.

I find myself agreeing with both accounts. Both accepted that the possibility of universal progress requires these presuppositions:

- Humanity as a unity
- Ordered and regular forces maintaining the world
- Gradual improvement in the past
- Anticipation of continued improvement in the future.

Bury could see that the idea of original sin undermines progress by taking us back to square one with the birth of every baby. Similarly the idea of eternal damnation is of such great significance for those who believe it that any this-worldly progress becomes virtually irrelevant.

Nisbet, however, spotted an additional ingredient. We can accept all four of those presuppositions and still ask why we would *want* progress. The answer will depend on what we mean by 'improvement'. Most modern answers have been in terms of new technologies or knowledge. What makes them count as progress rather than just change? The improvements, whatever they are, must be something we value. People who value new knowledge or technologies for their own sakes may think of them as progress, but progress tied to these aims is not guaranteed either to be universal or to continue in the future. If progress is to have a content which is more permanent than whatever a particular community desires for the time being, and if we are to expect this content to develop further and further in the future, we are in for a great deal of wishful thinking—*unless* we attribute some kind of overall design to the process. Nisbet therefore adds another presupposition:

- 'the image of progress as the unfolding through long ages of a design present from the very beginning of man's history'.[22]

It is the idea of universal design, continuing through the past and into the future, that gives universal progress its meaning. However, design implies a designer. Ancient polytheisms of divine conflict often provided designers, but not designs guaranteed to persist through time. Design adequate to justify universal progress is a distinctive feature of monotheism. Bury's strictures remind us that the coherent case for progress was established not by Christianity in general but by the monotheistic strand within it. More recently John Gray, who rejects the idea of progress, has blamed Christianity for the belief that human history has a meaning:

> Neither in the ancient pagan world nor in any other culture has human history ever been thought to have an overarching significance. In Greece and Rome, it was a series of natural cycles of growth and decline. In India, it was a collective dream, endlessly repeated. The idea that history must make sense is just a Christian prejudice.[23]

Is monotheism intolerant?

I now turn to the question of whether monotheism is intolerant. Critics often quote the eighteenth-century philosopher David Hume's comment that 'the intolerance of almost all religions, which have maintained the unity of god, is as remarkable as the contrary principle in polytheists.'[24] It is not that polytheistic societies were less prone to war but that, according to Hume and his successors, monotheism provides a reason for intolerance while polytheism rarely does.

Their most popular model of polytheistic tolerance is the ancient Roman empire. Rodney Stark makes much of it. To summarise his case, there was no obligation to honour any particular god and no limit to the number of gods one might honour. People were free to choose. Different gods were honoured for different purposes. One could adopt the cult of a new god without repudiating others. Veneration of any god could come and go, and get stronger or weaker, without any significant change of worldview or conversion experience. Priests might make a lifetime commitment to their god but there was no expectation that others would. Priests had a clientele, not a church. The general public patronised many gods, attending to one or another depending on their needs at any one time. There was no drive to convert others. Polytheistic societies could make great effort, but there were limits to what they would do on behalf of a god. Even when paganism was collapsing under the pressure of Christian missionary work, Stark notes, Graeco-Roman polytheism could not generate counter-missionaries. As for morality, there was much less interest in it. Instead the gods offered a variety of lifestyle choices. A Greek who valued drunken orgies might become a devotee of Dionysus; another, who preferred sobriety and a life of ordered moderation, might prefer Apollo; a warrior might honour Ares. People could in this way appeal to one god or another to justify their lifestyles. It was comparatively easy for worshippers to transfer allegiance. If an illness did not get healed by one god, they would try another.[25]

Taking this account as a measure, Stark finds monotheism intolerant. The god of monotheism can be offended, either by criticism or by the worship of other gods. Recently, indeed, there have been many reports of militant Muslims attacking critics of Islam. Stark argues that this is characteristic of monotheism:

> *Whenever a group within monotheism gains sufficient power, it will seek to silence all competitors* (other things being equal)... leaders of well-established religious monopolies will often tolerate minor instances of religious nonconformity—individuals and small groups that do not challenge their power and position. But real threats will bring real retribution.[26]

As a sociologist of religion Stark aims to describe the behaviour of monotheists rather than the logic of monotheism. Still, if this is what monotheism generates it raises the question of whether intolerance is an inevitable result. It is not. Stark is referring to the 'monotheism from above' described in Chapter 2. The offence is felt by the believers. They may be convinced that God feels offended too, but this only indicates the limits to their monotheism. A god who was offended by a lack of worship or the worship of other gods would be a threatened god. Such a feeling of offence would make good sense if God had defeated all rivals but was afraid of their continuing power. If there is only one god this is not the case. Moreover, if we have been created by the one and only god, our creator can hardly feel aggrieved at the way we have turned out.

Another criticism concerns the belief in election. Stark argues that each monotheist tradition claims to be the only true faith, and therefore rejects not only polytheism but also rival monotheisms:

> It is precisely God as a conscious, responsive, good supreme being of infinite scope—the One True God as conceived by the great monotheisms—who prompts awareness of idolatry, false Gods, and heretical religions. *Particularism,* the belief that a given religion is the *only true religion,* is *inherent in monotheism.*[27]

Where this comes from is no secret. As we saw in Chapter 3, the idea of a chosen race has its natural home in national polytheism. By identifying the supreme god of the world with the god of Israel, Second Isaiah was doing the same as the prophets of other nations. When people today associate monotheism with the idea of a chosen race, they are merely applying selective memory. We have forgotten the equivalent claims made on behalf of polytheistic nations.

The issue still arises. Evangelical Christians today often claim to be monotheists but argue that the Allah worshipped by Muslims is not the Christian God. Leaving aside the fact that 'Allah' is the Arabic for 'God' and is used as such by Arabic-speaking Christians, this is a conceptual muddle. Christians and Muslims both normally claim that there is only one god, so if Allah exists at all Allah must be God, and vice versa. Christians who describe Allah as an evil divinity simply reveal that they are not monotheists.

A more substantial point is what Stark describes as the *scope* of gods. In polytheism different gods have different scope. Some gods control a little, some a lot. Believers are willing to make greater sacrifices for a god of greater scope who can offer more. In monotheism the one god has infinite scope. This maximises the tendency for loyalty. As he remarks of ancient Jews, 'No running off to Baal if response to one's request is not immediately forthcoming'. The effect is increased if rewards in the next life are on offer. It is in monotheism, not polytheism, that martyrdom for one's faith is valued.[28] Monotheists think their beliefs are absolute truths which everybody needs to know:

> The armies of Rome, imperial China, or ancient Egypt did not march on behalf of divine will... Only One True God can generate great undertakings out of primarily religious motivations, and chief among these is the desire, indeed the duty, to spread knowledge of the One True God.[29]

Here Stark observes a real difference between polytheism and monotheism. Unfortunately, like other modern critics of monotheism, he seems to overlook the significance of the difference. These critics do not actually believe in the gods of ancient polytheism; they are simply using them as a stick with which to beat monotheism. They see no reason for intolerance because from their secular perspective polytheism and monotheism alike belong in the 'religion' bubble, irrelevant to all else. They therefore overlook the reasons not only for monotheism but also for the ancient polytheist practices they claim to consider superior. Those practices made sense within a conservative, pre-Axial theology where the many different forces of nature were expressions of different gods. Cultic acts were performed in the belief that they might persuade the relevant god to modify his or her behaviour. In other words, they were attempts to modify the forces of nature. We also attempt to modify the forces of nature, but in a different way. Whereas they associated natural forces with free divine agents who might be open to persuasion, we associate them with consistent regularities that can be understood and manipulated. If we are to compare ancient Roman paganism with a modern equivalent, therefore, the appropriate equivalent would be science and technology. One person researches possible cures for HIV, another develops a new strain of wheat. We do not debate whether they 'tolerate' each other because they are doing different things. In the same way, when ancient pagans worshipped different gods they were doing different things.

Because we today attribute natural forces to impersonal processes we look for ways to control them—to predict the weather, to find cures for illnesses. Our solutions are cumulative. We expect progress. When ancient polytheists believed the forces surrounding them were personal and unpredictable, there was no reason to expect cumulative progress. One of the reasons, therefore, why ancient Roman polytheists were tolerant of different lifestyles is that they did not expect future progress. It was not that nothing mattered, but that in the long run nothing could be changed. The way things were was the way things always would be. Hope for improvement was limited to persuading a particular god on a particular matter at a particular time.

This lack of hope was supported by the characteristic descriptions of the gods. They were in practice based on human models, so the logic was circular: the status quo was justified by appeal to gods who were themselves images of the status quo. The tolerance of different lifestyles, so often praised by opponents of monotheism today, was not so much approval of diversity as failure to expect that life could be any different. As Gray puts it:

> For pagans, history is modelled on natural processes. Growth and decline, death and rebirth—these are the categories pagans apply to history... In this pagan view, the life of each generation may have meaning, but history as a whole has none. It may well be doubted if a pagan could have thought of writing a history of mankind.[30]

Ancient Roman paganism therefore tolerated not just different lifestyles but conflicting ones: war, oppression, starvation and intolerance itself were all accepted as the way things were and always would be. When we today learn about the living conditions of ordinary people in the ancient Roman Empire we are likely to be horrified and wonder why more was not done to improve their lot. The answer is that, in their conservative polytheism, there was no expectation that things would ever change.

In the Roman Empire this conservative, pre-Axial theology was already declining. Paradoxically the decline provides evidence for Stark's case. Traditional practices often continue longer than the reasons for them. A modern parallel would be that over the last sixty years many Christian priests have had increasing doubts about whether they believe in God, or the Communion service. They have continued to conduct these services while privately wondering whether there is any point. In the same way, in the ancient Roman Empire, as the older beliefs declined many people continued their traditional practices while feeling increasingly doubtful about the rationale behind them. Such doubts can produce a kind of tolerance: one is not sure how much one's cultic act matters, or whether it matters at all, or whether it is really much the same as somebody else's apparently different cultic act. This is evidence not of a tolerant theology but of a declining tradition; after all, if the tradition had held all along that none of it mattered, they would never have worshipped any gods at all.

Stark's point about the different scope of gods therefore has much truth in it. For those who classify all religious beliefs as irrelevant, intolerance is a puzzle. Those, on the other hand, who think their beliefs about God are both true and important are naturally keen to spread the news. However there is nothing distinctively religious in this. It simply means that when religious beliefs matter to us, we treat them the way we treat everything else that matters to us. With its stronger roots in Axial Age values, monotheism is more committed to seeking change. Recognising the difference, the Egyptologist Jan Assmann argues that we tolerate an opinion when we disagree with it but are 'powerful or generous enough not to have to treat it as a threat'.[31]

Truth-claims threaten contrary truth-claims. In the case of science we take this for granted:

> The truths of science may well, for the most part, be relative and have a limited life span, but that does not mean that they are compatible with everything else under the sun, for they have their own criteria of validity, verifiability, and falsifiability, which they are obliged to meet. This has become so self-evident to us that it has become practically inseparable from our concept of knowledge.[32]

The analogy is apt. Tell scientists that evolution never happened or that the earth is flat, and they can become intolerant quite quickly, insisting that these false views should not be given equal treatment on television or in schools. Similarly, when our nearest and dearest are ill we do not adopt an airy tolerance of all possible beliefs about the causes and cures. We seek out the truth, drawing on whatever resources are available. If we get convincing information that the patient is taking the wrong tablets, we pass it on as convincingly as possible and we may get angry with people who disagree. Some beliefs matter to us too much to allow for an easy-going tolerance of contrary beliefs.

I am not seeking to defend the aggressive techniques of evangelism that have become common in recent times, among both Christians and Muslims, and have given religion in general a bad name. Stark rightly observes that these activities are performed in the name of monotheistic religions. Those who care about truth should take trouble to listen as well as teach, and expect to change their beliefs in the light of new evidence. However he and similar critics of monotheism make two errors. One is to fail to distinguish between true monotheism and the veneer of monotheism covering very different agendas. This leads them to blame the icing for the over-baked cake. The other is to overlook the real reasons for religious beliefs and practices.

Conclusion

Believing in gods is natural. To be more precise, reflecting on our circumstances, observing that we are maintained by forces we do not understand, and asking how we can make the most of life is natural; and answering this question in terms of the purposes intended by those forces is natural. Speculation about the divine therefore has an ethical element at its heart. The way we see fit to live will to some extent express the purposes of the divinities we believe in, though most of us are prone to plenty of self-delusion and inconsistency.

Beliefs about gods vary immensely. I have argued that the most ethically significant distinction is between divine conflict and divine harmony: between forces who create us to meet their needs and forces who create us for our own sakes. If we are created to meet the needs of the gods there are limits to what we can expect from this life. The limits will depend on what the gods have provided for us and what they want from us. These limits provide an agenda for human life: we have to meet the demands of the gods, and beyond that we have to work out how to minimise the misfortunes the gods leave us with. Life is what it is, and there is no expectation of long-term improvement. Characteristically the agenda is communal and consequentialist: the community works out how to protect itself from the various threats by judging the likely consequences of any course of action. In the process individuals may be sacrificed for the sake of others.

If, on the other hand, we have been created for our own sakes, as recipients of an act of blessing, the appropriate response is very different. What life gives us is designed to be good for us. Our gratitude to the divine, and our trust in the quality of what we have been given, are not limited in the same way. We can welcome our physical environment, our bodies and our mental capacities as just what we need, and celebrate them. The hardships and tragedies we experience are to be interpreted not as unavoidable limits to the goodness of life but as problems we can seek to overcome. To say that our lives have been given to us as a blessing is to say that every one of us has been created for a fulfilled and happy life. So every individual counts; nobody is to be sacrificed in the interests of another. The quality of a civilisation, from a monotheistic perspective, is to be judged not by competing against other civilisations, nor by overcoming the limits of our physical environment, but by how we care for each other and help each other to flourish. We can see this in the way the most disadvantaged and the outcasts are treated.

Thus divine conflict and divine harmony produce different accounts of how we relate to the divine, and these lead to radically contrasting ethical systems. One tells us we are pawns in the games of the gods, of little or no importance in ourselves, with a history that is going nowhere, while everything that matters happens on a divine plane that we cannot see. The other tells us we have been created for our own good, to flourish and be happy. We matter more. We have more responsibility. We can achieve more. We can make progress.

The difference between the two is of prime importance. They produce contrasting accounts of what we can do and what we ought to do. Although political, economic and military debates today are rarely described in these terms, the tension between them is still a major influence in generating the contrasting agendas of governments and their oppositions.

Every living faith tradition is to some extent a mixture of the two. The next chapter will illustrate how Christianity modified its monotheism with polytheistic themes, thereby provoking a more radical rejection of the divine.

Chapter 5. Christian polytheism

So far this book has focused on different kinds of gods people have believed in. Modern society offers another option, that there are no gods at all. This is often presented as common sense, a default position onto which religious traditions have added theories about gods. However, the history of atheism tells a different story. While earlier texts occasionally reveal individual speculation that the gods of their culture might not exist, popular atheism has a distinctive history. Together with secularism it began in reaction against some very pessimistic themes in late medieval western European Christianity. This chapter will describe these pessimistic themes, showing how their theological character is polytheistic rather than monotheistic. The next chapter will describe the secular and atheist reactions against them.

Early Christianity

We saw in Chapter 3 how some scholars believe that monotheism was not established until the early Christian era, with the debates between Jews, Catholic Christians and Gnostics. New Testament scholars today describe Christianity as diverse from the start. Many of its early debates were between monotheists and polytheists. Some distinguished between the god of the Old Testament and the god of Jesus. Such views were suppressed by the dominant tradition, but the debate left its mark. The New Testament contains many affirmations of monotheism. The created order is as God intended, secure and good. Paul's speech at the Areopagus in Athens, for example, is described by Eric Osborn as 'pure monotheism'.[1] In the Synoptic gospels we read about the goodness of nature, not just for humans but in its own relationship with God.[2] There is similar concern for animals.[3] Many of Jesus' parables use illustrations from nature and in the process presuppose its fundamental goodness as something to be enjoyed.[4]

The theme continued in early Christian writings. The second century bishop Irenaeus stressed it in opposition to Gnostics who believed the world had been made by angels contrary to the will of God:

> It will not be regarded as at all probable by those who know that God stands in need of nothing, and that he created and made all things by his word... He himself in himself, after a fashion which we can neither describe nor conceive, predestinating all things, formed them as he pleased, bestowing harmony on all things, and assigning them their own place, and the beginning of their creation.[5]

Responding to the claim that God was constrained by necessity to create a flawed world, he replied:

> It would have been much better, more consistent, and more God-like, to have cut off at the beginning the principle of this kind of necessity, than afterwards, as if moved by repentance, to endeavour to extirpate the results of necessity when they had reached such a development.[6]

This appeal to God's power and goodness was a live issue that distinguished the dominant 'early Catholic' Christians from Gnostics and polytheists. Later Christians have often tried to harmonise these texts with other, more pessimistic Christian doctrines.[7] The move is easily made since Irenaeus and his contemporaries were not always consistent. Unfortunately this means that the monotheism of these texts has often been overlooked by theologians of later ages.

Christianity began among the dispossessed and destitute of Galilee. John Dominic Crossan describes three ways the economically oppressed tend to respond to deteriorating conditions.[8] All three appear in the New Testament and the early Church.

One is to work for justice. This is a characteristic product of monotheism: if a good god creates a good world but gives us power to harm each other, then suffering must be caused by human wrongdoing rather than the divine realm or environmental factors. It remains the basis for many movements that seek to change social and political systems in order to improve conditions.

The second response is the ascetic one. Experience of life is so grim that hope of a better life here on earth is abandoned. Gnostics developed theories about how the world was made by evil or ignorant gods. Ascetics would aim to have as little as possible to do with it, and instead pin their hopes on a better life after death. This more pessimistic theology is influential in the Gospel of Thomas and scholars debate how much of it is in Paul and John. Most of the later New Testament epistles seem to oppose Gnostic theories of one sort or another.[9]

Historians usually tell us that the Catholics won the argument. Christianity subsequently denied the existence of evil gods, let alone evil gods who took part in creating the world. However the very negative evaluation of this world survived; later Christians have often described it as a 'vale of tears'. Why a good god should create an unpleasant world needs explaining, so the negative evaluation led to the persistence of polytheistic theories within Christianity.

The third response is the millenarian one. Here the oppressed find it impossible to believe that God will allow the oppressive situation to continue. A new age is beginning as divine intervention puts things right, or soon will. Jewish millenarianism was already well established by the time of Jesus. Many hoped God would begin a new age by driving out evil spirits. Some Jews were attracted to Jesus because they hoped he would be God's agent in this process. Mark captures the mood of excitement: one sequence of four miracles (Mark 4:35-5:43) seems to have been put together to express the comprehensive range of the victory: over the forces of nature, evil spirits, physical illness and death.[10]

All three of these responses appear in the New Testament. Once it had been canonised as Holy Scripture, they all had scriptural warrant despite the contradictions. The ascetic and millenarian ones affirmed the destitute Christian's experience of being oppressed by the forces governing the world. Extreme oppression often leads to a black-and-white sense of good and evil. This is expressed in the New Testament's frequent references to the devil. He usually performs the same role as the heavenly satans in the Old Testament, a role which can be translated 'test' or 'tempt': the Greek word can mean either. Compared with the Old Testament texts, though, he has become a single individual being and seems to have a freer rein. Occasionally he acts as an opponent of God, especially in Revelation.[11]

These two roles are contradictory: Satan cannot be both obedient servant and enemy to God at the same time. If he is God's servant, God is still responsible for evil. If on the other hand he is God's enemy, a cause of evil independent of God, the question arises as to why God allows him to operate in this way. God either colludes or is powerless to stop it. The contradiction has played an important role throughout the history of Christianity. It still allows Christian teachers to duck and weave in explaining evil. When asked why unbelievers are to spend eternity in hell they can tell us that this is God's justice—so Satan is God's obedient agent of punishment. When asked why there is so much wrong with the state of the world, God is not at fault; Satan is to be blamed.

The black-and-white judgements were also applied to spirits. Pagans thought they were surrounded by invisible spirits that varied in character. Wayne Meeks describes how the early Christians divided them into good ones and evil ones:

> The leaders of the Christian movement from the very beginning struggled to impose upon the common, helter-skelter picture of a world filled with unseen powers a bipolar division that was fundamentally moral. On the one side are God and his "messengers" or "angels"; on the other are Satan and his "demons."'[12]

In the thought world of the ancients, illness was usually caused by gods and spirits deliberately causing trouble. A persistent problem with monotheism was how to provide an alternative explanation. One Jewish view was that illness must be punishment for disobeying God's commands.[13] Needless to say people noticed that it comes to the obedient and disobedient alike. The book of Job elaborated its failure but did not provide a convincing alternative. I shall offer my own response in Chapters 13 and 14, but for now we should note that demons were the most common explanation.

As with the devil, God must be either responsible for their actions or powerless to stop them. However, spirits varied. Around the time of Jesus urban pagans believed in a variety of supernatural forces with a wide remit. Paul referred to some of them: 'principalities and powers', 'thrones and dominions', 'heights' and 'depths', 'the elemental spirits of the world'.[14] Rural society was different. Here the emphasis was on local spirits with limited power. It is these local spirits that we hear about in Mark's gospel. Matthew and Luke copied him.

Jesus' position is of particular interest to Christians today. The exorcism narratives in the gospels give the impression that Jesus must have believed in these local spirits. However there is a case to the contrary. The major philosophies of his day generally had little time for them. Paul may not have believed in them.[15] It would not have been unusual for Jesus to have disbelieved in them too.

Evidence to this effect comes from the gospels' descriptions of exorcisms. Other exorcists used formulas, incantations, lists of powerful names or complex liturgies. The logic behind them was partly magical, partly the belief that most evil spirits had limited intelligence and could be frightened into running away. Jesus' exorcisms dispensed with these actions. Characteristically, according to the accounts we have, he simply commanded the spirits to leave.

Mark took this to mean that they knew who Jesus was and capitulated quickly.[16] An alternative explanation is that Jesus' diagnoses were different. I find this convincing because I have been in this situation many times myself, summoned as a parish priest to get rid of an evil spirit or a ghost from a house. In most cases I found it easy to make a judgement about the real cause—faulty electrics or bad relationships. On the other hand it was usually impossible to persuade the people that the demons did not exist. Usually, therefore, I would perform some authoritative act designed to give them confidence that, whatever had happened in the past, there were no longer any evil forces present. The act would need to be bold enough to inspire confidence but not misleading. For all we know Jesus' approach may have been along the same lines. Of course we cannot be sure. Meier, after examining the stories of Jesus' exorcisms, remarks that 'we must admit how meager the data and therefore how fragile our judgments are.'[17]

Establishment

Three hundred years after the death of Jesus the Roman emperor Constantine put his trust in the god of Christianity. From then on bishops were to be high status officials acting on his behalf. At his request they produced a creed that is still recited in churches today.[18] In the process Christianity changed. It could no longer appeal to a higher moral authority that passed judgement on the emperor. It ceased to express the faith of the poor and dispossessed. Instead it became a 'monotheism from above'. Once again the supreme god would have to provide a model for a ruler constantly striving to maximise his power at the expense of his enemies. Garth Fowden writes of the period from the second to the ninth centuries CE that Europeans had a

> ...conviction that knowledge of the One God both justifies the exercise of imperial power and makes it more effective. Antecedents of this idea can be traced in the polytheist world of ancient Greece and Rome, but Constantine placed it at the center of Roman political ideology when he became a Christian.[19]

In this new dispensation the theologians of the fourth and fifth centuries needed to show that Christ had achieved a great victory and inaugurated a new age for the human race three hundred years earlier. Thus arose doctrines of the Work of Christ, or the Atonement. Theologians searched the Christian scriptures for information about Christ's achievement. What they found was a diverse range of images primarily concerned with other matters. These images were then turned into theories of what Christ had achieved. Often, Frances Young notes, conflicting theories were proposed by the same theologian:

> Traditional patterns of thought were adopted without a real appreciation of the contradictions involved. God is love; God is angry. God is ultimately responsible for everything; the devil is responsible for evil. God sent his Son to overcome evil; God was placated by his Son's sacrifice.[20]

The theories of what Christ achieved are usually classified into three types. Following this pattern I shall refer to the work of Jesus as Example, Victory or Substitution.

The Example theory is ethical. Unlike the other two it is in principle consistent with divine harmony. The concept of a person voluntarily dying for their city, friends and family seems to have been widespread at the time. For Jews the Maccabees provided a model. They had rebelled against the emperor of the day and been given exemplary punishments, death by torture. Jews later honoured them as heroes dying for the cause.[21] New Testament authors echo this tradition:

> For it is to your credit if, being aware of God, you endure pain while suffering unjustly. If you endure when you are beaten for doing wrong, where is the credit in that? But if you endure when you do right and suffer for it, you have God's approval. For to this you have been called, because Christ also suffered for you, leaving you an example, so that you should follow in his steps.[22]

It was a common theme among early Christians.[23] The best medieval exponent of the theory was Abelard, who argued that love and forgiveness enable others to love and forgive, and the suffering and death of Jesus was a supreme instance.[24] Hastings Rashdall's *The Idea of Atonement in Christian Theology*, 1919, reaffimed Abelard's view. Salvation works through human nature; Christ's death is significant not just in itself, but because of his life.[25] A more recent defender of this position was Marcus Borg. Whereas Rashdall argued that the death of Jesus should be understood within the context of his ministry, Borg drew on more recent research into the historical Jesus to add flesh to the bones:

> Jesus was not simply an unfortunate victim of a domination system's brutality. He was also a protagonist filled with passion. His passion, his message, was about the kingdom of God. He spoke to peasants as a voice of religious protest against the central economic and political institutions of his day. He attracted a following, took his movement to Jerusalem at the season of Passover, and there challenged the authorities

> with public acts and public debates.[26]

The second theory was that Jesus achieved some kind of victory over evil powers. From the New Testament to the fourth century, Young writes,

> …the Christian felt himself to be involved in the warfare between God and the devil, good and evil, light and darkness, life and death, righteousness and sin… The martyr felt himself at war with the opposing forces of evil when he died for his faith. With the powers of evil, God had to do battle or business, and the supreme moment of victory was the Cross of Christ.[27]

The victory was often associated with the idea of ransom. Paul had described people being 'slaves to sin', 'sold to sin' and bought with a price, the blood of Christ.[28] Mark 10:45 became an influential text:

> For the Son of Man came not to be served but to serve, and to give his life a ransom for many.[29]

The idea sprang to life in the fourth century.[30] However, as theologians speculated about what God had put right, they had to explain what had gone wrong in the first place. To answer this question they produced the idea of a primeval Fall. Christians today often confuse the doctrine of the Fall with the doctrine of sin. The idea of sin is that God has created us capable of doing good and evil, and allows us to do either. The Fall, on the other hand, was a single event: God originally created a perfect world but, contrary to God's intentions, it developed imperfections. Such a divine failure was common among polytheists, and Christian Gnostics produced a variety of creation narratives to explain which god did what. However the only references to a

Fall in the Bible are two passing mentions in Paul's Epistle to the Romans[31] while his focus was elsewhere. The third Chapter of Genesis, with the story of Adam, Eve and the serpent, does not mention it; it was the early Christians who first interpreted the story this way.

It was not till the fourth century that theologians developed the three-stage historical schema of creation, fall and redemption which is now often considered traditional Christian doctrine. At first God, being good, created a perfectly good world. Adam and Eve however sinned, either of their own free will or because of Satan's tempting. If Satan tempted them, Satan must have already fallen.[32] The problem was: whoever was responsible for the first sin, they must have been perfect before they sinned, so why did a perfect person sin? It was a matter of intense speculation. Augustine offered the most thorough analysis, inevitably concluding that God must have predestined the Fall right from the start.[33] The 'darkness' of the fallen angels, including Satan, 'although it had been a fitting part of the divine plan, was not a fit enough subject for the divine approbation'.[34] So God deliberately created the fallen angels in a manner of which God could not approve! Hick comments:

> They seem to have been in the same kind of discouraging situation as someone endowed by nature with irresistible criminal tendencies who discovers that a prison cell was reserved for him before he was born.[35]

It is this contradiction within Augustine's system which has bequeathed to western Christians a double bind. On the one hand we cannot help being the way we are because that is the way we have been since the Fall; on the other, it is still *our own fault*.

The Victory theory was the most common understanding of Christ's achievement from the fourth century until the eleventh when Anselm's supplanted it. It was revived in the 1930s with

Gustav Aulén's *Christus Victor* and more recently by N T Wright, who combines it with the Substitution theory. Wright attributes the lack of interest in it to 'an obvious credibility gap between such a claim and the realities of the world'. We can hardly deny that the gap exists. How, then, does Wright close it? He would need to show how the state of the world after the death and resurrection of Christ reveals less activity by God's enemies than previously. What he offers, though, is different:

> Somehow, the suffering of Christians in the present, as they share Christ's sufferings and groan in awaiting their final redemption, is to become the means by which the Spirit of God prays from within the heart of a world in pain, in order that the world itself might be redeemed. Somehow, the witness of the martyrs, as they live their lives and die their deaths in obedience to the gospel of Jesus, puts into effect the victory of the cross above and beyond the immediate impact that their witness may have on the actual observers.[36]

The passage continues with two more somehows. Clearly he does not know how, yet nearly two thousand years have passed since the victory was apparently achieved; by now, surely, we should be able to observe some results. Instead he tells us:

> It is not enough to analyze the causes of oppression and suffering in the world and to encourage people to stand up to them. Darker powers, unseen forces, are involved in these struggles... and only the belief that the principalities and powers have in fact been led as a bedraggled and defeated rabble in Christ's triumphant procession will provide the right foundation for a true Christian political activity.

On the one hand the darker powers and unseen forces are actively opposing us today, but on the other—on the same page!—they have been a 'bedraggled and defeated rabble' since the time of Christ. Aulén offers a similar combination.[37] It is as though the idea of Christ's victory has the same appeal as those television cartoons where the baddie is defeated every time but reappears, as strong and confident as ever, at the beginning of the next episode.

Mark's gospel expected a real this-worldly change: after Jesus had defeated the devil, life in this world would be different. Natural disasters, illness, death and demonic possession would be vanquished. It never happened. What did happen was that Mark's gospel was hallowed by its presence in the New Testament, convincing some Christians that a new age must have begun *somehow*. The tension remains in Christian discourse today.

The Substitution theory began as an analogy to the ancient practice of sacrificing an animal as a substitute for a human who deserved punishment. The pagan rationale was that angry gods demanded the death of guilty people but would accept an animal instead. Thus the sacrifice was a form of propitiation, re-establishing a positive relationship. The early Christians sometimes used the language of these guilt offerings as a way to describe the death of Jesus. Paul wrote that Jesus

> ...was handed over to death for our trespasses and was raised for our justification.[38]

The theory was affirmed by fourth century theologians along with the Victory theory. The first major analysis of it was Anselm's *Cur Deus Homo* (1097). In his day rulers saw it as their task to punish breaches of the law in order to maintain the system of rights and obligations. Anselm saw God as similarly responsible for punishing sinners to redress the moral balance. To be forgiven we must repay what we owe, but humanity is unable to repay all we owe to God. Anselm's resolution was that the repayment was made by Christ who was both human and divine:

> There is no-one... who *can* make this satisfaction except God himself... But no-one *ought* to make it except man; otherwise man does not make satisfaction.'[39]

The theory was developed further by Calvin[40] and has had many defenders in the last century. Emil Brunner's *The Mediator* provided an extensive analysis. More recent defenders include John Stott, J I Packer and N T Wright. It is a major influence in churches today. The Universities and Colleges Christian Fellowship's Doctrinal Basis, to which student Christian Unions in Britain subscribe, states that

> Sinful human beings [i.e. 'the whole of humankind'] are redeemed from the guilt, penalty and power of sin only through the sacrificial death once and for all time of their representative and substitute, Jesus Christ, the only mediator between them and God.[41]

Substitutionists stress the seriousness of sin, its incompatibility with God's holiness,[42] the necessity of punishment[43] and the inability of humans to make amends. Because Christ died for us, 'God's holy love was "satisfied"'.[44]

To many it sounds as though a sympathetic Jesus negotiated with an angry God and offered to sacrifice his life for the sake of humanity. This would clearly be a case of divine conflict, but substitutionists insist that atonement is God's work throughout; it is God in Christ who provides satisfaction. Nor is it a matter of God's justice being in conflict with God's love. God's love is just. Wright argues:

> God's wrath is the necessary outworking of his love. If God does not hate slavery, child-abuse, and the exploitation of the poor; and if God is not determined to condemn them and rid his world of them, then God is neither good nor loving.[45]

Nevertheless dualism is not so easily removed from the picture. It is one thing for God to hate slavery, another to subject slave-owners to afterlife cruelties far greater than they imposed on their slaves.[46] Divine conflict is unmistakeably present, albeit within the same god. Central to the theory is God's inability to forgive.[47] It is worlds away from the New Testament evidence that Jesus was a friend of 'sinners and tax collectors'.[48] Yet it is essential to the theory. Substitutionists, especially Brunner and Stott, often wrote as though they were furious and uncomprehending at the extent of humanity's sinfulness. The motive is clear: forgiveness has to seem unrealistic. Our sinfulness has to seem intolerable to God. Yet if we ask who established this intolerance, the only possible answer is that God did. If God created us the way we are, with our freedom to sin, the fact that we do can hardly be cause for surprise. If God is angry and intolerant, the problem is of God's own making. It would not be of God's own making if human sinfulness had been caused by some other deity like Satan, but then we would be back to a divine conflict with an enemy of God able to upset God's plans. In either case the Substitution theory depends on divine conflict.

It seems to parallel the Victory theory in an odd way. Defenders of the Victory theory claim that Christ defeated the spiritual powers of evil, but at the same time argue that the Christian's task today is to struggle against them. This leaves us wondering just how much of a victory Christ achieved. Similarly, defenders of the Substitution theory characteristically argue both that Christ's death on the cross paid the penalty for everybody's sins once for all, and that most of us will burn in Hell anyway. It is as though many people find their favoured theme too powerful to let it go. Whether victory or punishment, the psychological attraction of it leads its devotees to apply it both to their interpretation of Christian doctrine and to the state of the world in their own day. The result, in both cases, is a contradiction. It is as though some of us are just too competitive and some of us are just too punitive.

So over the course of the centuries the optimistic and bottom-up message shared by many Christians, albeit inconsistently, was overlaid by very different accounts of how humanity relates to the divine. The active roles of the devil, evil spirits and an angry, punitive God re-established divine conflict and made the condition of humanity once again tragic.

Christian pessimism

The most influential threat was Hell. As far back as the evidence takes us people have always believed in life after death. At some stage there developed a distinction between the after-lives of good and evil people. For Jews this seems to have first occurred in the second century BCE. Praising heroes who had been tortured and killed in the Maccabean wars, they felt there should be some reward for them. They also felt that their enemies should not share it. Perhaps this is typical of how the idea developed: a black-and-white division of humanity into allies and enemies, with intense bitterness towards oppressors. Early Christianity revived it when persecuted:

> Those who worship the beast and its image, and receive a mark on their foreheads or on their hands, they will also drink the wine of God's wrath, poured unmixed into the cup of his anger, and they will be tormented with fire and sulphur in the presence of the holy angels and in the presence of the Lamb. And the smoke of their torment goes up for ever and ever. There is no rest day or night (Revelation 14:9-11).

Other Christians wrote down their visions of Hell, describing in detail the most painful tortures they could imagine and looking forward to their adversaries enduring them.[49] Recent psychological tests have shown that many people are keen to impose suffering on their adversaries, even at great cost to themselves.[50]

In the early years of Christianity the persecuted felt the same. This was the Hell of the martyrs, embittered by persecution.

When Christianity became the established religion of the Roman Empire afterlives of eternal torture, instead of being forgotten, were universalised. Augustine's doctrine of Original Sin provided the justification. Adam and Eve had committed a very grave sin by eating the forbidden fruit. The whole human race was 'in' Adam at the time.[51] All humanity as his descendants deserve eternal punishment in Hell. In an influential passage Augustine explains why a minority will be saved:

> Mankind is divided between those in whom the power of merciful grace is demonstrated, and those in whom is shown the might of just retribution. Neither of these could be displayed in respect of all mankind; for if all had remained condemned to the punishment entailed by just condemnation, then God's merciful grace would not have been seen at work in anyone; on the other hand, if all had been transferred from darkness into light, the truth of God's vengeance would not have been made evident. Now there are many more condemned by vengeance than are released by mercy; and the reason for this is that it should in this way be made plain what was the due of all mankind.[52]

The idea took on a new significance later. For about three centuries, from the fourteenth to the seventeenth, there was a succession of devastating plagues across Europe. They made a difference to the way people thought of life. You may be young and healthy today, but you may be dead by next week: what will happen to you then? We today can look back on the appalling standards of hygiene at the time. A book of etiquette, published in 1558, advises people not to pick up excrement they observe on the street, show it to somebody else and invite them to smell it. There must have been people who did this. The book disapproves not for health reasons, but because it is not a 'very fine habit'.[53] At the time they found it easier to attribute the plagues to God's anger. A genuine terror of eternal damnation became widespread. We today are so familiar with Christians who claim to believe in Hell but adopt an easygoing complacency about it, that it may come as a surprise to reflect on what it must have meant to people who took it seriously. This was the age of the *danses macabres,* the witch hunts and stories of pacts with the devil. Visions of the afterlife and paintings on church walls made it clear that the sufferings of Hell would be extreme and eternal. According to Jacques Le Goff,

> Unless we bear in mind the obsession with salvation and the fear of hell that motivated the people of the Middle Ages, we shall never understand their mentality.[54]

Two confusions rubbed salt into the wound. One was about who would be saved. This applied to Protestants and Catholics alike. Salvation was only for those who accepted the doctrines of the true church, whichever one that was, or for those who lived good lives (the appeal of indulgences), or for those at peace with Christ at the moment of death, or for those whom God had predestined from eternity. The uncertainty meant nobody was quite sure.

The other confusion is the one already noted about the role of Satan. Was Satan God's obedient torturer or God's enemy? To think that God stands on the sidelines watching helplessly while Satan triumphs was unacceptable to Protestants and Catholics alike. Satan must be God's obedient servant, as he is in most New Testament texts. Yet to draw attention to this arrangement is to make God responsible for the eternal tortures of the majority. Belief in Hell remains credible when people are unclear about the relationship between these divinities.

Hell has practical implications. It was obvious to many

governments and military commanders that heretics needed to be suppressed, by force if necessary, to prevent them enticing other people to eternal damnation. Since no atrocity could be worse, every cruelty seemed worth the price.[55] If a just and righteous god was going to torture sinners, godly governments should too. A German newssheet of 1603 describes the execution of two teenagers found guilty of murder. After the gory details the moralising conclusion speaks volumes about the god they believed in:

> They began by stripping the two boys, then they whipped them in such a way that their blood abundantly covered the ground. Then the executioner stuck red-hot irons on their wounds, at which they screamed such screams that it is impossible to describe them. Next they cut off their hands... The execution lasted about twenty minutes. Boys and girls attended, as well as a great crowd of adults. In this torture, one and all admired the just judgments of God and learned from this example.[56]

By the end of the seventeenth century Hell was losing its centrality in people's minds: if God consigns the majority to eternal suffering, how can God be called good? However it was revived in the nineteenth century. In 1860 there was a major public controversy over the publication of *Essays and Reviews,* in which two Church of England clergymen confessed to not believing in it. The outcry was so great that it eclipsed the debate over Darwin's *Origin of Species,* published the previous year. A court case exonerated the unbelieving clergy, much to the disgust of most church leaders. The popularity of Christian belief in Hell at that time is illustrated by Joseph Furniss's books for children, first published in the 1860s. They contain descriptions of children suffering eternally for their sins, like this one about a girl wearing a bonnet of fire.

> It is pressed down close over her head; it burns into the skin; it scorches the bone of the skull and makes it smoke… Think what a headache that girl must have… She is wrapped in flames, for her frock is on fire… There she stands burning and scorched; there she will stand for ever burning and scorched! When that girl was alive… she cared only for one thing, and that was dress!... And now her dress is her punishment.[57]

These books sold in millions. In other words, millions of parents wanted their children to read them and be suitably terrified.

Another pessimistic element that developed within Christianity is self-denial.

> Man is born for work, for suffering, for fear, and—what is worse—for death.

So wrote Cardinal Lotario di Segni, later to become Pope Innocent III, at the end of the twelfth century, in his *De Contemptu Mundi*.[58] One negative assessment of God leads to another. Terror of eternal punishment after death does not encourage a happy and contented life before it; apart from the fear, a god willing so much distress hereafter cannot be expected to provide a bed of roses now. While a gloomy attitude to life is common enough, an attitude of 'contempt for the world' was encouraged in the medieval monasteries. The main components were a strong sense of guilt about sin, disapproval of the world, disapproval of the body and a sense of fleeting time. Delumeau describes how to Roger of Caen the fleeting joys of this life engendered eternal suffering; to Jean de Fécamp earth was an exile; to Philip the Chancellor flesh was a dungeon; to Peter Damian the senses were the pimps of sin. Throughout the Middle Ages monks and nuns inflicted on themselves acts of mortification which seem astonishing today. What is most frequently condemned is sexual activity.[59]

Every society seeks to discipline the sexuality of its members, but Christianity developed a negative attitude to it from early days. The first reference is 1 Corinthians 7 where Paul responds with ambivalence to Christians who thought they should renounce sexual activity for life. In the following century renunciation of sexuality came to be a sign of the new age brought in by Christ; death would become a thing of the past so there was no need for procreation.[60] On the other hand people continued to sin, get ill and die. Once again it was Augustine who turned a collection of inconsistent beliefs into a stable theological system. He did not disapprove of sexual activity in itself; it was the passions involved, and the loss of rational control, which he considered sinful. Any lover of wisdom, he believed, would prefer to beget children without the irrationality of lust,[61] but it occurred, he noticed, even in the sexual intercourse of baptised Christians.[62] Jerome went further in his disapproval of marriage, with long diatribes including the remark for which he is best known: 'Marriage populates the earth: virginity populates heaven'.[63]

So it was that medieval monks and nuns learned to think of sexual activity as sinful. Every stirring of desire would then seem like a reminder of their sinful condition.[64] This comes across strongly in the medieval penitentials, advice to priests on how to respond to the sins reported by penitents in the confessional. Although they varied, the trend was for every sexual act to be forbidden except heterosexual intercourse within marriage, with the man on top and the woman underneath.[65] Even that was severely restricted: no sex for the ten weeks of each year covered by Lent and Advent, or on Wednesdays or Fridays throughout the year. Different penitentials listed different additions. It is easy to imagine how difficult it must have been for priests in the confessional, struggling to suppress their own libido, to come to terms with the moral permissibility of sexual relations for others. Confessors were to ask so many questions about who did what with what and where, that their Victorian successors were shocked:

> Evil deeds, the imagination of which may perhaps have dimly floated through our minds in our darkest moments, are here tabulated and reduced to a system. It is hard to see how anyone could busy himself with such literature and not be the worse for it.[66]

Medieval Christians could argue that God must want at least some people to produce children. Luther's reaffirmation of marriage gave Protestantism a more positive view of it. By then, though, the superiority of celibacy had been so well established that defences of marriage depended heavily on the need for children. Even within Protestantism there remained a tendency to disapprove of non-procreative sexual activity. This was expressed, in the nineteenth and twentieth centuries, in the churches' opposition to contraception. Once contraception ceased to be controversial (even among Roman Catholics, despite the 1967 encyclical *Humanae Vitae* forbidding it) public disapproval of sex acts concentrated on homosexuality, which has been unfortunate for gays and lesbians but leaves heterosexuals freer from ecclesiastical disapproval than they have been for a long time—perhaps since ancient times.

Negative attitudes to sexuality affect us differently because we vary in the strength of our libidos, but they have set countless Christians at odds with their bodies. Each of us, in the privacy of our own thoughts, can be weighed down with a sense of guilt, about our desires if not our actions. It fits the polytheism of divine conflict: God has made us to be what God disapproves of.

A similar tension between God and the human mind took longer to develop. The early Christians engaged in open debate about their beliefs. Most of what we know about them is their arguments against pagans and each other. After the collapse of the western Roman Empire, educational standards declined and it was not till the eleventh century that their doctrines were seriously examined again. Anselm and his successors tried to prove by logic that God must be a trinity and must have taken human form. By the fifteenth century the search for logical deductions of inherited Christian doctrines had proved a failure. However, instead of examining why the early Christians had reached their conclusions, the late medieval solution was to treat them as direct revelations from God. The logical implications of this idea were not immediately apparent, but were worked out over time and are still influential in Christian circles today. If direct divine revelation was independent of human reason, it must have greater authority than any amount of human reason. It must 'trump' all our rational thoughts. There cannot, therefore, be any role for modifying or interpreting a revelation, let alone challenging it. Conceived like this, divine revelation provided absolute certainty.

This then set the scene for the Reformation debates. Catholics and Protestants alike argued that the only things we can know about matters of faith are what God has revealed. Owen Chadwick illustrates the approach of Counter-Reformation Spanish theologians:

> The Church tells me that valid baptisms regenerate. I know that I did fulfil the conditions laid down for validity when I baptized that baby. One might have supposed that my immediate knowledge of what I did was certainty—while the general proposition that valid baptisms regenerate, being dependent on an act of faith, was not without the touch of probability attaching to any act of human faith. For all these Spanish thinkers that is a precise reversal of what is true. The revealed proposition is certain absolutely: the human immediate knowledge is certain ('merely' certain) morally. Faith is a higher certainty than knowledge.[67]

Protestants developed the language of the 'clear', 'plain' teaching of Scripture; as a matter of principle it must be clear and plain because it is true and not to be interpreted. Luther taught that ever since Adam's sin natural human reason would be better described as unnatural.[68] Calvin taught that nature still offers us some awareness of God, but humanity is so conditioned by sin that we can no longer understand nature rightly.[69] Although a number of scholars have recently argued that Luther and Calvin allowed greater scope for reason, their influence in the sixteenth century was overwhelmingly on the side of minimising its value in matters of faith. Melanchthon did defend the idea of a balance between reason and revelation, but the main defenders of reason at that time were the Socinians, who were so unpopular that they were expelled from one country after another.[70]

These views were so extreme that they were soon modified, but a precedent had been set and later movements, in different circumstances, reaffirmed them. The protagonists in the Reformation debates used every rational argument available to them while claiming to accept divine authority and accusing each other of using mere human reason. Eventually the absurdity of these certainty claims became clear and the intense debates gave way to the Enlightenment, the Age of Reason.

In the nineteenth century human reason was once again demoted, but in a different setting: the threat of atheism. Reason tended to be understood more narrowly. Instead of encompassing human thinking in contrast to divine revelation, it was restricted to analytic and empirical processes—logic, mathematics and data collected through the senses. Conceived as the only reliable source of knowledge it produced a simplified, mechanistic account of the physical universe, lacking any spiritual or moral dimensions. It seemed that, to give any meaning to life, one would have to look elsewhere, to some non-rational source of information. It was then that the Vatican gave the word 'dogma', originally Greek for 'opinion', its present meaning of a divinely revealed truth, proclaimed as such by church teaching and eternally binding on the faithful.[71] Protestantism followed suit. The dominant theme of Karl Barth, the most influential theologian of the twentieth century, was that God is totally other: altogether unlike us, separated from us by our sinfulness, beyond our understanding.[72] Our knowledge of God must be restricted to the Bible and the Church; all secular philosophy

> ...is the classical point for the invasion of alien powers, the injection of metaphysical systems which are secretly in conflict with the Bible and the Church.[73]

Thus it was that, in reaction against the rise of atheism, leading western Christians, Protestants and Catholics alike, emphasised the non-rational, dogmatic elements of their beliefs. Today it is often taught, by both 'conservative' Christians and atheists, that Christianity is a matter of 'faith' *as opposed to reason*. People who self-identify as Christians often feel it is their duty to accept whatever their local church teaches, without thinking through the issues for themselves. For English Roman Catholics this duty was explicitly demanded by the *Joint Pastoral* of 1900. Noting that some Catholics had been 'infected by the critical spirit of private judgment' it urged them to develop 'a more docile spirit'.[74]

This has proved an effective method of control by church leaders. With the threat of Hell and a generalised sense of guilt in the background, Christians can be warned against using their own reasoning powers and urged to leave their questions to church leaders who know what the divinely revealed truths are. It was at this stage that atheists could describe themselves as believers in reason, thus implying that Christians were not.[75]

Many churches today inherit their character from these nineteenth century developments. The result is a sort of neo-Gnosticism, a sense of belonging to a group with superior knowledge derived from a spiritual source not available to unbelievers. By contrast the 'spiritual but not religious' movement attracts those who do want to think for themselves; or at least, they prefer not to be bound by other people's dogmas.

Inevitably, organisations that tell their members to believe only what their own tradition teaches struggle to respond constructively to new issues. This gives many churches a backward-looking feel. For many western Christians today, what characterises their Christianity is the things secular society rejects—churchgoing activities, restrictive sexual ethics, miracles. Such a collection is a scrappy remnant of what Christianity once meant. To take just one contrast, some of the medieval Mystery plays lasted seven or eight hours to perform and told the story of creation from start to finish: from God's first decision to create the world to the future Second Coming of Christ. These plays were full of the pessimistic themes described in this chapter and we cannot go back to that thought-world. Nevertheless they provided what we now lack: a coherent account of who made us, for what purpose, and how therefore we should live. Many churches today are unable to offer an equivalent because they continue to understand their role in the terms of those nineteenth century reactions.

Conclusion

Hell, self-denial and dogma: negative messages about our bodies, our minds and our destiny. Between them they tell us that everything about us is condemned by God. Psychologically they are unsustainable. Occasional individuals can go through life with such a poor sense of self-worth, but when whole societies try it they destroy themselves.

Christians today who believe in the pessimistic doctrines described in this chapter do not usually describe themselves as polytheists. However, the attempts to reconcile these doctrines with monotheism fail. Why do we deserve eternal Hell? Because we are riddled with sin, contrary to God's wishes. Why have human bodies and minds turned out to be such disastrous vehicles of sin and error? Because something went wrong with the way God made us. Somewhere along the line the explanations have to appeal to some evil force between us and God, something that undermines God's power and goodness.

With their attempts to defend the indefensible churches have gradually declined. In the next few chapters we examine the larger, more influential story, of how European society turned its back on church teaching and produced new theories of who we are and how we should live.

Chapter 6. Inventing religion

A few years ago I was in a hospital, with a tube being pushed further and further up my nose. The doctor explained: 'God has given us sinuses, but he also lets us create technologies to look inside them.' My immediate thought was that he must be a Muslim. His manner of speaking about God is *not done,* least of all in the state-run National Health Service where staff have been disciplined for offering to pray with patients. Hundreds of years ago it was normal, but in our secular society most of us have learned not to talk like that. God belongs in a category we call 'religion', and religion has been quarantined. It is a kind of taboo.

An analogy may help explain what I mean. Early modern scientists distinguished between primary and secondary properties. Your shoes have size, shape and weight. Those are its primary properties. Their colour is a secondary property because it does not inhere in the shoes; it is just how our brains interpret the rays of light coming from it. Imagine what it would be like if on that basis it became socially unacceptable to talk about colour, except when you were specifically discussing the nature of secondary properties. A conversation might go something like this:

'What did you buy at the shops?'

'I bought some red shoes.'

'Red?' Oh now you're being colourist. You're talking about colour. I'm not a colourist, I just wanted to know what you bought at the shops.'

It would be a clumsy taboo. It would artificially hinder communication. Yet societies often create taboos on what can be said in decent company. Paul Veyne tells us that in the Roman Empire 'It was indecent to point out that such and such a slave had been born free'; to mention such things was to raise a question about 'the barrier between humans and subhumans' which 'was supposedly impregnable'.[1]

This is the kind of taboo modern society has placed on all talk of God, prayer and life after death. The motive was to get away from the very pessimistic Christianity described in the last chapter, and to make progress in understanding the world without depending on church authorities in constant dispute with each other.

On public matters the solution was secularism. The chief exponent of the new arrangement was John Locke. Because 'True and saving Religion consists in the inward perswasion of the Mind', it followed that a church should be

> ...a voluntary Society of Men, joining themselves together of their own accord, in order to the publick worshipping of God, in such a manner as they judge acceptable to him, and effectual to the Salvation of their Souls... The hopes of Salvation, as it was the only cause of his entrance into that Communion, so it can be the only reason of his stay there.[2]

Conversely governments should have nothing to do with them.[3]

This speaks volumes about the state of Christianity at that time. Any other reason for churches, apart from securing a favourable afterlife, seems to have disappeared from view. This suited the separation: the churches would confine themselves to the hope of eternal life and nothing else.[4]

In Locke's day it was government that most needed liberation from church authority. What applied to government was gradually extended to other features of society. Scientists, lawyers, economists and philosophers all found it necessary to put religious disagreements to one side and conduct their affairs 'as though there was no God' as Grotius put it. They did not need to deny the existence of God, or life after death, or the truth of Christianity, but in the circumstances it seemed best to set them aside. In the long run, as different elements of society were separated from all reference to the things Catholics and Protestants disagreed about, people learned to manage without them.

On a more individual level the same reaction against pessimistic Christianity led to a search for alternatives, and the main one was atheism. Nowhere else in human history do we know of a movement determined to deny the existence of any gods at all; commentators have often described atheism as a specifically Christian heresy.[5] Scholars debate how many of the ancients, if any, disbelieved in gods altogether. The main focus of attention is classical Athens. To many in the rising class of educated Greeks, Homer's gods would have been incredible. Xenophanes and Heraclitus attacked them. Protagoras said—and this is all we know of his view—'Concerning the gods I am unable to discover whether they exist or not'.[6] At the time Greek cities were full of temples, statues, processions and sacrifices to these very same gods, and anybody who did not take part in the activities would be suspect. Publicly doubting their existence was dangerous; it was on this charge that Socrates was sentenced to death. As a result it is probably safe to surmise that a substantial proportion of the educated classes disbelieved in the Homeric gods, but we can only guess at what they believed instead. My guess would be that most of them, like Herodotus, lived with contradictions.

In the Middle Ages Christian culture judged dissident beliefs, like Judaism and Islam, as heresies. The English word 'atheist' first appears in the sixteenth century.[7] There are parallels to classical Athens. Again, a growing educated class considered the traditional theology too pessimistic to be credible despite immense social pressure to conform. Again, critics might challenge many traditional beliefs, but not necessarily all of them. Again, 'atheist' was a term used by accusers, who often saw such people as threats to society without necessarily being clear as to the nature of the threat, or which beliefs were being questioned.[8]

It was at the end of the seventeenth century that the word 'atheism' was narrowed to its present meaning of denying the existence of any god at all. Those who believed in a god but not in traditional Christian doctrines then came to be called 'deists'. As long as it was dangerous to declare unbelief, we have no way of knowing how many unbelievers there were.[9] Alan Charles Kors describes d'Holbach's *Système de la nature* (1770) as 'the first unambivalent, published, programmatic statement' of Enlightenment atheism.[10]

Today when atheists describe the history of atheism, they naturally like to present it as a logical next step in humanity's increasing understanding of reality. Church leaders like to agree: they would hate to think unbelief was provoked by the off-putting character of Christian teaching. However the intense conflicts of the Reformation debates and the religious wars left their mark. The most important single doctrine was Hell. Preachers declared, and many a church wall depicted, how after death the damned would suffer indescribably for eternity. Beiser points to evidence that it sowed the seeds of popular atheism: for those genuinely terrified the most convincing hope was that God might not exist.[11]

As secularism spread it excluded all references to God and Christian doctrines from public accounts of reality. Such matters were separate, irrelevant to this public world. A new word was needed to encapsulate them. Thus arose the modern meaning of the word 'religion'. Before the seventeenth century there was no distinction between the 'religious' and the 'non-religious' aspects of society because people had always believed their gods were involved in all aspects of their lives. The word 'religion' had had different meanings; in medieval Europe to be a 'religious' was to be a monk or a nun, and the word is still used this way in Catholic circles today.

Wilfred Cantwell Smith traced the changes to the way the word 'religion' was used from the seventeenth century onwards. One is the plural 'religions'. Until then it did not exist. 'Religion' was more akin to words like 'piety', 'obedience', 'reverence' or 'worship', which have no plural because they are about what is going on in our minds. The plural arises when 'religion' means a system of belief and practice as observed from the outside by someone who does not share it. The second change is the generic use of 'religion' to designate the total sum of all systems of belief, again as observed from the outside.[12]

Once this concept had been established it became possible to reinterpret the past. Secular philosophers, for example, can study Plato's philosophy in great detail while ignoring his many references to gods as though they were irrelevant. A similar fate awaited the populations of newly discovered lands. Their beliefs about gods, and associated activities, were classified as their 'religion'. Different religions were assumed to be hostile to each other, in what Peter Harrison describes as 'the projection of Christian disunity onto the world.'[13] In this spirit Europeans invented the words 'Hinduism' in 1787 and 'Buddhism' in 1801.[14] Maps of world religions were published, over-simplifying people's real beliefs and practices by dividing the world into contrasting religions.[15]

To illustrate the fluidity prevailing before these changes, Brent Nongbri tells the story of St. Josaphat.[16] In the later Middle Ages western Christians loved stories of saints and their miracles. One of the most popular was the story of Barlaam and Josaphat. Before the invention of printing these stories were passed on by word of mouth and different versions developed. According to the most popular western version Josaphat was the son of a king somewhere far to the east. Barlaam was a monk who converted Josaphat to Christianity. Josaphat became an ideal Christian king, but later retired to become a monk. There is a reference to the story in Shakespeare's *Merchant of Venice*.

Modern scholars believe that some medieval saints probably never existed. In the case of St Josaphat, however, they have traced the development of the story, with the help of newly discovered manuscripts, right back to a person we know about from other sources. The saint's name changed as the story spread from one language to another. Josaphat is the Latin version. It was translated from Greek, where his name is Ioasaph. The Greeks inherited it around the year 1000 from a Georgian version. The Georgian version came from Arabic, where the name is a bit different again, Yudasaf. In Arabic the letters for 'y' and 'b' look very similar. Earlier Arabic texts give the name as Budasaf. The Arabic was in turn a translation from Sanskrit, where the name is Bodhisattva. In this way, by putting together a variety of manuscripts scholars have managed to trace the story back to its origin. Saint Josaphat, officially canonised as a Christian saint by Pope Gregory XIII in 1580, can now be identified with a man known independently from eastern sources. So he really did exist. Today, however, he is better known by his other name: Buddha.

The story of this holy man had spread from country to country, with changes along the way, from people we now call Buddhists to people we now call Hindus and Muslims and from there to people we now call Christians. The dividing-lines between one 'religion' and another were not what they are now. Christians, Hindus and Muslims could celebrate the same holy man without telling themselves 'I am not a Buddhist so I cannot accept him'.[17]

By the end of the nineteenth century the modern idea of 'religion' had been established: a self-contained set of beliefs and practices with no bearing on society's public understanding of reality and therefore irrelevant to science, law, art, politics and all other aspects of human culture. Atheism, by its nature, implies that reality can be explained without any reference at all to religious concepts. It should therefore be possible to discuss anything at all in the real world without 'bringing religion into it'. So religion gets locked away in its own box. Though the reason is to be found in the atheist project, most church leaders at the time supported it because it enabled them to elaborate their 'spiritual' doctrines safely beyond the reach of scientific challenge.[18]

So it was that when nineteenth century atheists set out to show how the universe could be explained without invoking any gods, they faced the puzzle that every other society they studied did believe in them. If religion was error, why was the error virtually universal? Anthropologists and sociologists looked for answers in universal features of human life, either the human brain or the way societies function. Some mix of psychology and sociology would have to account for belief in gods despite the complete lack of evidence for them. They travelled round the world studying archaic societies and collecting data to develop universal theories. It was a major topic of research until the 1920s. The racist theories common at the time encouraged the view that the people they were studying were at an earlier stage of evolution, less intelligent or with less consciousness.[19]

Later anthropologists have of course corrected these errors, but some still argue that belief in gods can be explained as a particular phase of human evolution. It is not a good argument against the belief: after all, in principle it should be possible to classify *all* our practices and beliefs in this way. Similarly, psychological explanations of religion have often seen it as the product of brain processes while sociological ones have seen it as the product of social processes. 'Explanations' of these types simply describe some of the relevant processes; *all* our beliefs, whether true or not, correlate with some brain process or other and *all* our actions can be interpreted in terms of social processes.

Defining 'religion' turned out to be difficult. Countless definitions have been proposed but none has been widely accepted.[20] More recently anthropologists have accepted that in other societies, beliefs and actions relating to gods have been integral parts of a unified understanding of reality. Confirmation appears in statements such as these:

> One indicator of the problematic nature of the category 'religion' in Chinese history is the absence of any premodern word that unambiguously denotes the category.[21]
>
> Extant pre-Columbian Mesoamerican inscriptions do not contain words which can be rendered as "religion".[22]

Thus other societies had no concept of 'religion' until modern westerners introduced it. The failure to agree a definition is easily explained once we recognise that they were trying to define a concept which had only just been invented.

While confining it to its box, modern secular society remains strongly committed to its invention. On the one hand religion has no purpose this side of the grave. On the other it is very important to let everyone practice their chosen religion. The First Amendment of the US Constitution (1791) states that 'Congress shall make no law respecting an establishment of religion, or prohibiting the free exercise thereof'.[23] The United Nations Universal Declaration of Human Rights, 1948, Article 18, states:

> Everyone has the right to freedom of thought, conscience and religion; this right includes freedom to change his religion or belief, and freedom, either alone or in community with others and in public or private, to manifest his religion or belief in teaching, practice, worship and observance.[24]

The European Convention on Human Rights (1950) is similar.[25] These regulations make abundantly good sense from the perspective of a society that went through the religious wars and ended up redefining religion in the way described above. It is free of cost: since religion is only about the other-worldly, there is no harm in allowing free choice. It is presupposed that nobody would have religious reasons for refusing to pay their taxes or becoming a suicide bomber.

In the past, and still today where western influence is resisted, there is no compartmentalised 'religion'. Beliefs in gods are part of an integrated account of reality, along with beliefs about physical things. Together with these other beliefs they contribute to an overall understanding of reality, combining the factual with the evaluative so that judgements about how we should live are derived from accounts of who made us and for what purpose.

By making this division, putting all references to the divine into a separate box, and forbidding them to influence public life, secularism has created a new way to conceive of reality. Churchgoers often live with the contradictions; they use God-language in church meetings but avoid it in other contexts. More creatively, the 'spiritual but not religious' find workarounds, language on the edge which is not properly 'religious' or 'secular'.

These changes have taken time. In the eighteenth century only a small number of intellectuals positively denied the existence of God. Not even Voltaire went so far, and Hume's real opinion remains unknown. In the nineteenth century the numbers increased, but as far as we can tell they were well outnumbered by those who continued to believe in *something*: instead of God we get much talk of Providence or Fate or some kind of force in history guaranteeing progress. Many must have felt like today's 'spiritual but not religious': that there must be some transcendent mind but they were determined to distance themselves from the pessimistic doctrines associated with Christianity.

It is as though God gradually *slid* out of sight. As long as it was possible to affirm some kind of benign transcendence, the logic of atheism failed to appear in all its clarity. For those to whom it has appeared, things look very different; but a great deal of public discourse is yet to catch up with the implications of removing God from one's picture of reality. If we describe the integrative function of traditional spiritual beliefs as answers to three central questions, we can see how secularism answers them.

First, who made us? In an atheist account, no intending mind made us. We are the product of impersonal, automatic forces. In a secular account, we may privately believe that the creative forces knew what they were doing but we should not bring our belief into the public realm. On public matters we should treat the atheist position as though it were the true one.

Second, for what purpose have we been made? Again the atheist account is to be treated as normative. Even if in private we think our life has a purpose given to us, public discourse should be based on the presumption that it has no true purpose, point, meaning or value. We may invent these things for ourselves, but they are only our subjective inventions. This conclusion is not popular. Only very slowly have intellectuals come to appreciate that it is an inevitable implication of secular thought. Over the centuries ghostly substitutes for God have partly filled the gap: abstract nouns like Providence or Destiny have been invoked to give a continuing sense of purpose and direction to human effort. We shall look at the fate of human values in greater detail in Chapter 11.

Third, in the light of the above, how should we live? Again the answer is an empty one: since we have been created by unthinking, automatic processes, only humans have the capacity to conceive of moral norms. Right and wrong, good and evil do not exist objectively; they are only what we decide for ourselves, human constructs. This answer has also taken centuries to be acknowledged, and then only by a few intellectuals; but unlike the answers to the other questions it has immediate practical relevance to a wider range of people. Secular societies can postpone or ignore the deeper questions of life's purpose and meaning as they get on with their immediate tasks; but who says the immediate tasks, whatever they are, need to be done at all?

Meanwhile secular accounts of western culture usually ignore the positive contributions of monotheistic Christianity. Debates about postmodernism have often characterised religion as essentially dogmatic and anti-rational, while attributing reason, the unity of humanity and progress to Enlightenment values. Unfortunately social critics and philosophers rarely read any theology and are often misled into thinking these Enlightenment values are opposed to Christian thought. On the contrary it Christian monotheism from which the Enlightenment inherited them, albeit at a time when most church leaders preferred more pessimistic theologies.

Histories of the western churches often reinforce the error: sixteenth century good, eighteenth century bad, nineteenth century good. For Protestants Luther and Calvin are standard-bearers for their respective churches, while for Roman Catholics the Council of Trent plays a similar role. Then unfortunately came the Enlightenment. The churches declined and fewer people attended church services. Things got better with the nineteenth century revivals. Because western churches today still operate on the nineteenth century model, this picture remains popular. It has the effect of praising the worst elements of the Christian tradition and blaming the Enlightenment for the best. More realistically, in the sixteenth and seventeenth centuries church attendance was usually compulsory, and anyway the terror of Hell was motive enough. Once both were relaxed, fewer attended. Church leaders stopped being so passionately opposed to each other. Intellectuals once again felt at liberty to question inherited Christian teachings. As Dominic Erdozain has shown in his recent study *The Soul of Doubt*, they mostly did so without abandoning their faith; it is posterity that has chosen to classify people like Voltaire as Deists. With the rise of atheism in the nineteenth century church attendances rose again, but because of a new anxiety. The emptiness and meaninglessness of life in the absence of transcendent reality was more obvious when it was first popularised than it is today. As that fear declined, church attendances dropped again. Over the last few decades ministers of western churches have been inundated with advice about 'church growth', like the recent 'Renewal and Reform' programme of the Church of England.[26] We might summarise that the anxieties of church leaders were about eternal Hell in the sixteenth century, the meaninglessness of life in the nineteenth and a shortage of churchgoers today. The big spiritual questions about who created us, why, and how we should respond have long ceased to dominate the minds of most church leaders as they busy themselves maintaining their declining institutions.

There was no sudden break between Christian and secular society. Societies inherited practical agendas which had more or less Christian justifications, and over the centuries dispensed with the Christian elements. While secularising the reasons for doing them, they modified what needed to be done. Because these changes took place over long periods of time they were not immediately obvious. The next three chapters will offer examples of them.

Chapter 7. Taking control of the world

This chapter and the next four will explore what difference it makes to society's ethics and values when God is removed from our discourse.

For monotheists the universe is designed for our well-being by a god who knows incomparably more than we do about how to maintain it. We cannot control it, and do not need to because God does. Many ancient polytheisms understood the relationship differently. If the world was controlled by gods who only had limited concern for human well-being, perhaps it might be worth trying to improve the physical environment.

Modern secularism is closer to the polytheistic account, but takes it to an extreme. If there are no gods, and instead the universe is maintained by unthinking, determined laws of nature that do not decide anything at all, then deciding to control something is what only humans can do. If humanity is not in charge, nobody is in charge. Our survival and well-being depend on the best decisions being made and only we can make them. It would seem foolish not to take control of our situation, find out how the universe works and create a new way of living, designed by the best human minds in the interests of our well-being. In this way a radically different account of how we should relate to our physical environment became popular.

It has not been an unalloyed success. The scientific evidence of environmental destruction first attracted popular concern in the 1960s. One of the questions raised was how western attitudes to nature had become so destructive. The debate is often dated from the publication of an article by Lynn White in 1967.[1] White accused Christianity of encouraging human exploitation of nature on the basis that it was not sacred and did not deserve any respect in its own right. Subsequent commentators have contrasted this exploitative stance towards nature with non-western societies where spiritual perspectives have set limits to how the natural environment may be used. To this extent western Christianity seems to have failed where other spiritual traditions have succeeded. Why?

White dated Christian instrumentalism from the eighth century when new ploughing techniques were developed in western Europe. Subsequent commentators have focused on later developments. Much attention has been paid to early Enlightenment thinkers, especially Francis Bacon and René Descartes. I shall follow this account.

The project

The search for power over the natural environment became a major issue during the period of the plagues. Bacon, an English government minister in the early seventeenth century, gave a new twist to the tradition of contempt for the world. The dominant view from the fourth century onwards had been that when Adam and Eve had eaten the forbidden fruit humanity had fallen but nature had remained in a state of perfection. Bacon proposed the reverse: that the state of nature had been corrupted but humanity had the ability to restore its original state through science and technology.

> That the state of knowledge is not prosperous nor greatly advancing, and that a way must be opened for the human understanding entirely different from any hitherto known, and other helps provided, in order that the mind may exercise over the nature of things the authority which properly belongs to it.[2]

Eventually Bacon believed humanity should be able to exercise the 'dominion' over it mentioned in the Bible.[3] In describing how to proceed he used the language of the contemporary witch trials. Scientists would 'torture nature's secrets from her'. Nature had to be 'hounded in her wanderings', 'bound into service' and made a 'slave'.[4]

In this proposal Bacon combined three different evaluations. One was an extremely optimistic view of human capacities. The other two were about the natural environment: a negative view of it as something flawed and needing be corrected[5] and a neutral view of it as a potentially useful resource, valueless in itself but available to be used. The ancient Stoics had taught that the physical world was at the disposal of humanity and medieval Christians had occasionally agreed. This in itself would not have led to the idea of making radical changes to it without the more pessimistic value judgement of its current state.

Bacon inherited from Christianity, or rather his version of it, three ideas: that the environment had once been better and so could be again; that God had given us minds capable of understanding the physical order; and that God had given humanity the task of dominating nature. Thus arose what I shall call 'the control project'. Later versions, to be described in the next chapter, proposed to control society. To distinguish between the two I shall refer to the later one as 'the social control project' and Bacon's earlier one as 'the environmental control project'.

When God is removed from the project it changes. In its theological setting it was a limited exercise. The aim was to re-establish the original perfection. Once liberated from its theological roots it no longer envisages an end point. Instead it offers the prospect of never-ending development. The Garden of Eden is replaced by a treadmill.

Without God, Bacon's evaluations of nature lose their justification. Nature is no longer fallen; on the contrary scientists have elaborated an impressive account of physical and evolutionary change towards greater complexity. Neither is it provided for human use; it is *just there,* the accidental product of unthinking, unintending laws of nature, without purpose, let alone value. There is no command given to humans, either to venerate the natural environment or to transform it.

Neither, though, is there any reason for confidence that nature will continue to provide for our needs—that we will not, for example, be destroyed by another ice age or volcanic eruption. Instead all we have is a story—today, an evolutionary one—describing how we got to where we are; and since we can all find fault with the way things are, it is up to us to decide what to do with it. So the project acquires a new justification. We, who unlike the forces of nature can think and plan, should be able to do better. The dominant image becomes one of humanity-as-a-whole struggling to improve an unsatisfactory environment. Humanity against nature. It is presupposed in countless ways when the mass media tell us about accidental deaths, illness, floods and scientific discoveries.

To make the control project seem credible it was necessary to make some assumptions about both the world and the human mind. The basic presuppositions of science needed to be extended.

We saw in Chapter 4 how the two presuppositions of science—that the universe is ordered and that the human mind can understand it—were both based on monotheistic claims about the nature of reality. Removing God from the explanatory structure left secularists without any justification for them. Given that our ordinary experience of life provides plenty of evidence to the contrary, on what basis can we carry on assuming that the universe is ordered and comprehensible? In the absence of God's guarantee, the only possible answer becomes *humanity's* guarantee: order and comprehensibility will have to be something human knowledge can establish.

To illustrate the point we might contrast two theories about the end of humanity on this planet. In the first half of the seventeenth century many people believed the Second Coming of Christ was due imminently. It would have been an act of God, as planned from the beginning, part of God's order. Today astronomers calculate the probability of an asteroid hitting our planet and making it uninhabitable. On a godless account this would be completely without purpose, not part of any plan. To predict it would require a vast amount of astronomical expertise; to prevent it would require incomparably more still. By comparing the two we can see how godless secularism today puts us at the mercy of chance or mindless determinism; humanity is back to the radical insecurity of Homer's world, not knowing what will happen next—unless we understand it so well that we can control it. Three centuries ago the security provided by God was not simply abandoned. It was gradually transferred to the only possible alternative guarantor: humanity.

However humanity cannot provide this guarantee unless it *knows* the universe. It is no longer good enough to be ordered and comprehensible *enough* for human purposes in God's design; it will have to be *completely* ordered and *completely* comprehensible. God's omnipotence and omniscience will have to be transferred to humanity; otherwise we will have no reason for confidence that we know what we are doing. It is not so easy to dispense with the belief that somebody knows how things work.

Of course not even humanity as a whole, let alone any one individual, has so much power or knowledge. It therefore became a task to be achieved. Not long after Bacon, Descartes made this seem credible with his dualistic account of reality. According to his theory there are two realms: a spiritual one where the human soul relates to God and a soulless one made up of only physical matter. On this basis it became possible to believe that the physical universe could be completely known by human minds observing it and studying it as if from outside it. By the end of the seventeenth century, under Isaac Newton's influence, the universe was often being compared to a clock, ticking away as atoms pushed each other in obedience to impersonal and eternal laws of nature.[6]

A similar change was needed to the powers of the human

mind. Monotheism gives reason to expect that our minds are capable of understanding the universe well enough for the legitimate purposes for which we have been made. The control project needs *complete* understanding, known with *certainty*. Late medieval theologians had often claimed that humans could gain completely certain knowledge by means of divine revelation which transcends all human reason. Calvin had emphasised it.[7] The Enlightenment philosophers transferred certainty from revelation to human reason. Descartes is best known for this claim. He thought it would be possible build up an account of reality that was free from error by starting with a self-evident foundation—his 'I think, therefore I am'—and deducing other certainties from it.[8]

Empiricism, the evidence of the senses, would provide the data about the universe. For science to establish complete knowledge everything would have to be available for inspection by humans, at least in principle. It would have to be free of invisible and unpredictable agents, so an important principle was that there cannot be any unobservables. At first this was a matter of dispensing with angels and demons. It soon created difficulties for scientific research, which has always speculated about unobservables. When Newton first published his findings about gravity other scientists criticised him for proposing an unobservable, occult force;[9] the idea of denying unobservables was essential to the control project.

In these ways, putting together an exalted view of humanity's potential knowledge and a very simplified account of the universe, it seemed possible to develop complete and certain knowledge of it. Towards the end of the eighteenth century the French atheists Baron D'Holbach, Jacques-André Naigeon and Denis Diderot offered materialist accounts of reality with no room for anything empirical science could not establish. True knowledge of reality could only come through the physical senses. To increase happiness and minimise pain we should use our physical senses to observe how nature works and make changes accordingly. Locke had already argued that knowledge comes from the physical senses; what these atheists added was that we cannot know anything about anything which does not affect these senses.[10] They abolished Descartes' spiritual realm, arguing instead that everything that exists is physical. Instead of Descartes' two worlds, Naigeon argued, 'there is only one, and it is the *whole*.' Nature operates according to eternal and unchangeable laws and is indifferent to us. Even our thoughts and wills are products of these laws. The world 'could not be other than what it is', so 'Let us leave nature what it is, and not speak of its perfection, nor its wisdom, nor its goodness.' The universe offers nothing that can be praised or condemned, so it is meaningless to attribute moral qualities to it.[11]

The resulting picture of the universe was well expressed by what has come to be called 'Laplace's demon':

> Given for one instant an intelligence which could comprehend all the forces by which nature is animated and the respective situation of the beings who compose it—an intelligence sufficiently vast to submit these data to analysis—it would embrace in the same foundation the movements of the greatest bodies of the universe and those of the lightest atom; for it, nothing would be uncertain and the future, as the past, would be present to its eyes.[12]

Laplace's argument depended on two claims, both of which remain influential today. One was determinism. This claims that the universe is a mechanical system of cause and effect, with every state caused by a previous state, in accordance with exact and unbreakable laws of nature, going all the way back to the beginning of the universe. Nothing could possibly happen otherwise than the way it does.

The other was reductionism. In this theory everything can be understood by breaking it down into its parts and examining each part in turn. It applies to both entities and processes: every complex entity can be explained by examining its parts, and all processes can be explained by reducing them to a fixed set of laws of nature. Reductionists characteristically anticipate that it should be possible to reduce all the sciences to physics.

Putting determinism and reductionism together produces Laplace's image of an impersonal and unalterable process allowing for no deviation from the beginning of the universe to its end. To foretell the future like this seems like a control freak's dream. It is a bit like some of today's enthusiasts for robotics, who insist that robots will one day be able to do everything humans do. When we ask the obvious question—'Will robots have emotions like ours?'—the temptation is to redefine emotions so that they are nothing but something a computer can do. In the same way, the search for power over the environment led to the claim that the universe does not contain anything our minds cannot understand and manipulate.

To those seeking control, then, the universe had to be a self-sufficient and impersonal mechanism. Remaining gaps in the scientific account were to be filled by continuing the search for physical explanations.[13]

Thus arose the philosophy of knowledge known as 'positivism'. Philosophers rarely defend it today but in popular thought it remains influential as a way of claiming that only science produces true knowledge.

The term comes from Auguste Comte. Comte believed that the human mind had progressed through three stages: the theological, in which explanations are made in terms of gods; the metaphysical, in which they are made in terms of abstract concepts that cannot be shown to exist; and finally the positive or scientific, in which they are properly rooted in the study of nature and its laws. To Comte, 'Civilization consists, strictly speaking, on the one hand, in the development of the human mind, on the other, in the result of this, namely, the increasing power of Man over Nature.'[14]

The attractiveness of positivism was largely due to its systematic denial of everything to do with religion. Refusing to accept any unobservables became an absolute principle. As O'Hear remarked,

> ...it would be something of a disaster for the old-fashioned anti-religious positivism if it turned out that natural science made significant use of what appears to be non-observational knowledge.[15]

All truly scientific knowledge, therefore, was to be based on data observed through the senses. Every legitimate theory had to be empirically verifiable, or at least falsifiable. Hume had noted that we never observe one thing causing another; all we ever observe is repeated conjunctions of events. Positivists accepted that all talk of causes had to be reduced to constant conjunctions. Similarly all metaphysical theories, being unobservable, were to be rejected. This meant rejecting all deep explanations in science.[16]

The early positivists made ambitious claims for science. By gathering data through empirical observations they thought it would be possible to establish the laws of nature, understand how the world works and make predictions, without invoking any metaphysical concepts or unobservables. Comte and others hoped to establish a general account of knowledge which would integrate the laws of all the sciences into a single account of reality.[17]

After their confident, ambitious beginnings positivists worked through the logic of their theories to the point at which they were undermining science itself. You see something and you call it a table; but your senses only tell you that you are seeing a rectangular brown shape. To call it a table is to go beyond the observable evidence. By the end of the nineteenth century Mach was arguing that everything we see, along with all scientific concepts, are just bundles of sensory experience. It followed that concepts like 'force' and 'atoms' have no proper place within science.[18]

Positivism was revived in the 1920s in a linguistic form, logical positivism. This movement was based on the Verification Principle, which states that the meaning of a statement is its method of verification. There are two kinds of verification, rationalism (logic and mathematics) and the evidence of the senses. Any statement which fits neither type—like any statement about God—is not merely uncertain but meaningless.[19]

The theory did not stand the test of time. Its stringent criteria for meaning excluded not only God but mathematical formulae, scientific axioms, the rules of logic, statements about the past, statements of feeling and the existence of other people's minds.[20]

Nevertheless it remains influential at a popular level. It is the source of the idea of a sharp distinction between 'facts' which can be 'observed' and 'verified' as true knowledge, and on the other hand 'beliefs' and 'theories' which cannot. The *Guardian* newspaper still publishes an echo in a sidebar on its Opinion page,[21] a quotation from C P Scott, its editor in 1921: 'Comment is free but facts are sacred'.

Positivism flattens reality. By denying the existence of unobservables it tells us that the physical things we experience can no longer point to greater or richer dimensions of reality. In some forms it accepts that there is still much to be discovered, but nevertheless insists that whatever there is must be describable by the mental concepts we already have. No longer do we need diverse types of communication to express what is beyond our language and concepts—analogical language, dramatic and liturgical performances, narrative, poetry—because now there is nothing that words cannot represent directly.[22] As Louis Dupré puts it, 'The notion of transcendence lost much of its meaning when the mind itself had to define what, by its own description, totally surpassed it.'[23]

Arguments for atheism usually appeal to the interplay between positivism and science, where the positivist denial of unobservables is treated as scientifically proved. Historically, though, atheism came first. Positivism came later and was—and still is—invoked to justify atheism.[24]

These developments were accompanied by a strong sense of progress. Nisbet describes the period from 1750 to 1900 as a time when progress became the dominant idea of European society, setting the context for other ideas. Its proponents were determined to establish it on a foundation which excluded God:

> From Turgot's notable lectures and discourses in 1750-1 through Condorcet, Comte, Marx, Mill, Spencer, and others, there is a manifest desire to liberate progress from any crucial relationship with an active, guiding, ruling Providence. Throughout this period we find that system after system in philosophy and the social sciences was concerned primarily with demonstration of the scientific reality of human progress and of the laws and principles which make progress necessary.[25]

So progress, no longer explained by God, came to be seen as determined by the laws of nature. Before the nineteenth century the laws of nature were generally regarded as forces implanted in the world by God. Newton, for example, thought the nature of these forces was unknowable; but since God was responsible for them they could still be accepted as reliable, so observation and induction were still worthwhile activities. As long as they were considered forces, they could be described as governing events. Events *obeyed* them. By the end of the nineteenth century, however, with God emphatically out of the picture, later theorists like Ernst Mach recognised that 'force' went beyond the evidence; what scientific research revealed was regularities, nothing more. The laws of nature were descriptions, not forces. Maurice Mandelbaum has illustrated how the most influential proponents of deterministic progress, like Auguste Comte and Herbert Spencer, in practice treated progress as a fudge between the two models. Of Comte he writes that

> ...it was one of the basic tenets of his system to reject the theological interpretation of the laws of nature; he also rejected any employment of the so-called metaphysical concept of "forces." Yet, he did not cavil at treating scientific laws as if necessity could unquestionably be attributed to the particular sequences which such laws served to describe. Comte never examined or sought to defend the basis on which he held this view; like many of his contemporaries, he seems to have taken it for granted that once one abandons the appeal to God's purposes as a means of explaining phenomena, it becomes necessary to assume that the reign of law is absolute.[26]

This is neither one thing nor the other. To treat the laws of nature as anything more than the regularities so far observed, one needs a metaphysical theory—if not God, then something else. Yet despite the inconsistency, it remains a common belief. The dominant metaphysical substitute for God is now the laws of nature, technically defined as regularities but treated as though they were real forces. It is this contradiction that leaves the impression that the laws of nature explain how the universe works.

The apotheosis of humanity reached its height in the nineteenth century. In 1800 Fichte wrote:

> All those outbreaks of unregulated power before which human strength vanishes into nothing... can be nothing less

> than the last struggles of the rude mass against the law of regular, progressive, living, and systematic activity to which it is compelled to submit in opposition to its own undirected impulses; - nothing but the last shivering strokes by which the perfect formation of our globe has yet to be accomplished... This dominion of man over Nature shall gradually be extended until at length no further expenditure of mechanical labour shall be necessary than what the human body requires for its development, cultivation and health; and this labour shall cease to be a burden; - for a reasonable being is not destined to be a bearer of burdens.[27]

Lawrence Stepelevich described the view of Feuerbach, a major influence on Karl Marx:

> Feuerbach's goal was to press the consciousness of his readers to the point where they would fully understand that "Man is the true God and Savior of Man". His intention, as he stated it, was to change "the friends of God into friends of man, believers into thinkers, worshippers into workers, candidates for the other world into students of this world, Christians, who on their own confession are half-animal and half-angel, into men—whole men." But this humanistic truth was not to be found in abstract ideas, in philosophical speculation, but in immediate physical feeling, in a direct sensuous love of Man as Man-God.[28]

Failure of the project

The project of controlling the environment, for all that it is being pursued today as strongly as ever, has clearly failed. Of course it has produced innumerable new technologies, many of which have proved beneficial, but we cannot know how many of them would have been produced without it; technologies were developing anyway and no doubt would have continued to do so.

What has become clear is that, despite the control project's continuing popularity, especially in political circles, it is no longer scientifically credible.

On a practical level environmental destruction is undeniable. All living beings adapt their environment to some extent. Others, however, do it constructively. They take what they need and return it in a form that can be used by other species. Over the millennia human societies have done the same, changing their lifestyles and developing technologies to meet their needs. Before modern times, however, they did so with a more constructive philosophy: their adaptations were intended for living in harmony with the natural environment, not for turning it into something else—let alone bequeathing industrial deserts to future generations. The control project urges us to make permanent and irreparable changes, many of which have proved disastrous. It can only claim credibility by ignoring the destruction of everything it has not measured.

Popular environmental concern peaked in the late 1980s and early 1990s and systems were put into place to limit the damage. What was being urged was more than a set of technological fixes. It was also a change in values. To stop the destruction, what we need is not just to do the same things differently, but to do different things—and therefore to *want* different things, to judge our achievements differently. The things we have been trying to do are, it turns out, the wrong things to do.

While paying lip service to the concerns, in practice governments carry on with the destruction. To take one much-discussed example, in December 2015 at the end of the COP21 Climate Change conference in Paris, all 195 countries agreed to limit the rise in global temperatures to 2°C. This agreement, though it left every country to decide for itself how to implement it, was hailed as a great step forward. David Cameron, the British Prime Minister, said:

> Instead of making excuses tomorrow to our children and grandchildren, we should be taking action against climate change today. What we are looking for is not difficult, it is doable and therefore we should come together and do it.[29]

Yet within a week he had granted 93 licences for fracking, which adds greenhouses gases to the atmosphere.[30] Nobody was surprised. We all know that this is how governments operate: grand speeches while the world's media are attentive, followed by business as usual. It is as though we live in parallel universes: while climate scientists imagine that reality consists of physical things like air, water, plants and animals, governments are confident that it really consists of economic statistics.[31]

The control project has given birth to a culture that despises or ignores essential natural processes while glorying in new technologies. It has no shortage of proponents working on, or excited by, the prospect of ever more powerful machines making bigger and bigger changes to our environment. It is now so deeply embedded in our society that alternatives can be dismissed as absurd. To take just one example, car exhausts cause air pollution and contribute to various illnesses. Researchers study ways to reduce the pollution. The easiest solution would be to reduce the number of cars on the roads. This would require planning, but there is no law of nature telling us that the number of miles we each travel is bound to increase and increase. Yet only committed environmentalists consider reduced motor travel a realistic option: in the dominant narrative, to do that would be going backwards. If we ask: 'from what perspective would that count as going backwards?' the answer would have to be that going forwards requires ever-greater artificialisation of life, with new technologies taking us further and further away from harmony with our natural environment. This attitude, often dressed up as science, is in fact a value judgement, an appeal to the control project. It makes abundantly good sense if, and only if, we conceive of humanity as a whole being permanently at odds with recalcitrant nature.

Thus we reach today's absurdity: a society constantly excited by the latest technological artefacts while unthinkingly destroying wildlife which is incomparably more intricate and essential to the quality of life. We have driven to extinction the greatest number of species since the age of the dinosaurs, and are still doing it. Sun and rain, photosynthesis and pollination, are redefined as just accidental products of unthinking, impersonal laws of nature; but the latest mobile phone is a triumph of the latest technology and millions are spent advertising it. Of course we all know that humanity's knowledge is neither complete nor certain; but over-confidence convinces us that we know what we are doing. In 1991 an American mathematician even suggested blowing up the moon in order to enhance fertility.[32] Every time our efforts lead to disaster we tell ourselves we need more research.

The alliances have shifted. In the seventeenth century popular religious teachers warned that the end of the world was nigh while scientists described it as ordered and predictable. Now, the scientific community have swapped sides; they tell us that we are indeed heading for the end of human life on earth, or something approaching it. It is our politicians, economists, business leaders and the mass media who still urge us to produce and pollute more and more.

The scientific case for the control project has collapsed. Since Einstein's day the trajectory of scientific research has been clear: every time an uncertainty is resolved, new questions arise. Everything we examine, from the vastness of galaxies to the components of atoms, the mental processes of dolphins and the way bacteria respond to antibiotics, turns out to be more and more complex. Theoretical physicists, far from refusing to believe in unobservables, keep finding that they have to invent new words to describe new discoveries. Reductionism and determinism still have their defenders, but are no longer as convincing as they seemed in the nineteenth century. Even then Nietzsche could see the absurdity of making these extreme claims. In his famous passage declaring the death of God and describing 'all of us' as God's murderers, he asks:

> But how have we done this? How were we able to drink up the sea? Who gave us the sponge to wipe away the entire horizon? What did we do when we unchained this earth from its sun? Whither is it moving now? Away from all suns? Are we not plunging continually? Backward, sideward, forward, in all directions? Is there any up or down left? Are we not straying as through an infinite nothing?[33]

The belief that determinism and reductionism had been proved by science was always an illusion: they were *presupposed* because the control project would have been impossible without them. Keith Ward asks questions about their picture of reality.

> Is there nothing that really exists except elementary particles? Are all properties even of the physical universe subject to precise quantitative measurement? Can one ever exhaustively describe every feature of the universe, much less know that one has done so? Is there a finite and closed set of physical laws? Are these laws completely universal in their application, so that nothing lies outside their scope? Is every event in the physical universe completely predictable, even in principle? And do causes necessarily determine their effects, in such a way that nothing could happen except what does happen?[34]

Our scientific knowledge, though now incomparably greater than it was in the nineteenth century, now looks tiny compared with what we do not know.

The same has happened to the capacity of our minds. Studies of the human mind and brain have revealed that our mental processes are incomparably more complex than people believed before the time of Freud. Even so they have limits. Evolutionary studies have shown how our brains have developed for more immediate purposes like eating and reproducing, not for understanding the nature of the universe. To have some understanding of it is a bonus, but a complete understanding of it is beyond us. The fact that we make mistakes, and hold improbable beliefs while dreaming, should be enough to warn us against the fantasy that we can ever access certainty.

Our situation is a bit like that of Rover and the newspapers. Day after day, Rover lay on the mat waiting until it was time for walkies. He had to wait until his master finished reading the newspaper. Every day a new newspaper was bought and read, using up time which could have been spent running round the field. Eventually, unable to understand this obsession with black and white, Rover took a batch of old newspapers to an analytic chemist for testing. The result was that every newspaper consisted of nothing but paper and ink. So why spend so long looking at paper and ink? Why, also, buy a new newspaper each day, when it only consists of paper and ink just like all the others?

Rover's blind spot was to overlook the additional dimension of meaning provided by the exact shapes of the ink. The shapes provided information, different each day, which no amount of chemical analysis could reveal. It would only be revealed by a different kind of analysis. In the same way western society, still heavily influenced by positivist theory with its emphasis on facts generated from the physical senses, remains reluctant to acknowledge other dimensions of reality which it cannot measure.

As for the idea of progress, it had its natural home in monotheism with its senses of linear time, physical security and moral calling. When God was removed, linear time and physical security were retained and moral calling was reinterpreted in other terms like the control project. As determinism, with some kind of 'law of progress', replaced God, nineteenth century atheists convinced themselves that progress was inevitable. It is not. At any one time one can point to examples of increasing control which shows no sign of hitting any buffers, but there are others which have come to a stop. In the middle of the twentieth century the latest scientific evidence seemed to indicate that false teeth were better than natural teeth and bottled milk than breast milk. Subsequent research has refuted these claims for human ingenuity; natural teeth and breast milk are far more complex, more valuable to health, than our predecessors realised. Medical culture has adjusted accordingly. No doubt in fifty years' time our successors will look back at the exciting new technologies of today and distinguish between the foolish ones and the helpful ones.

Progress is a value term. It means not just change, but change for the better. In the absence of God, who decides what counts as better? What is there to progress *towards*, and who says we ought to? Secular theorists today often oppose the very idea of progress. An example is John Gray, who tells us it is an illusion driven by the assumption that we can only live well if we have the power to remake the world.

> Yet most humans who have ever lived have not believed this—and a great many have had happy lives. The question assumes the aim of life is action; but this is a modern heresy. For Plato contemplation was the highest form of human activity. A similar view existed in ancient India. The aim of life was not to change the world. It was to see it rightly… At the start of the twenty-first century the world is strewn with the grandiose ruins of failed utopias…[35]

Power in turn depends on knowledge. However, 'Knowledge

does not make us free. It leaves us as we have always been, prey to every kind of folly.'[36]

Gray is of course right to say the world is 'strewn with the grandiose ruins of failed utopias', but this is because of the *means* of progress, the belief that we do it by changing the world—the control project. Yet if there is no god telling us what to do, why do we need to do anything at all? Might the whole idea of progress be just somebody's way of manipulating us?

Conclusion

It was monotheism that first told Europeans that the world was ordered and comprehensible, and thereby made modern science possible. When God was removed from the picture, order and comprehensibility were transferred to humanity. This generated the need for humanity to know all about everything. Following Descartes, Europeans taught themselves to stop thinking they were part of nature. Instead they were minds, standing over against it and observing it, its enemy destined to become its master. Secularism also borrowed from monotheism the idea of progress, replacing religious moral norms with the drive to control everything around us. Atheism added that nobody knows how to do it better than we do. The onward march of science and technology has become the defining content of modern progress.

The control project was mistaken both in its deification of humanity and in its demotion of the physical environment. Humanity is not a single benevolent mind: it is billions of different people, each partly benevolent but also partly self-centred. It has neither omnipotence nor omniscience and never can have either. Imagining that it can, we have created a society that is better and better at knowing how to do things but has lost the ability to reflect intelligently on what needs to be done. Our attempts to improve on nature by creating more artificial lifestyles have now become the biggest threat to the continuation of human life on earth. Einstein aptly remarked:

> Our much vaunted progress in technology, generally of civilization, is like the axe in the hand of a pathological criminal.[37]

From a monotheistic perspective it is human behaviour that needs to improve, not the environment. The complexity of life needs to be respected as far more intricate, life-giving and essential than anything human technology can devise. We should respect it at the very least for our own sakes, if not also for the sake of other living beings. To save the environment for future generations, the governments of western nations need to face the fact that the damage is being done not by their failures but by their successes. What they have been trying to do has proved the wrong thing to do.

The change that is needed is therefore a cultural one affecting all industrial societies. There have been times when governments have made formal apologies, on behalf of their nations, to those they have wronged in the past—for imperialism, genocide or slavery. Such apologies establish a change of values: they now admit that what their ancestors did was wrong. The scale of the change needed is of this type. What we are doing now in our environmental destruction will leave our descendants wondering how on earth we could have brought ourselves to carry on, knowing the damage we are doing. We need to change our values. The achievements we now celebrate our descendants will lament; what we now despise they will rediscover how to venerate. The sooner we begin the reversal, the less damage we will do.

The change that is needed may seem demanding, and indeed it is—as long as we are determined to be in control of the world order rather than putting our trust in the forces that govern it. The difference can be illustrated by the image of a school trip. The control project has the character of the head teacher, knowing exactly what is supposed to happen, making sure everybody is in the right place at the right time and holding the right ticket. Everything should have been properly planned. There are to be no unexpected surprises. The monotheistic perspective is more like the children, jumping up and down with excitement. Unexpected surprises are precisely what they are hoping for.

Which of the two perspectives we take depends on whether we feel the need to be in control, or whether we trust somebody else to look after us. For those happy to live without certainty and control, willing to put their trust in the benign nature of things, the fact that reality is greater and richer than we can ever know is not a problem: on the contrary it is something to be excited about, something to celebrate. We do not know everything, and never will. However much we know, our lives have to be characterised by an act of *trust* in the forces maintaining the universe. Our hunter-gatherer ancestors were right after all.

Chapter 8. Taking control of society

In the ancient Sumerian city of Uruk archaeologists have found a tablet dating from the 3rd century BCE, listing the food to be given to the gods at the temple there. These gods were wooden statues, a dozen at most, about the size of humans. Somebody would put a plate of food on a table in front of the god. The god would be left alone to eat. Later somebody would remove the 'leftovers'. The meals consisted of drinks, grain, fruit and meat. The daily meat allowance was

> ...21 top-grade sheep, fattened and without flaw, fed on barley for two years; 4 specially raised sheep, fed on milk; 25 second-grade sheep, not fed on milk; 2 large steers; 1 milk-fed calf; 8 lambs; 30 *marratu* birds [wild bird, not identified]; 20 turtle-doves; 3 mash-fed geese; 5 ducks fed on flour mash; 2 second-grade ducks; 4 dormice [translation uncertain]; 3 ostrich eggs and 3 duck eggs.[1]

Over and above the question of how they could believe the gods ate anything at all, such an enormous appetite, including five whole sheep per god per day, needs explaining.

The dominant theory was that the gods maintained the world and ensured the continuation of life and fertility. When they were happy all would go well. When they were angry they could impose droughts, floods, plagues, military defeat and any number of hardships. To keep them happy the humans had to provide sacrifices. Knowing which sacrifices to offer to which gods for which purposes was a complex skill. The people trained in it were the priests.

The priests also had another role. It was they who disposed of the 'leftovers'. They ate what they wanted and sold the rest.[2] Since the priests were both the experts and the beneficiaries it is easy to imagine what happened. Over the thousands of years—Uruk was one of the world's first cities—the priests would have been tempted to keep increasing the gods' requirements. In this way the sacrificial system became a method for taxing the common people more and more in the interests of the temple hierarchy.

We can imagine what this must have meant to the ordinary peasant farmer. You struggle to eke out a living and put food on the table for your family; but however poor and hungry you are, you have to take your best animals to the temple for sacrifice. It would be better for your children to starve to death than for the world order to revert to the original chaos and all life on earth to end because the gods were dissatisfied. How many animals needed to be taken? The priests knew.

Today this story may seem astonishing. How could the people have been so stupid as to believe such nonsense and undergo such hardships because of it? It may perhaps reinforce our sense that we are more intelligent than our ancestors. However I shall suggest that what is happening today is very similar indeed. Today we still need experts. We need to trust them. Being susceptible to human failings, they are easily tempted to misuse the trust we place in them. The rest of us are easily fooled.

The social control project

The idea of taking control of the world, described in the last chapter, became possible at a time when European intellectuals thought their minds were independent of it. The separation was best described by Descartes, with his theory that reality consists of two realms: a determined physical one where atoms push each other in accordance with regular laws of nature, and a separate spiritual one where the human mind relates to God. The mind, located in one realm, would control physical matter located in the other. In this picture the human mind is not available for scientific examination. Educated Europeans got used to the idea that they were 'detached observers', looking at the world as though from outside it.

A century later the Radical Enlightenment, led by French atheists, abolished the spiritual realm. Instead of two realms there was only one, the physical one. How, then, could they account for the mind? There was only one option: it had to be part of physical reality. Not only our bodies but our minds as well must be part of the simplified, determined universe, wholly subject to its laws and capable of being understood.

Mental determinism is similar to physical determinism in that it insists that every thought is caused by something else. It accepts the difference between being constrained and being free to do what we want; the question is whether, when faced with a choice, the decision is fixed in advance. If I offer you tea or coffee and you choose coffee, was your choice inevitable in the circumstances? *Could* you have chosen tea? Did you have an 'open future'? We normally think we do have open futures, but if we do it will be impossible for science to predict our behaviour. Instead determinists argue that free will is an illusion: every thought is *caused,* and is therefore bound to be what it is. This means that if somebody knew enough about your past, and all the laws of nature, they would be able to predict every one of your choices.[3]

Over half a millennium, then, a single reality was divided into two and then collapsed back into one, but a much emptier one. For Thomas Aquinas in the thirteenth century, reality was a whole but only partly knowable. By examining what we knew we could make new discoveries about the unknown.[4] Under Descartes reality was split into two, the observable physical realm which was in principle completely knowable and the unobservable spiritual one. Later again the spiritual was abolished and reality returned to being a single whole, but this time completely knowable and emptier, nothing but atoms pushing each other in unthinking obedience to unintending laws of nature. Even human minds were part of it.

Once this belief was established, another possibility arose. Just as science and technology made it possible to manipulate the physical environment, they should also make it possible to manipulate human minds. It opened up the prospect of social engineering. This, in Barry MacDonald's definition, is

> The planning of social change according to a blueprint, and the associated technology of social design and manufacture… the force of the metaphor in modern times derives from a belief in the power of science-based technological thinking to solve social problems… In its strongest sense the term connotes a belief in the human capacity to invent a future which is discontinuous with the past… and explores the possibility of altering individual behaviour through manipulation of the environment, and eugenics.[5]

Thus the 'control project' was extended to include what I shall call the 'social control project'. The two kinds of control are closely associated. Both are part of the commitment to progress and often the same intellectuals have promoted both.[6] It is no coincidence that Auguste Comte who first coined the word 'positivism' also established the discipline of sociology. Positivist theory was to be applied to the social sciences as well as the natural sciences, to establish the laws determining how society functions. The elite who discerned these laws should then use them to run society. As befitted someone who believed the human mind was determined, Comte was contemptuous of liberty and democracy. His ideal new system would vest power in the hands of those at the top of his proposed positivist religion: sociologists.[7]

Like environmental control, social control had theological roots. Charles Taylor has explored the reasons why seventeenth century Calvinists energetically campaigned to make society more godly. Medieval Catholicism was in many ways a pre-Axial society, with no expectation that disorder and crime could be reduced. It was also spiritually hierarchical, with a higher Christian standard attributed to monks and nuns. For Protestants, abolishing the hierarchy meant that all Christians should aspire to the same standard, and especially for Calvinists this meant demanding higher standards from most.[8] Taylor suggests that what they aimed to do was unprecedented in European history, in two respects:

> …first, in that the aim was to do away with violence and social disorder altogether, leaving only individual crime at one end of the spectrum, and the legitimate violence of the state in war and the repression of crime on the other; secondly, in that the goal was to inculcate at least some of the norms of civility and a properly ordered life in *everyone*.[9]

So when we are shocked by urban violence today, this is because we have inherited the changes they made to social expectations. Even Augustine, the theologian they revered most highly of all, had not expected life in this world to change so much. What gave those Calvinists confidence in their ability to do so much more was a conviction that they were the elect chosen by God to rule society and impose godly discipline on it.[10]

When the project of changing society was secularised it needed a new justification. We might note three elements. One was process: how to achieve it? Calvinists found their instructions in the Bible. Secularists looked to science. Another was authority: why did they consider themselves authorised to do it? Calvinists thought they had been chosen by God. Secularists again appealed to science: the job was to be done by people who knew the answers, and they believed they did.

Given their determination to impose on other people what other people did not want, they needed to be confident that they could not be wrong—that people who disagreed were simply mistaken. Their confidence in science had to be absolute, their information complete and certain. Of course, science's account of reality was neither complete nor certain; but at the time enthusiasts thought it eventually would be, and felt they could preempt this outcome. Conceiving of science like this, secular social engineers in effect allocated to themselves the omnipotence and omniscience previously reserved for God.

The third element could not be justified by science. Central to the project was a value judgement: that the new social order would be *better*. Calvinists thought that what they wanted must be the right thing because it was what God wanted. What made secular social engineers equally confident? They might prefer their proposed new social order to the society they already had, but that was just their value judgement and a minority one at that. If they were to work towards it they needed to believe that they had everybody's best interests at heart. How, then, could they justify their preference? There never was a satisfactory answer. Because they thought science was giving them the facts, it was easy to imagine that science was giving them the values too. In practice they inherited the hopes of their Christian predecessors and gradually adapted them. God slid out of sight only slowly; God's standards slid out of sight more slowly still.

Thus they needed to appropriate to themselves not only God's omnipotence and omniscience but also God's benevolence. It is a characteristic human weakness to believe that we ourselves are benign and have everybody's best interests at heart even when others tell us we do not. Faith traditions offer systems of meditation, confession and prayer to help people reflect on the quality of our values. Secularism rarely develops successful equivalents. What makes social engineering such a devastating force is the ability of the powerful to hear the voices of only the people who agree with them, and remain deaf to others. It is reinforced by the twin beliefs that their knowledge is certain and that those who disagree are certainly ignorant.

As we saw in the last chapter, monotheism provided a basis for hope in future progress. Nineteenth century secularists inherited it, but once God was removed from the picture the question arose as to why they should expect it. The dominant replacement for God was determinism: progress was guaranteed by some kind of inevitability. It was in this form that the idea of progress reached its apogee in the nineteenth century. Saint-Simon expressed it: 'Our intention is to promote and explain the inevitable'.[11] Comte believed that social change was governed by law and proceeded in a uniform progressive direction. Herbert Spencer interpreted these beliefs in the light of evolutionary theory:

> Progress... is not an accident, but a necessity. Instead of civilization being artificial it is a part of nature; all of a piece with the development of an embryo or the unfolding of a flower. The modifications mankind have undergone, and are still undergoing, result from a law underlying the whole organic creation; and provided the human race continues, and the constitution of things remains the same, those modifications must end in completeness. As surely as the tree becomes bulky when it stands alone, and slender if one of a group; as surely as a blacksmith's arm grows large, and the skin of a laborer's hand thick;... as surely as a clerk acquires rapidity in writing and calculation;... as surely as a passion grows by indulgence and diminishes when restrained, as surely as a disregarded conscience becomes inert, and one that is obeyed active; as surely as there is any meaning in such terms as habit, custom, practice;—so surely must the human faculties be moulded into complete fitness for the social state; so surely must evil and immorality disappear; so surely must man become perfect.[12]

Of course there is no such law of inevitability. The belief in it was a remnant of Christianity, adapted for other purposes.

The content of social engineering

Some projects have been abandoned. An influential nineteenth-century social engineer was Jeremy Bentham, with his simple utilitarian theory. If everybody appreciated the need to maximise pleasure and minimise pain, he argued, the greatest happiness of the greatest number would be attained without intervention by government or reforming agencies. However only the enlightened understood the principle. He therefore proposed to reconstruct the social order so that even the unenlightened pursuit of happiness would produce the greatest happiness for the greatest number.

The most noteworthy Benthamite reforms were in penal policy. To reduce crime, potential criminals should be deterred by harsh punishments. If the punishments failed to deter they should be increased. On this basis Britain produced a draconian system of deterrents far more severe than any retributive policy could justify. Over 200 offences attracted the death penalty and huge numbers were sent to Australia for lesser offences. There was even an honoured place for deceit: the greatest happiness for the greatest number might be achieved by not hurting the criminal but convincing the public that stiff penalties had been imposed. Bentham and his disciples discussed this as a serious proposition.[13]

Racism was another early version of social engineering. It has received such a battering since the Second World War that it is easy to forget how scientifically well-established it once seemed. European progressives were confident that some races had evolved further than others and theirs had progressed the most. They felt confident that, just as they had nothing to learn from the past, they had nothing to learn from other nations. Nisbet comments:

> The reports Marco Polo made to his fellow Westerners in the thirteenth century did more to interrupt Western man's fascination with himself than did the torrential literature on the peoples and cultures of the world in the seventeenth and eighteenth centuries. For by then the spell of the idea of progress - and with it the Eurocentric view of the entire world - had grown to such proportions that little if anything in the world could be considered in its own right. Everything had to be seen through the West and its values.[14]

Arthur de Gobineau's *Essay on the Inequality of the Human Races* (1853-55) produced the idea of an original Aryan race. His racist theories of human progress became increasingly popular for the rest of the century.[15] Given enough time, the argument ran, eventually the inferior races would progress to the European standard. It is not so long since it was being publicly argued that black Africans would not be ready for self-government for a thousand years; I myself have listened to people propounding this view. However, a contrary proposal was available: why wait the thousand years? For those who believed that evolution meant natural selection through 'the survival of the fittest', there was no shortage of scientifically-minded imperialists to recommend genocide in the interests of racial progress.

Another candidate for social engineering is the education of the young. In 1910 G K Chesterton, looking back to 1870 when the British Government accepted responsibility for providing schools, observed that social engineering had been an important part of the justification. Children would grow up to be servants of the state; otherwise, left with their parents, they would become no better than their parents:

> In the lower classes the schoolmaster does not work for the parent but against the parent. Modern education means handing down the customs of the minority, and rooting out

> the customs of the majority.[16]

Later Ivan Illich's *Deschooling Society* (1971) argued that schools were inefficient systems for educating children but good at maintaining the status quo by training children to accept their place in society.[17] This may seem an extreme position, but official government policies offer plenty of examples. A UK Government report of 2007 describes

> ...our long-term vision to make Britain one of the best places in the world for science, innovation and research, and ensure our nation has the skilled workforce needed to compete in the global economy of the 21st century... We will encourage individuals to participate in learning in order to improve their prospects, encourage employers to invest in the skills of their workforce, and develop a world-class system for delivering skills training that meets their needs... We need to change the culture in this country around skills, so that when someone complains that they are in a low-paid, dead-end job, people ask them what they are doing to improve their skills, and when an employer complains about the skills of their employees, others ask them what they are doing to train them. We need to break down the barriers that prevent adults from improving their skills, getting a job and progressing in work, and ensure that in a fast changing world there is opportunity for all.[18]

In this text the purpose of education is clear: to turn individuals into useful contributors to the project being pursued by the governing class.

These examples illustrate how the control project, once extended to include control of society, has produced an élite which considers itself competent to impose its will on others regardless of opposition. It is significant that, once the appeal to

God was excluded, the people who set out to reform society were self-appointed. Elitist confidence was easily transferred from intellectuals to generals and dictators. Hitler, Stalin and Mao had their personal ambitions, but they were also able to draw on a tradition of people who thought they knew how to improve society.

I now turn to economics, the form of social engineering which dominates western society today. Most of us tend to take for granted the dominant features of our society because we are used to them, and may find it difficult to imagine what life without them would be like. As a result we often accept the restrictions placed on us by social engineers without realising how we are being manipulated.

Before the eighteenth century economics was a branch of ethics. The Catholic Church laid down rules for just prices and wages, restricting the profits to be made by the capitalist classes. This changed when it became common to believe that human behaviour was completely determined, governed by unbreakable laws. It then seemed possible to treat economics as a science, establish the laws of economic behaviour and use them to manipulate society. This proposal is not the result of economic theory; on the contrary economists are often mocked for their failures to predict outcomes. It results, rather, from the belief that human actions are determined so economic behaviour *ought* to be predictable. Today economists are not necessarily committed to determinism, but predictability still plays an important role.

A class of economic experts is established. Financial experts, business leaders and governments work together to develop theories about what we all need to do, devise incentives for us to do it and expect us to trust their expertise. Defenders of modern capitalism, especially in its currently dominant neo-liberal form, characteristically claim that it is the best way to balance the conflicting preferences of individuals. We shall return to individualism in the next chapter, but at present we should note that the claim is based on social engineering: economic success is judged not by meeting the subjective desires of individuals, but by maximising outcomes that the experts judge desirable and measure.

The nature of economic success therefore depends on what gets measured and who does the measuring. Especially since the invention of computers, we all need to fill in more and more forms. Information not recorded on them will not be known to the experts and so, in positivist manner, will be classified as unobservables, only fit to be discounted. The society being improved by the experts turns out to be a society consisting only of what the statistics reveal.

It is a created narrative, a long way from being self-evidently true. To accept their conclusions about how well off we are is to accept that the data on which they base their claims is more informative than our own subjective and unmeasured judgements. It is as though they know our interests better than we do. To maintain this assessment we need to be constantly reassured that we are a lot better off than we would have been otherwise—that life must have been dreadful before refrigerators, flushing toilets and mobile phones. We get used to new technologies and feel sorry for people who do not have them. Still, personal experience is often very different. The common observation 'you can't stop progress', in the 1960s a paean of praise for western technology, now more often takes the form of a lament.

Being no better than ordinary humans, social engineers are faced with an enormous temptation to benefit from the trust placed in them. Since 2008, for example, there have been proposals to prosecute those responsible for the financial crash. However, very few have been prosecuted. Instead, those at the top of the finance industry continue to receive salaries and bonuses out of all proportion to the incomes of the overwhelming majority. For a few years, while substantial prosecutions still seemed likely, public debate was for peppered with threats to emigrate. These responses are a clear sign that public opinion had come to think of these people as indispensable—that we really did depend on them to know what is good for us and tell us how to live.

This is what I mean by describing the present situation as similar to ancient Uruk. The priests of Uruk claimed to know how to propitiate the gods. The worst possible outcome would be that the gods would become so dissatisfied with the sacrifices offered that they abandoned their creation and allowed the world order to revert to the original chaos. Although that had not yet happened lesser misfortunes often did. Illness, bad weather and military defeat were caused by the gods, implying each time that the sacrifices were inadequate. The obvious human response was to find out where they had failed. The priests were the ones with the specialist knowledge.

Today once again we are being told that our whole society is threatened. Once again we depend on a class of experts to tell us what needs to be done. Once again our experts disappoint us time and time again as predictions fail; and once again we respond to the failures by seeking more of the same. Even the language is similar: there is much talk of the need to make 'sacrifices' to ward off the threat of economic 'chaos'.

The two cases are based on similar presuppositions. According to the surviving literature, the ancient Mesopotamians believed that humans had been created to meet the requirements of the gods. The essential moral tasks were to burn sacrifices and maintain temples. Everything else we did was less important. As long as we performed our cultic duties the gods did not care what happened to us so we could do what we liked. Monotheism replaced this picture of humanity's condition with a radically different one. God *does* care for us, and has put us in an environment which is good for us. Our relationship with the divine realm is based not on fear of what God will do next but on gratitude for God's generosity. The moral task is not to offer sacrifices to God but to care for each other as God cares for us. Secularism, in rejecting monotheism, goes back to ancient Mesopotamian polytheism—and beyond. Once again no divinity cares what happens to us, so there is no sense in which the world has been designed to be good for us; but this time there are not even self-interested gods with a vested interest in maintaining the human race. We are completely on our own. The need for knowledge and control is even greater than it was for them. It follows that our dependence on experts is even greater, so the case for a hierarchical society is even stronger.

Comparing the expertise of those ancient priests with today's economic experts, the details are different but the pattern is similar. At one level—I think of it as the 'bottom' level—is the empirical research. A sheep is sacrificed to a particular goddess and the illness subsides. Interest rates are increased and thereafter more people save money and fewer borrow it. In both cases the data are recorded and a cause-and-effect connection is assumed. At the next level is the theory which recommends the action and is open to modification if the results are not as expected: that sacrificing a sheep to the goddess responsible for this particular illness is what persuades her to desist, that interest rates affect levels of saving and borrowing. At the highest level is an overall worldview, an account of the human condition which makes sense of the theories: that events on earth are controlled by the gods, that we all do whatever maximises our personal wealth.

From our present-day perspective the ancient Mesopotamians were completely wrong at the 'highest' level, with the result that all their cause-and-effect connections were mistaken. We would not say the same of economic theory. Nevertheless, at this 'highest' level economic theorists make generalisations about humanity which only express a small part of what we are like. In the abstract we may want to maximise our wealth, but this is very much an abstraction from a much wider set of desires, most of which do not get measured at all. When economic theory dominates public policy the abstraction comes to be treated as our dominant feature, the one that needs to be addressed at the expense of others. An example would be recent trends in employment conditions for nurses and teachers in the UK. Under the 'Welfare State' ethic, the expectation was that most people in these professions were motivated to serve other people. It therefore made sense to give them adequate salaries and training and trust them to do their best. Under neo-liberalism, on the other hand, financial incentives are considered necessary to motivate them. Some have their pay increased, some have it reduced. The decision-makers possess economic hammers so the rest of us must be economic nails.

As in Uruk, the human condition is characterised by a struggle against hostile forces. Once the population accepts the judgement of the experts that the forces governing the world are not sympathetic to human well-being, the purpose of human life can be presented as a permanent battle against them. Market forces, in a limited world where we cannot all have our own refrigerator, computer and motor car, are depicted as a tragic feature of the way things are. The ruling classes present themselves as our leaders in a shared project of ameliorating the tragic features of the natural order.

Morality is redefined accordingly. Just as the ancient Mesopotamians believed that their overriding obligation was to serve the gods, society's chief obligation today is to serve the economy. Often today the word 'morality' is restricted to personal behaviour, but let us not allow that to mislead us. If we simply ask what, in public discourse, our society most of all *ought* to do, the economy has overriding importance. 'It's the economy, stupid', originally a catchphrase in Bill Clinton's 1992 presidential campaign, has become a cliché characterising elections in developed countries. The implication is: *of course* people will vote for jobs and money for themselves without regard for wider issues.

Thus morality is taken over by the economic agenda. Other moral issues continue but are less important. What is good becomes whatever promotes the economy. What is to be condemned is whatever hinders it. Spiritual traditions have usually encouraged people to be content with their material possessions when they have enough, but modern economic discourse tells us the opposite: we *ought* to be constantly striving to earn more and spend more because it is good for the economy.

The purpose of life is redefined in the same way. The ancient Mesopotamians believed it was to serve the gods. Secularism teaches that human life has no purpose given to us, though we can create our own. Capitalism does the creating for us: because of the economic threats we are to commit ourselves to serving the economy. Naomi Klein cites a survey of USA college freshmen. In 1966, 44% of them said that making a lot of money was 'very important' or 'essential'. In 2013 the percentage had jumped to 82%.[19]

Once this is established the value of each person's life comes to be judged by their contribution to the economy. Because some people make greater contributions to it than others, some lives are counted as more valuable than others. Just as a Mesopotamian farmer who produced more sacrificial animals was of greater value than one who produced fewer, so today a person with a higher paid job serves the economy more than a person paid less. In practice the low-paid often contribute a great deal to the well-being of their communities, as do those who bring up their children and care for elderly relatives, but this disappears from view as it does not contribute to the economy. Those without paid jobs are seen as a burden on society, with the implication that the rest of us would be better off if they did not exist. In the past the accumulation of wealth by the rich had limits, but today's international financial culture encourages the practice of using money to make more money, without limit and without having the slightest idea of the practical effects on other people—who may be anywhere in the world. What matters now is not how much we serve other people but how much we serve the economy; and we serve it better by having higher paid jobs. The economy has become an end in itself.

The rich get richer. For the priests of Uruk every drought, plague, flood or military defeat meant more sacrifices should be offered. Today, when the economy grows the stock market goes up and increases the wealth of those who can afford to invest in it. When it stops growing there is a loss of jobs as some people are made redundant. This is then treated not as a failure to distribute work and wealth fairly, but as a temporary crisis; until we get the economy moving again, we have to tighten our belts. Rarely is the moral of the story pointed out: that, whatever else happens, the top priority is always for the rich to get richer.

A good example is the speech by George Osborne, UK Chancellor of the Exchequer, to the Conservative Party Conference on 8th October 2012. At the time government policies were encouraging the polarisation of wealth. The richest were getting richer while welfare benefits for the poorest were being cut and the queues at the food banks were mushrooming. The media headlines[20] picked out his claim that 'We're all in this together'. The speech was peppered with statements like 'Everyone will have to play their part'. It was a well-timed claim precisely because at the time it was more untrue than it had been for over seventy years.[21]

In these ways modern capitalism has recreated the exploitative processes of ancient Uruk. Like those ancient gods, the economy is a superhuman force which has to be obeyed whatever the cost. It threatens chaos unless we do what we are told by the experts with their technical knowledge. Because it is often hostile it must be repeatedly propitiated. Again, the sacrifices are made by the common people; the ruling classes, with their experts who claim to know how what needs to be done, are the real beneficiaries. Again, economic exploitation is maintained by a myth about superhuman forces.

In one respect the present cult of the economy is even more oppressive than the cult at Uruk. The ancient Mesopotamians were obliged to provide the sacrifices demanded by the priests, and over the millennia the demands increased; but they had no principle demanding continual increases. Today's cult of the economy does. A permanently growing economy is declared necessary. This means that the total amounts of money everybody receives and spends must keep increasing without limit; we must produce more, earn more, spend more and consume more each year than we did the previous year.

Work, therefore, loses its limits. We might compare current expectations with those of forty years ago. In the 1970s there was much excitement about the development of computers. One day, enthusiasts told us, they would be small enough to be installed in an ordinary house. They would save so much work that perhaps the retirement age would be reduced to fifty, or we would all do a twenty-hour working week. Since then the technological advance has been even greater than expected but, far from producing the social benefits, it has led to the exact opposite. With the incessant demand for a growing economy, working hours have increased. The amount of economic growth, electricity and new technology needed is to keep going up and up. Since we live in a finite world this is of course impossible. The impossibility is then presented not as a refutation of the theory but as justification for the continuing siege mentality—the need for the population to support the experts in their battle against harsh economic circumstances. So obedience to the ruling powers is essential for the foreseeable future until our economic problems are solved; and because of the way we have defined them they never can be solved. There will always be many things that need to be done before we can relax and enjoy life. It puts us in a state of permanent crisis, as in George Orwell's *1984*. We have become wage slaves, obliged to work harder and harder to do things which previous generations saw no need to do.

Thus a philosophy of humanity that prevailed in ancient Mesopotamia has been recreated in modern secularism. It looks as though a society that gets rid of all its gods ends up creating new ones. Ironically, a control project which offered to free us from all constraints has tied us up with new chains. Our slavery continues because, and only because, enough people believe the myths recited by the priests of modern economic theory.

Flaws in the project

These unfortunate results of the cult of economics are not caused by capitalist economic theory, or indeed any economic theory. They are the product of a society that has already accepted the idea of social engineering.

Each programme of social engineering depends on the control project with its belief in progress, and the élitism which attributes to experts the ability to improve society regardless of the preferences of those affected. Élitism is therefore central to all such programmes. Every society needs experts and depends on their expertise, but social engineering demands more. Normally we seek advice and help from experts while retaining the right to decline their offers. What makes the social control project so much more ambitious is the use of force: the population's lives are to be changed regardless of their wishes. Force is defended on grounds inherited from Auguste Comte's positivism, with its anti-democratic account of humanity. It is not just that each expert knows more than the general population about the subject of their expertise, but that the population is divided into two classes, those who know the scientific facts and those who must be coerced for their own good.

The reason for the division can be seen by comparing control of the mind with control of the environment. The environmental control project was simpler: the physical world ticked away like a giant clock, every event causing a subsequent event, while the human mind looked on from outside. When the Radical Enlightenment abolished the spiritual realm, there was no longer any outside. The human mind had to be part of this clock, ticking away just like everything else. The theory became self-referring: if I think the mind is determined then I must think *my* mind is determined. The social control project therefore treats the mind in two ways. As knower it is omnicompetent, in principle capable of uncovering every secret. As known, it must be simple enough that we can understand it. Perhaps eventually we will be able to explain why it thinks what it thinks and predict its future thoughts.

The question is: can both descriptions be true of the same mind at once? It is easy enough to believe that the people we disagree with hold their opinions because their minds are determined. Thought 1 is caused by Thought 2 which is caused by Thought 3, and so on all the way back to the day they were born. If it is true of everyone, then everything everybody has ever thought is part of a causal sequence going all the way back to the Big Bang. This is a useful way to dismiss the opinions of other people. The trouble is, if it is true at all it must be equally true of our own minds. We find it harder to believe that our own minds are determined. We hold opinions because we really think they are true. However, if the thoughts of our minds are part of a causal sequence going back to the beginning of the universe, so that none of our opinions could have been other than they are, then we have no way to stand outside our minds, look at our beliefs objectively and use reason and evidence to assess whether they are true. We can never find out whether any of our beliefs are true.

Neurologists and philosophers still debate mental determinism. What resulted in practice was a dualism between the élite who learn how the mind works and the people whose minds are determined. The élite carried on looking at the world as though from outside, calculating how best to govern it, while treating the minds of their subjects as determined. This dualism allowed them to ignore the wishes of the majority. It still characterises ruling élites and their disciples, people who want to convince themselves that they know what is best for others. Rulers learn to live with an easygoing confidence in their own understanding and benevolence. Usually neither is justified, but the belief is needed if one is to lay down the law for other people whom one has never met.

We are left, therefore, back where we started. Our minds are capable of knowing a lot, but not everything. Just as our advancing knowledge of the physical environment reveals complexities far greater than we will ever fully understand, so also our advancing understanding of human society reveals that it is far too complex for any experts to understand it fully. The quality of our lives—our pleasures, happiness, hopes, disappointments, fears—are immeasurable. Each of us as an individual knows how we feel; nobody else can tell us our life feels better or worse than we think it does. Just as the attempt to control the physical environment has caused immense destruction, so also the attempts of social engineers to produce their utopias end up benefiting themselves at the expense of other people.

What made the social control project seem viable was a moral flaw that all spiritual traditions warn against. One of the first principles that young children need to learn is that other people's minds are similar to their own. The idea that we know things while other people's minds are determined is easily interpreted as a reason to unlearn it.

In the last chapter we saw how secularism, by dispensing with God, led to the conclusion that the physical environment was the product of unthinking processes and therefore could not be trusted. This led to the project to take control of it and alter it in humanity's interests. It would have been better if we had retained our trust in it. In this chapter we have seen a parallel project: of the leaders of society struggling for mastery over recalcitrant *human* nature. It might have been closer to the older spiritual idea that we need to change ourselves rather than changing the world around us, had it not maintained the opposition between those who do the changing and those being changed. Again, the possibility of doing more harm than good has not been taken seriously enough. Social scientists, and the people powerful enough to try out their proposals, are human beings with characteristic human weaknesses. In a culture that strives after an omniscience that it no longer attributes to God, those too confident that they know what is best for us have enslaved populations to their chosen agendas. Most of us would like some help and advice from experts over one thing or another, but we do not want them to control our lives. Our own individual judgements about what makes us happy are usually more reliable than anyone else's, however many forms we fill in. However often we get things wrong, handing over control to a class of experts is not the answer. We need to live with an act of *trust* that we have within us the capacity to live well. When we make this act of trust, we want freedom from control by others. We are right to want it.

Chapter 9. Freedom from control

The control project described in the last two chapters is communitarian in both its environmental and its social forms. God no longer gives purpose and direction to our lives; instead, humanity does. The individual's place in society is retained; it is society's place in the wider scheme of things that is re-engineered.

Another, more logical response to godlessness was available. If there is no god to tell us to have, or not have, dominion over nature; if there is no authority telling us how, or even whether, to make any kind of progress; if nobody has full knowledge about how we and the world work; what should we do? The answers must be found in whatever is left after this emptying out.

What is left is individual people. Assuming, as Descartes taught, that other animals cannot evaluate, all values are invented by the individual human being with his or her various hopes and fears. So in a tradition very different from what we have seen in the last two chapters, the individual human came to be seen as both subject and object of all valuing. All our valuing depends on staying alive, so nothing is more valuable than the individual human life. If anything else has value, it has value because, and only because, humans value it. This philosophy lies behind the tradition of liberal politics.

These thoughts arose at a time of debate about the legitimacy of governments. The seventeenth century produced a new interest in the origins of laws and governments. If the will of God does not legitimate them, what does? What would life have been like before they existed? Thomas Hobbes thought people in the 'state of nature' would have been self-seeking individuals fighting each other for resources. They would have been in a permanent 'war of all against all' so life would have been 'solitary, poor, nasty, brutish and short'.[1]

It was John Locke's account that became the most influential. To Locke, in the state of nature everybody had equal freedom. Nobody was subordinate to anyone else.[2] No governments had yet laid down laws, but there was a law of nature:

> The state of nature has a law of nature to govern it, which obliges every one: and reason, which is that law, teaches all mankind, who will but consult it, that being all equal and independent, no one ought to harm another in his life, health, liberty, or possessions: for men being all the workmanship of one omnipotent, and infinitely wise maker; all the servants of one sovereign master, sent into the world by his order, and about his business; they are his property, whose workmanship they are, made to last during his, not one another's pleasure: and being furnished with like faculties, sharing all in one community of nature, there cannot be supposed any such subordination among us, that may authorize us to destroy one another, as if we were made for one another's uses, as the inferior ranks of creatures are for our's.[3]

Locke believed that this original state of nature really had existed and continued to exist in his day in two classes of people: the rulers of independent states, and each individual until by their own consent they made themselves a member of a society.[4] The trouble with the state of nature was that each individual was biased in their own interests and there was no impartial arbiter. The result was conflict. They therefore agreed to create a civil society, establishing a social contract to uphold each other's rights. To make sure it was enforced they gave power to a political authority. Natural rights, universal and inalienable moral norms, had already existed in natural law but were to be enforced by the social contract.[5]

The idea of a social contract was Hobbes' way of justifying absolute monarchy and Locke's way of defending the expulsion of James II and the reign of William III. What they had in common was that governments are legitimated not by God but by the consent of the people.

Of course there is no evidence that it ever really happened. Our current evolutionary account of the history of humanity makes it look unrealistic; all primates, for example, have hierarchical societies. What has been invented is another example of Mircea Eliade's 'primeval time' when the conditions of life were established. If nineteenth century anthropologists had discovered it in Indonesia they would have classified it as a myth and wondered at the ignorance of people so foolish as to believe such things. Nevertheless it served the purpose that popular myths do: it provided a justification for a set of shared values. The idea that government was justified by an original contract between free and equal individuals provided a theoretical argument against both the divine right of kings to rule and the communitarian agendas described in the last chapter. It also reflected the interests of the rising commercial classes of the time.[6] Political liberals today do not need to believe it happened to be influenced by its values.

The theological origins of liberalism

For Locke, God was an essential part of the argument. The passage quoted above inherits two beliefs from Christian monotheism. One is that the divine creator has designed us for our own well-being and cares for every single one of us. The other is that there are moral truths which God enables us to perceive through our ordinary rationality.[7] God has created us as individuals (albeit in community), has endowed us with freedom to obey or disobey the natural law, loves all humans equally and gives us moral laws that are the source of rights. As long as this theological background was maintained the central principles of political liberalism could be derived from them.

The emphasis on individualism was a product of the fear of

Hell in the Reformation debates. It was each individual, with an eternal destiny, who stood under the judgement of God and would be saved or damned. So it was individuals, whose primary relationships were not with society but with God, who should between them determine government policies. Inheriting this picture, the story of the original state of nature conceives of the individual as historically prior to society, and therefore morally prior as well. The theological origins of liberalism are unaffected by the fact that religious authorities were often its strongest opponents.

Liberalism, as its name suggests, affirms the importance of freedom. As a gift of God, given in the state of nature, it took priority over political institutions. Which freedoms the individual should have, and the proper limits to them, could be derived from one's theology.

The idea of equality is largely a product of monotheism, as we saw in Chapter 4: all humans are created by a single god who cares for them equally, so worshippers of that god should respect their equal rights to life and fulfilment. Locke inherited it: the state of nature was

> ...a state also of equality, wherein all the power and jurisdiction is reciprocal, no one having more than another; there being nothing more evident, than that creatures of the same species and rank, promiscuously born to all the same advantages of nature, and the use of the same faculties, should also be equal one amongst another without subordination or subjection, unless the lord and master of them all should, by any manifest declaration of his will, set one above another.[8]

Here Locke is opposing the ideas of natural subordination which characterised medieval feudalism and the divine right of kings. Political liberals today continue this tradition by opposing inequalities for undeserved differences. This remains the basis for demanding equality of treatment for women and black people.

The other central element was rights. The western concept of human rights has a distinctive history. In ancient Roman law justice was seen as giving everyone their right—*ius suum*—what was due to them, whether it was positive or negative, a benefit or a punishment. Still today, some languages have just one word to cover both 'right' and 'duty'. Finnis suggests that we might translate it as 'due'.[9] In the later Middle Ages *ius* gradually came to refer only to the positive due. Thus Summenhart argued that birds have a *ius*, a right, to collect seeds and build nests. These rights were based on a natural gift from God. Unlike birds, humans can act against God-given norms, but this was not seen as a right.[10] A right, then, was something people should be allowed to do because God had designed them to do it.

This is the tradition Locke inherited. Every individual, he believed, had natural rights derived from 'natural law'. Two centuries before the 'science and religion' split, natural law combined two ideas which we now think of as separate: the scientific 'laws of nature' and the moral laws we perceive through our ordinary thinking and perceiving. These natural laws, physical and moral alike, were given by God. Locke added that natural law existed in the state of nature, was prior to any social organisation and took moral priority over any group or society. Thus he believed that basic rights really existed, as part of God's moral provision, commanding that 'no one ought to harm another in his life, health, liberty, or possessions'.[11] This view characterised much Enlightenment thought. In 1776 the American Declaration of Independence appealed to God as a higher moral authority than King George III:

> We hold these truths to be self-evident, that all men are created equal, that they are endowed by their Creator with certain unalienable Rights, that among these are Life, Liberty

and the pursuit of Happiness.[12]

Secularised liberalism

When the authority of God is withdrawn from these principles they change. The changes are rarely noted today because defenders of political liberalism tend to forget its theological roots while remembering the opposition it received from church leaders.

They became harder to justify. The story of the original state of nature and the ensuing social contract offer an account of human nature much thinner than either its theological predecessors or the evolutionary theory that arose later.

As long as principles are derived from a higher authority they can be justified in terms of it and their practical implications can be derived from it. Thus Locke could use his theology to explain what he meant by rights and equality. When they are reinterpreted as first principles they can no longer be justified by a higher principle. They thereby lose their justifications. Characteristically the principles of liberalism came to be understood as self-evident truths. When this happens they become versatile, capable of being reinterpreted to mean anything the speaker's language allows them to mean.

So the individual seeking salvation is replaced by the individual seeking whatever he or she seeks. The role of governments then becomes protecting the freedom of individuals to pursue whatever interests they may have. What the individual *wants* becomes the basis for all public morality. Hobbes, Hume and Bentham all took for granted that people are essentially self-centred. Bentham added that it was morally justified: 'Nature has placed mankind under the governance of two sovereign masters, pain and pleasure. It is for them alone to point out what we ought to do, as well as to determine what we shall do'.[13]

Secularised freedom becomes the principle that, since value is located in each individual, there are no legitimate goals except those of individuals. Each person's freedom to achieve their own goals becomes foundational for all other goals. In the state of nature we *are* free so now we *ought* to be free. As freedom ceases to be a resource for other uses and instead becomes an objective in its own right, ethical debate becomes less about how to use our freedom and more about how to maximise it. Alternative interpretations of it have generated the left-right split of modern politics.

Isaiah Berlin analysed the difference between negative and positive accounts of freedom.[14] The early liberals Hobbes, Locke, Adam Smith, Jeremy Bentham and John Stuart Mill defined it negatively, as freedom from interference. The principle here is that, because the only legitimate preferences are those of individuals, the state should avoid making judgements about what individuals should do. Instead it should limit itself to protecting their freedom to pursue their own interests and only intervene when their freedom is threatened.[15]

Negative liberals characteristically define freedom as the absence of coercion by other people. According to Berlin,

> I am normally said to be free to the degree to which no man or body of men interferes with my activity. Political liberty in this sense is simply the area within which a man can act unobstructed by others.

The point here is that deprivation of freedom is caused by the actions of other people, not by other restrictions:

> If I say that I am unable to jump more than ten feet in the air… it would be eccentric to say that I am to that degree enslaved or coerced… You lack political liberty or freedom only if you are prevented from attaining a goal by human beings.[16]

A more extreme view is that coercion by others only deprives a person of freedom when it is physical. If I hold a pistol to your head and say 'your money or your life' you may change your mind about whether you want to keep your money but you are still free to choose.[17] Few have argued this, but it does raise the question of where to draw the line: when does a constraint become a denial of liberty? The main area of debate is poverty caused by an economic system. Berlin notes:

> It is argued, very plausibly, that if a man is too poor to afford something on which there is no legal ban—a loaf of bread, a journey round the world, recourse to the law courts—he is as little free to have it as he would be if it were forbidden him by law.

However, Berlin disagrees with this judgement. It seems like a lack of freedom because of an assumption about the causes of poverty. Comparing the inability to buy bread because of poverty with the inability to run because of lameness, he replies that

> ...this inability would not naturally be described as a lack of freedom, least of all political freedom.

Therefore, Berlin concludes,

> It is only because I believe that my inability to get a given thing is due to the fact that other human beings have made arrangements whereby I am, whereas others are not, prevented from having enough money with which to pay for it, that I think myself a victim of coercion or slavery. [18]

This argument has characterised the proponents of twentieth-century neo-liberal economists.

Positive liberals differ from negative liberals by arguing that to be truly free we need an adequate degree of power over our circumstances. Many factors, including inequalities of wealth and power, limit our freedom. Thus we need some kind of welfare state ensuring that everybody has the basic necessities of life, including an education.

Part of the case for positive liberalism is the recognition that what the individual wants is not basic. People can want things because they are misinformed. Political and commercial forces manipulate preferences to suit their own interests. Studies have shown that impoverished people often give up even wanting things they know they cannot acquire.[19] As well as external restrictions on meeting our desires there are internal ones, like impulses and obsessions, which limit our freedom rather than expressing it. We have not just desires for possessions but also desires about desires, like the longing to give up smoking. People in desperately unhappy circumstances develop desires for things like hard drugs which they would not otherwise have wanted.[20] Positive liberals therefore argue that true freedom needs some welfare provision: governments should ensure that everybody has the resources—the money, the health, the education—to be truly autonomous.[21] 'Putting first thing first, bread and health for all before cake and circuses for anybody', proposed William Beveridge, the architect of the British Welfare State in 1944.[22]

Negative liberals reply that this expects governments to take a view about what is in people's real interests, thus imposing its own values and betraying the basic principles of liberalism.[23]

We should be clear what this argument for negative liberalism is doing. It is defining the word 'freedom'. Defenders of negative freedom draw the line at intention: if some people motivated by profit drive others to impoverishment, freedom is not removed because the intention was the profit, not the impoverishment. Even if the deprivations are foreseen as inevitable, they are not to count as taking away freedom; they must be described in other terms.[24] To follow the argument one has to bracket out the ethical question of whether such poverty is acceptable and focus simply on the meaning of the word. However, once negative liberals have established their preferred meaning of the word 'freedom', it then gets treated as ethically normative.

Compared with most religious accounts of morality this is a massive change. It tells people they do not need to care about the effects of their actions on other people, provided that they do not *intend* to harm them. So moral responsibility for other people is restricted to avoiding deliberate constraint, while freedom gets diluted to the point at which the only people who are not free are the ones intentionally constrained by other people.

The idea of negative freedom has the virtue of clarifying how much secularism dispenses with. A secularism that denies all transcendent moral authorities cannot uphold any public moral norms without contradicting itself; all it can do is defend the freedom of individuals to decide their own norms for themselves. We noted in the last chapter that one of the central arguments for neo-liberal economics is that it is the best way to balance the conflicting preferences of individuals. The point of the argument is that since there are absolutely no moral norms that transcend individual preferences, neo-liberalism offers a *technique* for meeting more preferences than other techniques do. This claim on behalf of neo-liberalism is undermined whenever its supporters argue that it is morally better than alternative economic systems—thus implying that there are, after all, moral standards higher than individual preferences.

Equality gets diluted in a similar way. To say that we are equal sounds like a statement of fact but clearly is not. We are not equally muscular, tall or intelligent. Perhaps we are all equally valuable or important: but to whom, if not God? The political discourse of equality characteristically uses it as a moral claim: we *ought* to treat each other equally. However, a moral appeal to a non-existent moral authority is meaningless.

In effect the appeal to equality has come to mean two contradictory things. For some, what is needed is equal access to resources. We have the bodies we were given at birth. If people should not be rewarded for being white or male, why should they be rewarded for being muscular or intelligent? Our ability to work hard is also unequal: because of the bodies we have, some can do more than others. Opponents reply that once we go down this path we end up negating all moral responsibility.[25] Instead, everybody should have the *opportunity* to do well for themselves, but some will make more of it than others. Inequalities will then reflect what people deserve. Desert, in this way, becomes a basis for inequality.[26]

Rights also lose their force. When secularised they simply *exist*, as features of moral reality, issuing commands. We might think of them as invisible shields in the sky, granting individuals moral protection from harm. In this form they have to be self-justifying foundational first principles for moral claims. Two questions then arise, which did not arise for Locke: which natural rights, if any, exist, and why should we pay any attention to them?

Because there is no way to observe which rights exist, let alone to explain why we should obey them, rights discourse today is something of a free-for-all. Popular discourse now claims rights for countless purposes. For one there is the baby's right to life, for another the woman's right to choose; for one the right to privacy, for another the public's right to know. Corporations can have rights. Popular indignation can be aroused when rights are abused. Western governments often condemn other governments for not respecting them, while consigning countless refugees to the bottom of the Mediterranean as though they had no rights. It is not at all surprising that many critics have denied their existence altogether. Among the early sceptics were Burke, Bentham and Marx. Bentham described them as 'nonsense on stilts' and 'anarchical fallacies, metaphysical entities which could not be shown to exist'.[27] More recently Alasdair MacIntyre has argued that 'the truth is plain: there are no such rights, and belief in them is one with belief in witches and unicorns.'[28]

Responses to critics

Secular critics of liberalism find the emphasis on the individual a major weakness. Marxists stress that human nature is a historical product, largely formed by the means of production, so it is the competitive and self-interested character of capitalism that makes people behave like isolated individuals. For communitarian critics the emphasis on the individual's autonomously chosen way of life excludes different conceptions of the good based on our communal nature. Feminists stress how masculine liberal individualism is: women are often better able to 'think through the body' and express the unconscious, the subjective and the emotional as well as the structural and intellectual.[29]

These critics argue that the emphasis on the individual misdescribes what humanity is like. It treats us as interested in other people only to the extent that we can get something out of them, and rational only in the sense that we calculate how to achieve our selfish desires. On the contrary we are essentially social. As well as liking to be cared for we like to care. As well as liking to receive we like to give. We have evolved with both competitive and altruistic tendencies. This means both that we have shared interests—so that there is such a thing as the public good over and above the interests of individuals—and also that individuals are often not the best judges of their own interests. A government that designs its institutions on the basis that we are all self-centred will inevitably encourage self-centredness—for example by trying to motivate public servants with financial incentives rather than encouraging a service ethos. Governments that recognise and encourage the altruistic, caring elements of our nature are likely to produce a more altruistic society.

Liberals have often explored the tension between liberalism

and the kinds of communitarianism described in the last two chapters. Some have argued that there is no such thing as the common good: since individuals are more real than collective entities it makes no sense to talk about the public interest except as an aggregate of individual interests. Reductionism is applied to society: if physical things can be understood by breaking them down into their constituent parts and examining each one, so can society. Jeremy Bentham considered the concept of society a fiction.[30] Friedrich Hayek and Karl Popper used similar arguments.[31] The claim that 'there is no such thing as society', often today associated with Margaret Thatcher, stands in this tradition.

Other liberals accept the idea of the common good and try to reconcile the priority of individual interests with it. The best known example is Adam Smith's 'invisible hand of Providence', arguing that there happens to be a happy coincidence between the two.[32]

The compatibility of individual self-seeking with the good of society is of course no more than an act of faith. Smith's word 'Providence' was a suitably vague term, covering the kind of faith capitalists often still have today that individual self-centredness *somehow* ends up doing more good than harm.[33] What remains more characteristic of liberal individualism is the individual's freedom to pursue his or her preferences *without* communitarian obligations. Thus the *faith* in an automatic benefit to the common good becomes a *moral justification* of an individualistic self-centredness that all the major religious traditions judge to be immoral. John Maynard Keynes recognised the weakness in the idea:

> Let us clear from the ground the metaphysical or general principles upon which, from time to time, *laissez faire* has been founded. It is *not* true that individuals possess a prescriptive 'natural liberty' in their economic activities. There is *no*

> 'compact' conferring perpetual rights on those who Have or on those who Acquire. The world is *not* so governed from above that private and social interest always coincide. It is *not* so managed here below that in practice they coincide. It is *not* a correct deduction from the Principles of Economics that enlightened self-interest always operates in the public interest. Nor is it true that self-interest generally *is* enlightened: more often individuals acting separately to promote their own ends are too ignorant or too weak to attain even these. Experience does *not* show that individuals, when they make up a social unit, are always less clear-sighted than when they act separately.[34]

Another approach is to retain the rhetoric of liberalism as a disguise for social engineering. In the last chapter I referred to neo-liberal economic theory as a form of social engineering. What I mean is the way freedom ends up being defined in such a way as to justify an economic programme largely disconnected from the actual preferences of individuals. We have seen how negative liberalism, claiming to be based on maximising individual freedom, redefines it in such a way as to treat people as free in circumstances, like extreme poverty, where their options are severely constrained. In this way exploitative economic relationships are removed from critical scrutiny. Such a definition of freedom raises our suspicions as it seems purpose-made for those who wish to make money without regard for the effects on other people. However, neo-liberals claim that it is important to define freedom like this because it needs to be objective. If all values are to be determined by individuals, they argue, governments must not take it upon themselves to interpret people's preferences or apply their own values. The freedom they defend must therefore be an observable, objective freedom.[35]

In no real sense is this position either liberal or individualistic. The real subjective preferences of individuals are ignored; the only preferences that will count are ones that are objectively measured by governments. The ones they measure, through price fluctuations in the 'free market', are then treated as the only preferences they need to defend. We are fully back to a communitarian project of social engineering, with an élite of positivists discounting all unobservables in their project of creating a new and different society. If neo-liberal governments really wanted to respond to the real preferences of individuals, instead of depending on economic statistics they could ask direct questions through social surveys and referenda. In effect, the liberal tradition's failure to provide an adequate account of how society can balance the real preferences of individuals has left the door open for social engineers to take over.

So we live with a strange inversion of individual and community. The ruling classes of capitalist societies govern on the basis that we are all selfish individuals and judge progress on the basis of how much we have bought and sold. This kind of liberalism, as Schaar puts it,

> ...extends the market-place mentality to all the spheres of life. It views the whole of human relations as a contest in which each man competes with his fellows for scarce goods, a contest in which there is never enough for everybody and where one man's gain is usually another's loss.[36]

Individuals, on the other hand, overwhelmingly believe in society, care for the common good and spend large amounts of time on unselfish activities for the sake of families, local communities, domestic pets and social engagements. When, for example, a person abandons his or her ambitions in order to care for a disabled relative the decision may be made out of love or duty or financial pressure; whichever it is, freedom is one of a number of elements balanced against each other. We rarely treat it as an absolute principle. We give and receive different freedoms according to our priorities at any one time. A better account of freedom's role, therefore, would be that it interacts with other values in a manner much more complex than the foundational narrative of liberalism can explain. What we need is a richer account of the priorities we have, why we have them and when we ought to have them.

Liberalism without God

Moral philosophers have often commented on the gradual reduction of the norms proclaimed by secular liberalism.[37] My claim here has been that the removal of God from the explanatory structure is a major part of the reason. Individual freedom, equality and rights all began as aspects of a God-given natural law which had been overshadowed, during the Reformation debates, by claims for divine revelation but had survived well enough to be reaffirmed, albeit in a weakened form, by early Enlightenment thinkers. At first they were simply careful not to attribute more than necessary to God for fear of stoking the flames of religious disagreement. Later, God was replaced by ghostly substitutes. Self-evident rights and duties, Adam Smith's 'invisible hand of Providence' or the 'destiny' of imperialists and social determinists seemed for a time adequate to fill the gap. When it became clear that they were not, liberal principles had no moral grounding at all. They were absolutised, turned into self-evident first principles which ought to be obeyed at all times. As absolutes, they suffer the fate of biblical texts in the hands of fundamentalists: each interpretation is proclaimed as the uninterpreted truth.

Principles which can be interpreted in countless different ways have a habit of being defined for us in ways that suit the dominant voices. Freedom, equality and rights therefore come to mean what governments want them to mean. You are homeless, helpless and starving, but free because nobody is physically attacking you. You are equal because you can apply for highly-paid jobs, even though nobody pays you anything. Liberal principles, once weakened by the removal of any consensus about their moral authority, became available for manipulation by the powerful.

The practical effect on ethical norms has been immense. Initially, it is easy to see why liberals saw fit to reject the moral norms emanating from church authorities. The exaltation of celibacy, the obligation to attend church services, the sales of indulgences and the threat of Hell could all be abandoned with no noticeable harmful effects and a great many beneficial ones. Unfortunately, when the older moral norms were rejected, what remained as the basis for morality was individual humans with their freedom, equality and rights. With every right comes a duty; if you have a right to be left alive others have a duty not to kill you. Earlier moral theory, using the same word *ius* to describe both positive and negative dues, had maintained a closer connection between rights and duties. Liberal discourse, by treating the individual's preferences as basic, has emphasised rights at the expense of duties, thus contributing to a culture where one demands one's rights without caring about any negative effects on other people.

In this liberal tradition, whatever the individual wants has been turned into the highest moral standard. For Locke the idea of humanity as a set of free and self-centred individuals was constrained by the natural law given by God. Take God out of the picture and there is nothing to use our freedom for, except to pursue whatever we happen to want. If we behave like this we inevitably reproduce Hobbes' 'war of all against all' since self-centredness is posited at the beginning of the theory.

Religious traditions characteristically treat individual wants very differently. They are not such basic facts about us. We think about what we ought to want. There are some things we want and wish we did not want. What we want for ourselves as self-centred individuals is an important part of moral reflection, but for the opposite reason. When we want what we morally ought to want, ethical issues rarely arise. Characteristically, they arise precisely at the times when we ought to do one thing but want to do another. When liberals tell us—as Bentham did and much neo-liberal economic theory still does—that what we want is the basis for calculating what we ought to do, it inverts the ethical tradition. The practical result may well be, and often is, that they tell us to do precisely what previous ethical traditions forbade us to do—like, for example, accumulating wealth without checking whether we are impoverishing other people. Self-centredness, which had previously been the classic instance of moral evil, has thus been turned into the foundation of moral good.

What undermines the liberal tradition of morality most comprehensively is the lack of any good reason to accept its principles. The early idea of an original state of nature followed by a social contract succeeded as a social myth because it combined two elements: an account of what human nature is like and a moral appeal derived from it. The account of human nature, though over-simplified, could be adapted as time went on; but why should anyone accept the moral appeal? Self-interest does the job in some situations but not all. If the originating myth had been literally true we might think it in our interests to respect other people's rights so that they respect ours; but sometimes there is the option of being a free-rider, and anyway in the unequal conditions of society today the extremely rich and powerful do not need, and rarely want, to treat the poor as equals; they have nothing to lose by trampling on their rights.

The alternative is to appeal to some kind of moral authority. However, moral authorities mean nothing unless the need to obey them is accepted. The authority of God, while still accepted, did at least provide reasons for obedience. If, on the other hand, nobody has authority to tell us which moral norms to accept, then any attempt to persuade us that we ought to respect any moral norms at all is just one more version of the experts telling us they know what is best for us.

From the start, secularism simplified. Just as the communitarian emphasis on humanity as a whole working towards a common agenda disguises the fact that most of our conflicts are with other people, the liberal emphasis on our individuality disguises the complex relationships between individuals and their society. Describing us as self-centred disguises the complex interplay between our selfishness and our altruism; describing our freedom, equality and rights as absolute principles which morally ought to be protected at all times disguises our ordinary everyday give and take as we sacrifice one priority for the sake of another.

It is not that the seventeenth century liberals were starting from scratch with the first attempts to describe human nature. On the contrary, Descartes' rationalism and Locke's empiricism in their different ways expressed the belief that they *ought* to start from scratch. Millennia of reflection on human nature had produced a rich tradition but the pessimism of late medieval Christianity had soured it. Going back to the beginning seemed the best option.

Later on, evolutionary psychologists and biologists developed much richer descriptions of humanity, recognising the complex interactions between individuality and community memberships. Both the earlier liberal accounts of freedom, equality and rights, and the communitarian notions of humanity striving against its environment or itself, can now be seen as anachronisms. Nevertheless they continue to exert massive influence on western society and culture.

The removal of God from the moral structure created a dilemma. As long as God was part of the story it was possible to relate the individual to the community in interactive ways: the proper roles of community and individual could be understood as parts of God's provision. When God is removed, and humans become the only beings capable of evaluating and thinking through what to do, then humanity takes over the role of God. But is this the whole human race acting in concert, or an élite of experts, or each of us as an individual? For those committed to a shared project, the characteristic need is for technical knowledge. Here we are, thrown into a world which, far from being conducive to our well-being, is a bit like the alien world of ancient Gnostics and Manicheans—except that our 'gnosis' will be not about how to escape from it but how to alleviate its worst effects. In order to find out how to do this we need to learn how it functions. Science will lead to improving technologies. For this to be effective we need division of labour with a class of experts. The experts will tell us what to do and how to live. The rest of us will be well advised, or perhaps forced, to obey.

For individualists, on the other hand, what they should do is up to them. In practice nearly everyone has strong feelings about some things being right or wrong. Many people put effort into opposing what the communitarian experts tell them is good for them—fracking, perhaps, or a new industrial development that will spoil the countryside, or experiments on animals; there are countless causes for which dissidents oppose what experts say will be of benefit.

Thus arises the dilemma. If we begin with the community, we end up with inadequate protection for individuals. Individuals get enslaved and exploited, forced to work towards somebody else's objectives. On the other hand, if we begin with the freedom and rights of individuals we end up with inadequate processes for resolving disputes. This tension between communitarianism and individualism is an inevitable result of secularism. On the one hand it gives an account of values without reference to God; on the other it attributes as much authority to its values as they would have had if they had come from God. The effect is to retain the impression of a moral authority that transcends humans, but attribute it to humans—whether to humanity-as-a-whole, an élite or each individual.

The practical result is paradoxical. By rejecting divine authority secularism points to a value-free conclusion. There is no purpose to life and therefore no progress towards it. There are no obligations on us. Yet we live as though the exact opposite was true. If there is one indisputable characteristic of modern western society it is that we are busy, and constantly being urged to be busier still. Fritz Schumacher proposed that

> The amount of real leisure a society enjoys tends to be in inverse proportion to the amount of labour-saving machinery it employs.[38]

We have become better than ever at knowing how to do more and more, but have lost the ability to reflect on what needs to be done. It is as though we are driving down a motorway to attend a wedding, when we hear that it has been cancelled; so, not knowing what to do, we just carry on driving. Eventually we shall have to decide what to do instead, but we have not reached that stage yet. Meanwhile we avoid the question by focusing on the immediate jobs.

Before the days of secularisation, the big questions about what society should do were referred to God. When God was removed from the picture it became humanity's task to answer the questions. After a few centuries of struggling with them, the answers have become increasingly clear: quite simply, in a godless world there are no right answers. As the earlier accounts of 'monotheism from above' indicate, a society that believes in one god can affirm the values of inequality and oppression in the same way as a secular society can. Public debate today shows that in most controversies believers and unbelievers alike can be on both sides. However their predicaments are not identical. Believers can appeal to objective moral truths that transcend the ruling classes. When unbelievers do the same, they betray their unbelief.

If we really are just self-centred individuals, each with our own preferences in a godless world with no intrinsic values, then any values we have can only be our own creations. Every appeal—whether to share in a common humanitarian project, or to accept the advice of experts, or to honour other people's rights—is only to be respected if we make a free, arbitrary decision to respect it. If there are to be any values at all, we shall have to create them for ourselves, and nobody has any business telling us which ones to create. This reduction of morality was inevitable from the start. The next chapter will explore how it dismantles all moral discourse.

Chapter 10. On creating one's own values

The last three chapters have described how secular society, over the last few centuries, has developed God-free systems of morality and values. For some, humanity-as-a-unity remained a dominant concept while being redirected to other aims. Others believed in a class of experts who understood how we should live and could guide individuals and societies. For others again the freedom of each individual was paramount. These are secularism's dominant ethical standards, laying down its most important moral rules: that we ought to co-operate with humanity-as-a-whole in a globalising project that we ought to obey experts who know how we should live, that we ought to treat other people as autonomous holders of rights.

They all share the secular principle that governments should be neutral between religious beliefs; so even if there is a transcendent authority giving our lives a purpose and moral guidance, it would be up to individuals rather than governments to respond to it. Society itself, and its representative governments, bureaucracies and agencies, are to be neutral regarding any such beliefs.

We have seen how each of these traditions had an earlier home as part of a Christian account of who we are and how we should live. As society gradually learned to detach its commitments from Christian theology, these different secular traditions retained different remnants. Each remnant, once detached from its earlier home, lost its earlier rationale. Eventually, each was bound to wither and die. The reason is the same in each case. For all that secular society at its best avoids discriminating against people with religious beliefs, it does discriminate against the belief that society should be governed in accordance with any transcendent authorities. This means that the only ethical authorities are people. Once this becomes clear, all those accounts of how we should live lose their force. What remains is that, when you reflect on what you should do, whether as an individual or as a member of a community, there is no moral authority higher than you. Equally, there is no moral authority higher than the neighbour who disapproves of everything you believe in or plans to burgle your house.

Replacing God

The decline of moral realism has been slow. At any one time it is largely hidden. Abstract nouns like 'morality' and 'freedom' can also be fluid in their meanings. God-substitutes can be treated as more or less real according to taste.

An example is the 'Euthyphro dilemma', so called because of Socrates' argument in Plato's *Euthyphro*. Secular defenders of objective morality draw on it to argue that if a thing is right only because God says so, God is being arbitrary rather than good. On the other hand if God says it is right because it is right anyway, then the fact that God says so makes no difference. In either case God has nothing to offer as a moral authority.

This argument makes sense within Plato's structure of reality. Plato was responding to a tension within traditional accounts of what the gods commanded. We have seen how earlier texts saw the commands of the gods as a matter of attending to the temples, statues and sacrifices, rather than relationships between humans. Gradually opinion changed and moral rules about human relationships were attributed to the gods. The *Euthyphro* reflects on the relationship between the two in the context of the traditional Greek gods. Plato's theory of the Forms treats moral standards as independent of the gods; they were there, in his theology, before the world was created. Thus he separated morality from the gods.

In a sense modern secular moral philosophy does much the same: just as Plato tried to establish a realist account of morality which did not depend on the vagaries of Homer's gods, modern secularists have tried to establish objective moral truths independent of the god of Christianity. In both cases divine agents with wills are replaced by more ghostly entities, invisible sets of ethical instructions. The trouble is: once they cease to be agents giving us reasons for obedience, why should we obey them?

Early Enlightenment moralists retained the authority of God: the Cambridge Platonists believed that God had implanted in us an awareness of the moral good, and Shaftesbury and Hutcheson agreed.[1] Later Kant, inheriting the tradition in a less believing age, inverted its logic: rather than beginning with God and deriving the moral sense from trust in God's provision, he began with the sense of moral duty provided by the mind and on this basis argued that humans, as rational autonomous beings, exist as ends in themselves and therefore have equal worth.[2] He treated this as justification enough, even though he also believed in God as the source. His successors, however, followed through the logic of dispensing with God. It then became possible to argue that we get our values from the structure of our consciousness and project them onto the world. Our values express what our minds do, not what the world is like.[3] If this is the case all our moral judgements, whether interpreted as rights or duties, are no more than human constructs and do not reflect any deeper moral truths.

This view characterises secular ethicists today. For example, defenders of rights theory no longer appeal to the self-evident rights of the American Declaration of Independence. Instead they argue that, in the absence of any real transcendent moral authorities, the language of rights is a constructive way for society to create moral limits to how any one individual should be treated.

The theoretical change had a practical effect, but its significance took time to become clear. Historians have often noted how the rejection of Christianity by nineteenth-century intellectuals was driven by commitment to traditional Christian moral standards: as Nietzsche noted,

> You see what it was that really triumphed over the Christian God: Christian morality itself.[4]

Hell was the main issue, though sexual repression and dogma contributed; this oppressive god contradicted all the standards of Christian morality. Nevertheless once God, and any imagined God-substitutes, have been excluded from the moral structure, those Christian moral standards lose their justification, leaving the individual human as the only possible moral authority. All ethical systems will therefore have to be built upon human evaluations. Whenever we decree anything right or wrong it is right or wrong because, and only because, we so decree it. If we are to have any moral values at all, we can forget about all the moral teachings inherited from the past. *We create our own values.*

The belief that we create our own values is very common today, but it can mean different things. In religious discourse it is often taken to mean that we work them out for ourselves rather than deriving them from an authoritative religious text. In that context 'create' is often taken to mean 'discover', so that rather than accepting moral rules from an authority we discover them for ourselves. This is an intra-religious debate relevant to the dogma described in Chapter 5. In this chapter I focus on a different and more popular meaning: that in the absence of God, there are no true values to be discovered. It follows that if we are to have any values at all, we will have to create them.

On public values, societies need to develop a consensus. To take a perennial example, is the nation's success to be judged according to providing for everybody's needs, or according to a communal goal like victory over enemies, or economic growth, in which individuals are expendable? In the absence of God, if society is to produce a consensus on public values, or even an informed debate about them, it will depend on individuals producing persuasive *proposals* for the values society might create for itself.

It is in this spirit that secular moral philosophers work today. Characteristically they accept most of the moral judgements dominant in modern western society, and debate how to justify them. When the justifications change some of the moral judgements are likely to change too, but the emphasis is on searching for a theory to justify the moral norms we already think are correct. Moral philosophers inherit the concepts derived from western philosophy since the Enlightenment—rights, equality, freedom, duties, utility and so on—transplant them into the framework of social constructs and set about showing how they produce, perhaps with one or two exceptions, the ethical judgements we already hold. In the absence of God, their various theories are proposals for systems of morality that they think would work well.

The most influential recent account of social ethics in this tradition is John Rawls' *A Theory of Justice*. Rawls accepted that there is no agreement about social and economic ethics, and developed a modernised version of social contract theory which, he argued, could lead to agreement on the values a society should have.

He offered a thought experiment. We are to imagine that we are all behind a 'veil of ignorance' not knowing which role we will play in real life. In this situation, he argued, we would vote for an egalitarian society. From this he concluded that a relatively egalitarian society is what we should aim for. He allowed an element of inequality but only to the extent that it benefited the least advantaged.[5] Thus he stood in the tradition of positive liberalism.

This 'veil of ignorance' is a good example of a recent God-substitute. For religious believers God views all our lives and cares for us equally. The veil of ignorance replaces God with humans and provides an artificial technique to prevent us favouring ourselves at the expense of others. The most obvious problem in transferring authority from God to humans is thereby solved. Others, though, remain: the limits to human knowledge, the likelihood that some would rather gamble than vote for the safest option. In a sense the popularity of Rawls' proposal shows how difficult it is to do without a God's-eye-view. We know that all humans are flawed. If all our values are created by humans, they too will be flawed.

Critics of liberal individualism complain that the theory still speaks the language of self-centred individuals negotiating against each other for personal advantage. Others argue that we are not behind a veil of ignorance, we know what we have got, and some would rather keep it this way. In his later writings Rawls accepted that his theory did not have universal application:

> Justice as Fairness presents itself not as a conception of justice which is true; but one that can serve as a basis of informed and willing agreement between citizens viewed as free and equal persons.[6]

Critics have argued that this undermines his earlier claims. Thus John Gray replies:

> Rawls takes as his point of departure, not a general theory of human nature, but what he calls 'the public culture of a democratic society'—roughly speaking the intuitions common among American East Coast liberal academics. The upshot of his theorizing is not a political conception of general human interest, but an apology for American institutions.[7]

This is inevitable. In the absence of any transcendent moral truths, *whatever* any moral philosopher proposes is only their proposal. If the only basis for morality is the attempt to meet people's preferences, every account of justice will meet opposition because every account will suit some people at the expense of others.

The problem is familiar to those who have followed the postmodern debate about metanarratives and incommensurability. A metanarrative is an overarching account of reality, the way we understand reality as a whole. It functions as a supreme authority. When two theories conflict, an agreed metanarrative provides a framework, a rational structure for resolving it. For example, the metanarrative of modern secularism affirms the existence of human rights and laws of nature but has no place for miracles, fairies or statements that contradict themselves. Some postmodernists argue that metanarratives are nothing more than modernism's attempt to privilege its own beliefs and rationalities; instead, they say, different societies have different rationalities and nobody is in a position to judge between them. We cannot stand outside them all, like Rawls' individuals behind the veil of ignorance, and make unbiased judgements about which one is best. From this it follows that the different rationalities of different societies cannot be judged against each other: they are incommensurable. All we can do is commit ourselves to one, and from our chosen perspective judge the strengths and weaknesses of others.[8]

In this way the incommensurability theory takes seriously the implications of removing God from our ethical standards and values. Denying that there is any standard higher than what the individual human thinks, it leaves us with a permanent plurality where there are no right answers. Every value, every claim that something is morally right or wrong, merely expresses one point of view and is no more legitimate than others.

Some postmodernists have defended incommensurability as a way of resisting the metanarratives of oppressive governments. However it is a weak argument. All it can claim is that when dissidents disagree with the ruling classes there is no neutral standpoint from which to judge which of them is right. It deprives them of any way of claiming that their values are better. By denying that there is any higher authority, therefore, the incommensurability thesis cannot support the oppressed. The best it can do is to draw attention to other societies with other values. In general, therefore, it suits the status quo.

If we look for the source of modernism's commitment to a metanarrative, we shall find it in monotheism. The one supreme god knows how the universe works and how we humans should spend our lives. By approximating to the mind of God through prayer, study and godly living, we can learn how to direct our lives. What empowers the poor and oppressed is a vision of a different society which is better, not just from one particular point of view, but absolutely. For a claim like this to make sense, we need to believe there is an ethical authority that transcends even the most powerful human institutions.

The idea that we create our own values is very common, as it is an inevitable deduction from the theory that only human minds are capable of creating them. However it is misleading.

It turns the authority structure upside-down. We expect our values to guide us in our decisions and in this way we grant them authority over us. To say that we create our own values, on the other hand, is to say that when they guide us we are only hearing the echoes of our own voices. For example, if I believe that telling lies is immoral, and if I believe it because the immorality of lying is a value I have created, then when I am tempted to tell a lie the only moral restraint is one I have imposed on myself. There and then there is nothing to stop me changing the moral standard I have given myself. If there really are no values that transcend self-created ones, there is absolutely no reason why I should not.

The idea of creating our own values can also give the impression that we once lived without any at all, a bit like the early liberal 'original state of nature', but then decided to create some. This may appear a common situation, but in fact it never happens. To take an example, when the 1967 papal encyclical *Humanae Vitae* forbade the use of contraceptives, Roman Catholics increasingly decided to make their own decisions. This may seem an example of creating one's own values. However, they already had values. What they were doing was acknowledging a tension between different values and judging for themselves which values would take priority for them.

Our most basic values are built into our nature, like the desires to experience pleasure and avoid pain. We inherit other values, at first from our families and later from society. Societies similarly inherit values. Neither individuals nor societies are ever in a value-free condition. If we were, we would have no reason to create any. When we become aware of conflict between our values we alter some of them to bring them into line with our more deeply held values. When we are not aware of conflict between them we have no reason to alter them.

So we never create our values out of nothing. We never *create* them at all. The original source of all our valuings is not a free and arbitrary decision made in a value-free situation, either by ourselves as individuals or by society. There never was a value-free situation. As soon as we left the womb we valued milk. Values are intrinsic to us, not created by us.

That we inherit values, rather than creating them, is in principle consistent with godless evolutionary theory: we have in practice turned out with some basic values, and we develop them into greater complexities as we go through life. However we are not like the blackbird who (presumably) values building a nest but does not have the brain capacity to reflect on why. When humans have values we believe in them. Religious believers can attribute our built-in values to God, perhaps through an evolutionary method. If, on the other hand, they are merely products of impersonal laws of nature, the question arises: why should we value our built-in values? Why not treat them the way the control project treats the physical environment, and set about changing them? Sometimes this happens. Soldiers are trained to repress their feelings of revulsion at killing people. The employment system trains parents to value going to work when they would much rather stay at home and play with their children. Resistance to social engineering projects is often motivated by a desire to retain inherited values and resist the replacement values social engineers propose. Usually, we value our values. They are things we think we ought to keep.

We

So let us examine this immensely influential idea that we create our own values. It becomes important to ask: who are 'we'? If there are no objective right answers and it is up to us to decide which values to live by, it matters greatly who is to do it. After all, when the school bully declares that we are free to do whatever we want, the other children know it is time to be afraid.

Chapter 7 described a tradition in which 'we' are humanity as a whole pitted against recalcitrant nature. Chapter 8 describes this 'we' as experts on society. The rest of us can identify with the experts or feel threatened by them. In Chapter 9 'we' are each individual. In practice the 'we' who create our values is a 'we' in continual interplay between individuals and societies. Individuals may associate their values with the nation state, or a geographical area within it, or its ruling class or its experts or a special interest group or a dissident group; but nearly all of us associate our values with some kind of 'we', some kind of society. Societies are made up of individuals with values, and individuals are in turn influenced by the values of their society. While at any one time most people broadly accept the values with which they have been brought up, change happens. Some independent-minded individuals spot what is wrong with the dominant values and promote alternatives. Others follow, more or less slowly. Others again dig their heels in. We are seeing this now, for example, in the changing attitudes to same-sex partnerships and the growing opposition to neo-liberal economic policies.

Every society has some dominant values and tolerates some diversity. We need some dominant values because societies need some cohesiveness and governments need to make decisions on their behalf. On the other hand we also need processes for change, especially change contrary to the interests of the ruling classes. Sometimes dominant values are successfully challenged and a minority position becomes dominant. It usually happens slowly and only after much effort. Still, challenges occasionally produce a new consensus—like the abolition of slavery—which later generations applaud.

In the interplay between society and individuals, some people are more influential than others. Those who control the provision of information—the owners of newspapers, television channels and the main social media—have their ways to tell us which values to adopt. By presenting their own values as though they were normal they make it easier for others to accept them and harder to resist them. It gives them immense power.

So in a society that believes that we create our own values, it is important to recognise that 'we' are, predominantly, the controllers of mass information. Russians believe the Russian media, Americans believe the American media and the British believe the British media. In most cases the providers are a tiny number of people authorised by their respective governments. The result is a positive feedback loop. Since the end of the wars of religion the duty of governments has been understood as doing the will of the people governed. Once in power they can usually control how information and ideas are disseminated, so the will of the people sounds much like echoes of their own voices. Meanwhile the poor and powerless in deprived communities, with no means of contact with decision-makers or opinion formers, rarely reported in the mass media, all too familiar with the immense gap between their own experience of life and the lifestyles presented on their television screens, are forced to accept whatever the powerful throw at them. In our communities of the impoverished, the 'we' who create the dominant values are emphatically 'they'.

This great power of the ruling classes to influence our values is hardly new. In itself it is as old as history. Just as the kings of ancient Assyria and Babylon could believe that the purpose of their lives was to wage war against each other, aspiring rulers today struggle for power to impose their values. This is what we have come to expect of politicians.

However the idea that we create our own values adds a powerful extra weapon to their armoury. Those Mesopotamian kings claimed that their role as warlords had been given to them by their gods. Their activities were explained in terms of the purposes for which the gods had created them. Closer to the present situation is Thrasymachus' answer to Socrates' questioning in Plato's *Republic*: 'I define justice or right as what is in the interest of the stronger party'.[9] Thrasymachus saw justice not as a fixed system of order imposed by the gods, but as an order which can be defined by the most powerful in their own interests. This is the double bind we are in today. The governing values are those the ruling classes prefer, not only because in practice they have the greatest power to influence public opinion but, more radically, because they are now the *creators* of values. In the absence of God there is no higher authority than them. They not only define what progress, freedom, equality and rights are to mean: they also define good and evil, right and wrong, moral and immoral. Just as Calvin taught that whatever God decrees is right simply because God decrees it, so also secularism, by denying any authority above the ruling classes, produces the result that whatever the ruling classes decree is right simply because they are the 'we' who create our values. Thus the Government creates the moral rules as well as the legal rules. As Jeffrey Russell puts it, 'In a world without objective values absolutely no criteria remain by which to judge the values of the Leader'.[10]

Fascists understand this only too well, but I doubt whether most people really believe that the highest values are by definition whatever the ruling classes of their own society decree. The idea that 'we create our own values' therefore disguises a dilemma. If 'we' are society as a whole, the dominant values are almost inevitably those of the ruling classes. It remains unclear why any one individual should accept them; in the absence of any transcendent authorities, it must be up to each individual to decide for themselves whether to accept them.

So the 'we' who create our values can therefore be understood as each individual. If the universe does not in fact contain any values, in order to give some meaning to our lives each of us 'creates', or rather accepts, some values for ourselves.

Secular morality, relativised in this way, recreates some features of ancient polytheism. In many ancient traditions divine conflict was understood as an inescapable part of reality. Different gods might make different demands on humans, or their battles with each other might threaten the conditions of human life, or they might serve as role models for conflicting human lifestyles. In these ways divine conflict could not only explain human conflict, but make it seem inevitable. Monotheism resists this conclusion. Instead it presents a divine harmony which both challenges the inevitability of human conflict and offers a contrasting role model. Secularism reverts to the conflict model. Once again there are many different moral authorities in conflict with each other. However, compared with the ancient pantheons with their few dozen major agents, every human being now counts as a value-creator with personal interests likely to conflict with other people's interests.

In this way morality is reduced even further than it was in the theories described in the last chapter. Those theories presuppose a population of self-centred individuals. When we add in the belief that we create our own values, it becomes inevitable that even if we were not self-centred, individuals and societies would still end up with conflicting values and objectives. In societies where this is the dominant belief, the hope of resolving conflict is bound to seem even more unrealistic. So one conflict replaces another as we fall out over different things, taking for granted that as long as competing power blocs, with different priorities, consider themselves competent to determine the values people should live by, there cannot be peace.

Ultimately, therefore, the idea that we create our own values reduces to a free hand for every individual to establish their own norms; even individuals committed to accepting society's norms do so on their own authority.

It follows that your values mean no more than you create them to mean, and the same for everybody else. It begins to look as though all morality is a pointless fantasy. I shall describe two such theories which have been popular over the last century.

Morality as an evolutionary trick

One is the moral determinism proposed by evolutionary biologists towards the end of the twentieth century.[11] There is now a consensus that self-deception can have evolutionary benefits. Some argue that all moral beliefs are of this type. For E O Wilson, 'morality has no other demonstrable ultimate function' than 'to keep human genetic material intact'.[12] Similarly Richard Alexander argues that our behaviour is controlled by our genes, but if we interpreted it like this our genes would be less successful at getting us to procreate. He grandly proposes a 'general theory of behavior':

> Society is based on lies... "Thou shalt love thy neighbor as thyself." But this admirable goal is clearly contrary to a tendency to behave in a reproductively selfish manner. "Thou shalt give the impression that thou lovest thy neighbor as

thyself" might be closer to the truth.[13]

Similarly, to Michael Ruse, 'ethics… is an illusion fobbed off on us by our genes to get us to cooperate'.[14] To Richard Dawkins, 'anything that has evolved by natural selection should be selfish'.[15] To Michael Ghiselin,

> Given a full chance to act in his own interest, nothing but expediency will restrain [a person] from brutalizing, from maiming, from murdering—his brother, his mate, his parent, or his child. Scratch an "altruist" and watch a "hypocrite" bleed.[16]

There are two claims here. One is that our moral beliefs are complete errors, misleading us into thinking we are choosing between right and wrong when there are no such things as right and wrong. The other is that, in any case, we are not really choosing at all because we have no free will. Our actions are determined by the way we have evolved. Our feelings of gratitude, resentment and anger presuppose that other people could have acted otherwise than they did. Since they had no real choice, these feelings are misplaced.

This evolutionary determinism, treating evolution as the cause of our moral beliefs, demands too much of it. The very same evolutionary biologists draw our attention to weaknesses in the theory. After Wilson has, as above, spelled out in its stark emptiness why all our morality is nothing but techniques for reproduction, he tells us to behave differently—for *moral* reasons! We are to 'favor diversity in the gene pool as a cardinal value', along with regarding 'universal human rights… as a primary value'.[17] It turns out that

> Human nature can adapt to more encompassing forms of altruism and social justice. Genetic biases can be trespassed,

> passions averted or redirected, and ethics altered.[18]

Most of his disciples agree. To Alexander,

> To say that we are *evolved* to serve the interests of our genes in no way suggests that we are *obliged* to serve them... Evolution is surely most deterministic for those still unaware of it".[19]

George Williams urges that

> An unremitting effort is required to expand the circle of sympathy for others. This effort is in opposition to much of human nature.[20]

The best-selling *The Selfish Gene* by Richard Dawkins urges: 'Let us try to *teach* generosity and altruism because we are born selfish'.[21]

Oh. So are we not determined after all? What seems to be going on in the minds of these authors is that we are selfish by nature, but when we know it we have the ability to override our selfishness and do something morally good instead. If this is what they mean, they are only saying what Confucius, Plato, the Bible and countless others said thousands of years ago. It is hardly new.

The contradiction is twofold. First, by making moral appeals they are abandoning the determinism with which they began. The whole point of those theories is that our ethical beliefs and practices are determined. Their moral appeals urge us to escape from this determinism, even though they themselves have built their careers on telling us we cannot. The other contradiction is that, after insisting that all morality comes from evolution, they then appeal to different moral standards which they consider better. Where, we ask, did they get these moral standards from, since they have taken so much trouble to assure us that all our moral beliefs are erroneous?

Each of these contradictions is, on its own, fatal to the theory. Holmes Rolston comments on Dawkins' argument:

> Dawkins laments this bad human nature. But Dawkins can do this only because he has found some vantage point from which he can recommend that altruism be taught in culture, educating us out of our beastly nature. If so, then he himself has reached a more comprehensive ethics—one in which he has escaped, or at least knows that he ought to escape, the biological legacy... Meanwhile, he can take himself seriously as an ethicist, and we can take seriously what he morally advocates, only if he and we are exempt from the theory that he is advocating as a scientist about how ethics works.[22]

Why have so many scientists been willing to turn a blind eye to these rather obvious contradictions in their publications? The answer seems to be that they were standing fair and square within a tradition of social engineering which had virtually forgotten that their theories about humans would apply to themselves. Perhaps a more interesting question is: why did public opinion lap them up with such uncritical enthusiasm? It seems that an extreme moral reductionism was exactly what many people wanted to believe. Perhaps there is a parallel with the rise of atheism: just as seventeenth century church teaching on Hell drove people to dispense with God, maybe the dominant ethical norms of twentieth century western society, obsessed as they were with limiting sexual activity, drove people to dispense with morality as they had inherited it and make a new start with intuitive moral standards. It seems that many people were delighted by the idea that all morality is error, but at the same time determined to believe in transcendent moral values that needed to be upheld.

Morality as emotional manipulation

The theory of emotivism has been much more influential. If each of us creates our own values, what are we really doing? From a positivist perspective morality cannot mean anything at all unless it can be observed and measured. Nobody has measured moral rules or truths. What is left?

The classic analysis of emotivism was Charles Stevenson's *Ethics and Language* (1944). Stevenson argued that each moral statement is a combination of a factual statement with an imperative. 'This is wrong' means 'I disapprove of this; do so as well'. All moral talk, he concluded, is really nothing but psychological manipulation.[23] It is an inevitable result: to people convinced that they have created their own values, it follows that we first create our values and only later do we think about how other people fit into them—in which case other people can quite rationally be treated instrumentally. Conversely, whenever we are influenced by other people's moral judgements, there is no truth behind them; we are just being manipulated.

Of course most people find this conclusion unacceptable. When we say something is morally right or wrong, we believe it really is. We feel sure that the latest terrorist murders are evil. But what makes them evil? In the absence of any authoritative moral standards, saying they are evil is nothing but a description of our gut feelings. In that case, Stevenson was right: morality is the product of the individual's hormones and all our moral assertions are nothing but attempts to persuade others to adopt our feelings.

MacIntyre's *After Virtue* describes the development and influence of emotivism. Published in 1981, it is even truer now than it was then. MacIntyre describes how, for Kant and most moral philosophers of his age, morally good behaviour is characterised by treating people as ends in themselves; to treat someone as a means to one's own end, on the other hand, is to treat them in an immoral manner. In emotivism, on the other hand,

> ...evaluative utterance can in the end have no point or use but the expression of my own feelings or attitudes and the transformation of the feelings and attitudes of others. I cannot genuinely appeal to impersonal criteria, for there are no impersonal criteria. I may think that I so appeal and others may think that I so appeal, but these thoughts will always be mistakes. The sole reality of distinctively moral discourse is the attempt of one will to align the attitudes, feelings, preferences and choices of another with its own. Others are always means, never ends.[24]

The result can be seen in the way public moral debate so often descends into endless propaganda battles. Because the only possible justification for any moral standard is the individual's feelings, proponents of every viewpoint can feel confident that their cause is justified by their own feelings; what remains is to manipulate the feelings of others. So public debate overwhelmingly appeals to emotions. Pro-abortionists and anti-abortionists, rather than spending time with each other analysing their differences, direct their energies to advertising their feelings. Photographs of starving African babies generate more donations to charities than economic analyses do. Anti-poverty campaigners, peace campaigners, animal rights campaigners, medical research campaigners and countless others devote their efforts to advertising their cause, persuading others to join them and lobbying politicians. Informed research is replaced by shouting matches, with the proponents of different positions trying to outperform their opponents in attracting attention but having very little to say in rational defence of their views.

In this chapter I hope to have shown why this is the inevitable result of secular ethical theory. If there is no higher authority than the individual's preferences, nobody's value judgements can be said to be wrong. This applies whether or not the individual's preferences are well-informed. There is therefore no place for rational analysis. Instead we get the endless tennis match of statistics being thrown from one side to the other, citing opinion polls on what percentage support which policies. These statistics have become the nearest approximation to a moral authority capable of judging between alternatives. They keep changing because in practice many of our opinions are ephemeral; but the theory insists on treating whatever we want at any one time as though it was a foundational feature of our values. We have gut feelings and we try to manipulate other people to share them. Rational debate has been replaced by simple slogans on Facebook and Twitter. Thus public moral discourse is now dominated by emotivist rhetoric.

As a result power is achieved by those who are most successful at this kind of manipulation. In a culture that thinks it creates its own values the feelings of individuals, however ill-informed, become supreme authorities on society's values. If this is the best we can do, we shall always be in conflict with each other for no better reason than that we have different hormones.

There is of course a proper role for feelings. They are essential ingredients in our values. They can protect us from rulers disguising their vested interests as rational, or 'the facts'. It is unpleasant to watch a whale being slaughtered or walk past starving people begging in the street. Our heartstrings can awaken us to the need to question the policies of the establishment. When we think about whether to support a cause a variety of factors are likely to play a part: as well as our feelings, the data available to us, the views of those we trust and our own ability to think through the values we hold and analyse what they imply in any given situation. However, if our values express nothing but our feelings, resolution of our disagreements is as impossible as making everybody's feelings identical. Conflict becomes as inevitable as it was when the kings of Assyria and Babylon declared war on each other, both claiming the authority of the supreme god.

Conclusion

So secular theory leaves us with a dilemma. On the one hand nobody attributes supreme moral authority to the ruling classes of their society. Some things, we think, are just plain wrong even if the government approves of them. This is to presuppose a higher moral standard. On the other hand, secular society denies that there is any such higher standard. As a result, when we accept secularism we cannot explain what we mean when we call our governments wrong.

Over time we have learned to live with this contradiction. When people devote years of their lives to campaigning for a change of government policy about something, they do so because they think the policy is wrong: absolutely wrong, wrong however much the government thinks it right. Beliefs like this contradict not just incommensurability theories, but more generally the idea that we create our own values.

This contradiction makes it harder to reflect on our moral values. Individuals can think through the values they hold and why they hold them. Specialist institutions may produce rational defences of their values. Small groups can discuss them; in a local political party meeting or church group the level of information and discussion may be high. These processes, important though they are, only function well in small groups. In wider public debate the taboo on transcendent authorities suppresses honest and informed discussion of the real reasons why people have the moral convictions they do.

This encourages us to live schizophrenic lives. We are born with some values and acquire others from experience, in our families, our neighbourhoods and workplaces. On national and international issues we depend on the mass media with their own value systems, shaped to suit the media's owners. So we oppose the immigration of refugees from a long way away, content for them to be treated in ways we would never tolerate for local people we knew. Our employer obliges us to work longer hours for less pay, but we vote for the government that constrained the employer to do so because they tell us the economy is improving. We approve of cuts to benefits for the disabled while being horrified by the lack of statutory support for a disabled neighbour. We live with the contradictions.

Theory and practice have well and truly parted company. Theory may tell us that we create our own values, but in practice when engaging with issues we care about, we treat our values as more than just our own creations. We appeal to moral standards as though they were real truths, not just expressions of feelings. When an anti-abortionist appeals to the unborn baby's right to life, or a taxpayer denounces a tax for depriving people of their rightful earnings, or one government accuses another of human rights abuses, they are presupposing that the right in question has moral authority over the law of the land: that governments *ought* to respect those rights as transcendent authorities competent to pass moral judgement on human actions. The contradiction is so deeply embedded in western culture that we usually fail to notice it; but it is there, powerfully confusing us about right and wrong. If modern western societies are to rediscover some way of working out what we ought to be doing, we will need to reaffirm a source of moral truth which is more than just what 'we', whoever 'we' are, have created.

Chapter 11. Value-free values

In 1879 Leo Tolstoy underwent a personal crisis which he describes in his *Confession*. He had been brought up in the Orthodox tradition but was no longer a believer. After becoming famous for writing *War and Peace* and *Anna Karenina,* he found questions cropping up in his head, at first occasionally and later persistently.

> Before I could be occupied with my Samara estate, with the education of my son, or with the writing of books, I had to know why I was doing these things. As long as I do not know the reason why, I cannot do anything. In the middle of my concern with the household, which at the time kept me quite busy, a question would suddenly come into my head: "Very well, you will have 6,000 desyatins in the Samara province, as well as 300 horses; what then?" And I was completely taken aback and did not know what else to think. As soon as I started to think about the education of my children, I would ask myself, "Why?" Or I would reflect on how the people might attain prosperity, and I would suddenly ask myself, "What concern is it of mine?" Or in the middle of thinking about the fame that my works were bringing me I would say to myself, "Very well, you will be more famous than Gogol, Pushkin, Shakespeare, Molière, more famous than all the writers in the world - so what?[1]

He found himself unable to attach any meaning to any of his actions. One day he would be dead and his deeds forgotten. Why, then, live at all? The question 'brought me to the edge of suicide when I was fifty years old'.[2]

It is possible to live only as long as life intoxicates us; once we

> are sober we cannot help seeing that it is all a delusion, a stupid delusion! Nor is there anything funny or witty about it; it is only cruel and stupid.[3]

This chapter continues to explore the idea that we create our own values, but extends it beyond morality to other values. We naturally feel that our lives have some kind of *meaning*. We find the birth of our own baby meaningful. If we try to explain *how* it is meaningful—what meaning it has—we find we cannot. The production of this new life, every bit as human as you and me, draws our attention to the wonder of life. If there is a fact there that we can explain, it is that life is more meaningful than we can explain. This sense of indefinable meaning keeps recurring at births, weddings and funerals, but also in lesser ways throughout our lives.

The sense of meaning is closely allied to a sense of *purpose*. We naturally feel that there is a point to life. We may not be able to say what it is, but most of the time we feel motivated by it. A few people do buck the trend and convince themselves that their life has no purpose, but this is when suicide rates reach their highest.

These two features of our normal assumptions about our lives give us a sense of direction. The meaningfulness makes us feel our lives have *value*, and the thought of working towards a purpose opens up the prospect of *progress*. Having a direction for our lives means that we judge positive contributions as good and hindrances as bad. This gives us a sense of right and wrong, so we can make sense of moral values. These values matter to us even when we do not think about them; they guide us to do what we do and avoid what we avoid.

Our values have a social as well as an individual dimension. Societies contain individuals with divergent values, so our desires conflict; but societies also do things, so they need to establish a consensus about some values. When, for example, the government of Britain or Turkey explains why it is accepting these refugees but not those, some of its values become apparent.

Purpose, meaning, value and morality are concepts shared by polytheists and monotheists. They have often disagreed about what the purposes, meanings and moral norms are, but they do not take them to be merely products of the human mind. Secular theory does, at least when consistent: in the absence of God, they cannot have any other source.

As a matter of fact, we do evaluate. It does not follow that we *ought* to. Any such 'ought' would be a value imposed on us from outside, which is precisely what people are denying when they say that we create our own values. So we do not have to create values; it is just that, in fact, we do.

If the only values are the ones we create, then until we create some there are no standards by which to judge which ones to create. Once we have created some, they are *by definition* the right ones. Whether we conceive of the value-creating as individual or social, the values we create are the right values *for us,* as they must be because we have created them.

If this is what our values are, it seems that they are nothing but fantasies; in a world with no real values we are imagining values and treating them as real.

Existentialism

A strictly God-free account of values has been explored by existentialists. The word 'existentialism' refers to the idea that existence comes before essence: there is no essence to the universe or to us, no nature of things that expresses the point of life. We just are what we are. Being what we are we create values, but they only seem important to us because we choose to treat them as such. Really, life is completely pointless, meaningless.

A few years after Tolstoy's *Confession,* Nietzsche wrote in his notes:

Ultimately man finds in things nothing but what he himself

> has imported into them: the finding we call science, the importing—art, religion, love, pride.[4]

What Nietzsche could see was that, with the 'death of God', much else had to die too. If there are no transcendent authorities competent to judge any of our choices right or wrong, we can make any choice at all and there is no sense in which it was the right choice compared with alternatives. Schopenhauer reached a similar conclusion, as Paul Edwards summarises:

> The final "judgment of nature" is destruction by death. This is "the last proof" that life is a "false path," that all man's wishing is "a perversity," and that "nothing at all is worth our striving, our efforts and struggles." He concludes: "All good things are vanity, the world in all its ends bankrupt, and life a business which does not cover its expenses".[5]

The thought that absolutely nothing at all matters in the slightest strikes many people as unattractive, if not terrifying. Some, however, welcome it. Aldous Huxley described how he and his young contemporaries welcomed it in the 1920s. They longed for two kinds of liberation: from the norms of sexual ethics, which inhibited their desires, and from the political and economic system which seemed unjust.

> The supporters of these systems claimed that in some way they embodied the meaning (a Christian meaning, they insisted) of the world. There was one admirably simple method of confuting these people and at the same time justifying ourselves in our political and erotic revolt: we could deny that the world had any meaning whatsoever.[6]

It is easy to see why people suffering sexual repression, or driven to oppressive poverty by processes publicly proclaimed as right and proper, would welcome this nihilism. When our society's dominant values oppress us, we would rather do without them.

Once this step is taken it seems that we decide for ourselves the purpose of our life, and what counts as meaningful and valuable to us, if anything does. In the 1960s Jean-Paul Sartre's *Being and Nothingness* argued that in the absence of God or any external constraint, we create values because we need them. What makes them exist is the free act which recognises them as our values. It follows that

> …my freedom is the unique foundation of values and that *nothing*, absolutely nothing, justifies me in adopting this or that particular value, this or that particular scale of values. As a being by whom values exist, I am unjustifiable.

We therefore know that we are always free to choose different values. Our values are never justified. This makes them absurd and produces anguish.[7]

> The possibility of these other choices is neither made explicit nor posited, but it is lived in the feeling of unjustifiability; and it is this which is expressed by the fact of the *absurdity* of my choice and consequently of my being.[8]

So what we think, say and do is justified by our values. Our values, on the other hand, are not justified by anything; they are merely produced by our free choice. The justification trail always breaks down here. Ultimately, everything about us is unjustified. There is no point in anything we do.[9] By his time many secularists had developed theories of morality without God, but Sartre rejected them too. The non-existence of God is to be lamented, not celebrated, because when everything is permissible 'as a result man is forlorn'.[10]

Even more dramatically, his colleague Albert Camus

declared:

> There is but one truly serious philosophical problem, and that is suicide. Judging whether life is or is not worth living amounts to answering the fundamental question of philosophy.

Why? Because

> The principle can be established that for a man who does not cheat, what he believes to be true must determine his action. Belief in the absurdity of existence must then dictate his conduct. It is legitimate to wonder, clearly and without false pathos, whether a conclusion of this importance requires forsaking as rapidly as possible an incomprehensible condition.[11]

To understand the issue is to see why they struggled. If all our values are our own creations because there is nobody else to give us any, there is literally no point in living. All our emotions rebel against the idea, but on an intellectual level we are left with no reason to believe anything at all is worth doing.

A more recent reflection on this absurdity is an influential article 'The absurd' by Thomas Nagel. It makes a number of relevant points. One is his proposal that the absurdity is there and we should just live with the emptiness. We live, he tells us, with two perspectives on life. In our ordinary daily lives we do things and want things, and apply energy and attention to them. 'We *pursue* our lives, with varying degrees of sloth and energy.'[12] At the same time, however,

> Humans have the special capacity to step back and survey themselves, and the lives to which they are committed, with that detached amazement which comes from watching an ant

> struggle up a heap of sand. Without developing the illusion that they are able to escape from their highly specific and idiosyncratic position, they can view it *sub specie aeternitatis*—and the view is at once sobering and comical... We see ourselves from outside, and all the contingency and specificity of our aims and pursuits become clear. Yet when we take this view and recognize what we do as arbitrary, it does not disengage us from life, and there lies our absurdity: not in the fact that such an external view can be taken of us, but in the fact that we ourselves can take it, without ceasing to be the persons whose ultimate concerns are so coolly regarded.[13]

Our instincts drive us to live as though our lives are full of meaning. The conclusion that they are not seemed to Nietzsche and Sartre to have devastating implications but Nagel, like other more recent philosophers, reassures us that there is no need to worry. Nagel's reason is 'irony'. We have no choice but to live our lives as though they were not absurd. Knowing the absurdity, we can reflect on it but then

> ...we return to our familiar convictions with a certain irony and resignation. Unable to abandon the natural responses on which they depend, we take them back, like a spouse who has decided to run off with someone else and then decided to return; but we regard them differently.[14]

So when we question the seriousness of life, and look at ourselves 'without presuppositions',

> We then return to our lives, as we must, but our seriousness is laced with irony. Not that irony enables us to escape the absurd.[15]

What effect does this have on our lives? It makes us spectators:

> In viewing ourselves from a perspective broader than we can occupy in the flesh, we become spectators of our own lives. We cannot do very much as pure spectators of our own lives, so we continue to lead them, and devote ourselves to what we are able at the same time to view as no more than a curiosity, like the ritual of an alien religion.[16]

Nagel sees no problem with this:

> If *sub specie aeternitatis* there is no reason to believe that anything matters, then that does not matter either, and we can approach our absurd lives with irony instead of heroism or despair.[17]

Nagel's '*sub specie aeternitatis*' is another usurpation of a God's-eye-view, like Rawls' veil of ignorance. The claim—that from the perspective of eternity there is no reason to believe anything matters—does indeed fly in the face of our normal daily experience. It would be difficult to exaggerate the practical significance. Nagel's 'irony' is, in effect, a matter of training ourselves to remember that despite our emotional responses to the ups and downs of life, nothing matters in the slightest. From his perspective, 'without presuppositions' as he puts it (!), there are no real ups and downs. The 'curiosity' of our lives carries on pointlessly. It is as though our own life has become a novel or a television programme, a piece of entertainment to be looked at by an outsider. He is certainly right to note that this 'irony' would be a replacement for heroism. If nothing matters, nobody will put themselves out for anything; after all, nobody would suffer or die for an imaginary character in a soap opera. In a sense it is also a replacement for despair, Nagel's alternative to Camus' suggestion of suicide. As Julian Young puts it,

> ...we become, not passionate and committed human beings

> capable of pursuing our projects through hardship and disappointment, but rather *actors*, ironically detached from the roles we play at any one time, ready to swap roles if and when the whim takes us.[18]

Because Nagel's logic is sound, he reveals just how much is at stake. His 'irony' is in effect advice to live a lie: from the detached observer's view we know the truth that our lives are absurd, but in practice, as we get on with our lives, he advises us to behave as though they are not absurd.

It is a radical challenge. Faith traditions offer rich accounts of the purpose of our lives, with ethical and spiritual dimensions in which we can grow. Just as studies of the physical world can (and used to) speculate about the actions of God, so also theological ethicists can respond to moral questions by relating their understanding of God's will to difficult situations. Furthermore this life may be part of a longer story, if death is not the end. Letting go of God left us in a material universe where everything, including ourselves, is just a combination of atoms obeying impersonal laws of nature. Nothing has any purpose or meaning. There is less to life than we thought.

Thus over time, from Nietzche to Nagel, the implications have been analysed and have led to the conclusion that nothing matters. It is as though the tradition has grown comfortable with the absurdity of life. Instead of contemplating suicide with Camus, we allow our lives to drift along pointlessly without expecting anything else from it. It becomes another case of reductionism: values, like physical processes, can only consist of what the rational human mind can explain.

If it is true that nothing matters and nothing has any purpose, then there is no reason why anybody should put themselves out for somebody else. Pleasure and pain remain but not value, meaning, purpose or morality. We may want to feed our crying baby, but if we are content for the baby to cry we would be mistaken in thinking that we *ought* to provide food; any such moral judgement, or indeed any longing we may have for the child to grow and flourish, would be part of the absurdity. We may as well live out our days with beer, heroin, art galleries, Russian roulette or whatever takes our fancy.

These arguments do not characterise popular culture. Even the most committed atheists usually take their values to be more objectively true than these arguments suggest. We do not try to live with absurdity: we rarely find life absurd at all.

Self-created values

So we hang onto our values. In the absence of God, we treat values as the products of human creativity. This can mean different things. At its most basic it means that as a matter of fact we believe some things to be meaningful or valuable, and these beliefs come to us through our minds rather than being imposed from outside. This is certainly true; even those who believe that true values come from God can agree that they are mediated to us through our minds. We can add, still uncontroversially (except for evolution deniers) that evolutionary psychology can trace how this capacity to have values developed. But none of this tells us whether our values are true. Are the things we consider meaningful really meaningful? Are the things we consider valuable really valuable? In a godless universe with no intrinsic value, the answer seems to be no; all that has happened is that our *beliefs* in values have evolved as a survival mechanism.

To avoid the sense of absurdity, some secular philosophers argue that the meaning we attribute to things is all the meaning there is, and suffices; we should not expect more.[19] Philosophers often discuss the life of Sisyphus as a way of exploring the issue. According to the ancient Greek myth, Sisyphus offended the gods and was punished by being made to roll a stone up a hill. Every time it got to the top it would roll down again to the bottom, and he would have to descend and start pushing all over again. He was obliged to carry on for eternity, performing this pointless task. Philosophers use the story to illustrate a completely meaningless life. What would it be like? Was his life completely meaningless, and is our own life equally meaningless? What would have to change to make it meaningful? Richard Taylor makes creative use of the story by offering three versions. The first is the traditional one, with Sisyphus laboriously pushing the stone up the hill knowing that he will be doing so for eternity.

> Now in this we have the picture of meaningless, pointless toil, of a meaningless existence that is absolutely *never* redeemed.[20]

In the second he suggests that the gods implanted in Sisyphus a compulsive desire to roll stones.[21]

> Exactly the same things happen as before. The only change is in Sisyphus' view of them. The picture before was the image of meaningless activity and existence. It was created precisely to be an image of that. It has not lost that meaninglessness, it has now gained not the least shred of meaningfulness.[22]

Our lives, he argues, are much the same as that of Sisyphus. We strive to achieve goals of transitory significance, and whenever we gain one we immediately start on the next.[23]

> Each man's life thus resembles one of Sisyphus' climbs to the summit of his hill, and each day of it one of his steps; the difference is that whereas Sisyphus himself returns to push the stone up again, we leave this to our children.[24]

In his third version of the story Taylor tells us that Sisyphus once again dislikes rolling stones, but wants to build a temple. This gives meaning to his life. Eventually he completes it. He contemplates his achievement, does nothing ever again and becomes bored.

> Where before we were presented with the nightmare of eternal and pointless activity, we are now confronted with the hell of its eternal absence.

The conclusion he draws is:

> Our second picture, then, wherein we imagined Sisyphus to have had inflicted on him the irrational desire to be doing just what he found himself doing should not have been dismissed so abruptly. The meaning that picture lacked was no meaning that he or anyone could crave, and the strange meaning it had was perhaps just what we were seeking.[25]

He concludes:

> The meaning of life is from within us, it is not bestowed from without, and it far exceeds in both its beauty and permanence any heaven of which men have ever dreamed or yearned for.[26]

Taylor's point is to contrast the temple-building in his third account with the stone-rolling in his second. The stone-rolling refers to nothing beyond itself. The temple-building does refer to something beyond itself, namely the completed temple. Somewhat arbitrarily he stops there, apparently forgetting that nobody builds a temple just for the sake of building it. People build them because of the things they want to do in them. Nevertheless Taylor's point is clear enough. Looking at reality as a whole from an atheist perspective, it lacks any given values. The idea that life has meaning is a fiction that humans create. Still, there are some things we like to do, and we experience them as meaningful. This is all the meaning there is, and he argues that it suffices.

Critics argue that this is too reductionist. If Taylor's second account of Sisyphus explains what meaning is, and if as he tells us the only difference from the first account is that he likes to do it, then his illustration implies that the meaning of life is nothing but pleasure. This is not what we normally mean by saying something is meaningful. Semantically, the meaning of the word 'mean' is reference to something else: for example the word 'hat' means something worn on the head. In the same way, when we say that we found a film or a conversation meaningful, we do not mean only that we enjoyed it: we mean that it directed our attention to something beyond the event itself. Often when we call something meaningful we are not sure what this something beyond is. We just have an undefined sense that we are being directed to something significant. When we try to explain *how* something is meaningful, or valuable, or purposeful to us, we often describe it in terms of its wider impact or the future. Typical examples might be the following.

'I'm not parting with that tea set even though it's chipped.' 'Why not?' 'Because my husband gave it to me and it reminds me of him'.

'Why do you keep reading Shakespeare's plays?' 'Because I find them meaningful'. 'What meaning do you find in them?' 'They help me understand human nature'.

'Why do you spend so much time studying?' 'I want to pass my exams.' 'Why do you want to pass your exams?' 'I want to qualify as an architect.'

In this kind of way we characteristically think of our values as embedded in wider values. Performing a valuable action is valuable because it contributes to a larger project which is also valuable. Similarly when we describe events or actions as meaningful, we point to something wider. By committing ourselves to a cause we consider meaningful, we feel our own lives have meaning.

These are justification trails. We explain one value by another, and that by another again. Usually the trails are pretty short because we do not need to think very far. We understand why the tea set's owner wants to be reminded of her husband. When the youngster has been an architect for twenty years, what then? This question has no answer because it does not need to be thought about yet.

Many secular philosophers agree with Taylor that the meaning of life cannot be explained by these justification trails. Paul Edwards illustrates the point:

> A man with a toothache goes to a dentist, and the dentist helps him so that the toothache disappears. A man is falsely accused of a crime and is faced with the possibility of a severe sentence as well as with the loss of his reputation; with the help of a devoted attorney his innnocence is established, and he is acquitted. It is true that a hundred years later all of the participants in these events will be dead and none of them will *then* be able to enjoy the fruits of any of the efforts involved. But this most emphatically does not imply that the dentist's efforts were not worthwhile or that the attorney's work was not worth doing. To bring in considerations of what will or will not happen in the remote future is, in such and many other though certainly not in all human situations, totally irrelevant.[27]

Certainly not in all, as Edwards recognises. Many people devote their lives to objectives which will not be realised in their lifetimes. They would not do so without a sense of long-term purpose transcending individual lives. But might not that also apply to his two examples? What if the men with the toothache and the false accusation are also devoting their lives to long-term causes—the future careers of their children, if not more besides?

The dentist and the attorney have helped them continue their work. Most people in paid employment prefer to feel that their work makes a positive contribution, even if they only have a vague idea of the cause to which they are contributing.

But not all do. Here lies the important distinction to which Edwards has drawn our attention. Not everybody sees their life as part of a larger purpose; but some do, and society would be much the poorer without them. If they were persuaded that Edwards is right, they would have good reason to abandon their efforts and adopt more self-centred lives.

Nagel agrees with Edwards and pursues the argument in more detail.

> No further justification is needed to make it reasonable to take aspirin for a headache, attend an exhibition of the work of a painter one admires, or stop a child from putting his hand on a hot stove. No larger context or further purpose is needed to prevent these acts from being pointless.[28]

This is perhaps rather odd, since it occurs in the same article as the one cited above, which accepts the absurdity of life and recommends 'irony'. Nevertheless Nagel makes two points about these justification trails. The first is that every trail has to end somewhere; otherwise we would have an infinite regress.[29] In practice,

> What seems to us to confer meaning, justification, significance, does so in virtue of the fact that we need no more reasons after a certain point.[30]

While this is true in itself, to say we need no more reasons after a certain point is not to say that there are no further reasons. When the architecture student is asked what her role will be in twenty years' time she does not know; but that future role, although she cannot describe it, is already a reason for the studying she is doing now. Similarly, when people march on a demonstration against cuts to benefits for the disabled, they do not know how their efforts will benefit any particular disabled people. All they know is that they are contributing to an action which, they think, may have a positive effect *somehow*. This is characteristic of our justification trails. As we justify our values in terms of other values, the trail ends not in the unjustified but in the unknown.

Nagel's other point is that every justification must be something we can understand:

> Those seeking to supply their lives with meaning usually envision a role or function in something larger than themselves. They therefore seek fulfillment in service to society, the state, the revolution, the progress of history, the advance of science, or religion and the glory of God. But a role in some larger enterprise cannot confer significance unless that enterprise is itself significant. And its significance must come back to what we can understand, or it will not even appear to give us what we are seeking.[31]

The exclusion of values we do not consciously think about and understand also reflects Nagel's belief that as there are no objectively true values, the only values are whatever humans think. This also misinterprets the popular, everyday understanding of values. It is belief in a larger purpose, for both the world and our own lives, that inspires people to devote their efforts to causes greater than their own personal happiness. Edwards and Nagel, believing that the only values are the ones humans create, have to truncate these justification trails at the point where people stop thinking about them. We justify valuing x by appealing to the value of y, and we justify valuing y by appealing to z; but because we have not thought enough about z, the justification trail has fizzled out before we get that far. Since they think values are human creations, the fact that we have not got round to accounting for the value of z implies that z has no value. Looking at this as a logical sequence, we must surely conclude that x and y cannot be justified this way. Their account of justification, far from being adequate, gets us to the point where absolutely nothing has value.[32]

The practical results are disastrous. If I convince myself that nothing really matters even though I am obliged to live as though I myself matter, I make an exception of myself in a manner something like that described by Nagel's irony. I do not matter any more than other people do, but in the case of other people I find it all too easy to live as though they do not matter. When I feel hungry my instincts make me look for food. When starving refugees feel hungry I find it easier to do the logical thing and just accept that their starvation has no significance at all. To watch on television slum dwellers in other countries living in appalling conditions comes to feel like reading a novel about distressed people who never really existed at all. A society that encourages people to think like this makes it less likely that anyone will so commit themselves to a cause that they end up being imprisoned or tortured for it. Thus the secular account of values, while not necessarily making us selfish, makes selfishness seem the most rational lifestyle to adopt.

Summary

Secular theories of value have failed to account for ordinary people's values. They reduce them to errors; we value things, but calling them valuable only means we attribute to them a quality they do not have, except in our minds. If we return to Edwards' illustrations, what we are left with is the anguish of the person falsely accused, the pain of the toothache and the instinctive desires of the others to help. We might yet describe those instinctive desires as values, but they can no longer be justified.

Far from expressing any truth about value, they are just the actions of people driven by instincts.

This is very different from what we normally mean. If our values are nothing but instinctive responses, or expressions of desire for pleasure and happiness, then they are merely alternative ways of talking about instincts, pleasure and happiness. Some value a walk in the park, others a fix of heroin, and it becomes meaningless to say that heroin is bad for you despite the pleasure.

One underlying reason for this reduction is the positivist assumption that nothing can be more than what we can explain. This has led these secular philosophers to reduce all values to the point where they are effectively abolished.

If Tolstoy could come back to life and hear them, he would of course recognise the point immediately. What they are describing is the situation as he saw it at the time of his crisis. All they have done is to widen the definition of 'meaning' to include what he counted as meaningless. What they offer is precisely what drove him to consider suicide and made Camus and Sartre describe life as absurd. But we have moved on: these newer philosophers are content with it. We have ended up with a dramatically *reduced* account of meaning. It is as though the deeper significance of our lives, which religious traditions once provided, is gradually being erased.

Tolstoy himself was not so easily satisfied. He observed how his peasants did not share his problem. They understood it and answered it 'with unusual clarity' by drawing on the resources of their traditional Christian Orthodoxy. He regained his faith.[33] It is religious traditions that can make sense of the justification trails Nagel struggled with. Our justifications for our values end not in the valueless but in the supremely valuable beyond human understanding.

Public secular discourse thus lives with a contradiction. Overtly claiming that we create our own values rather than deriving them from God, it nevertheless treats them as authorities that transcend ordinary human preferences. We hear this every day in appeals to human rights that transcend government decrees, and in arguments that some things are just plain wrong even if governments or international organisations decree otherwise.

What I hope this chapter has shown is that, if we followed the logic of those who believe all values are human creations, our lives would descend to the anguished distress expressed by Sartre and Camus. In practice very few people do. Instead western societies cling to many of the values we have inherited from our religious past, still assuming that they are more than just our own inventions. Somehow, in some way we have forbidden ourselves to think about, we matter to a transcendent 'beyond' which bestows meaning, value and purpose on us.

Chapter 12. Secular and monotheist ethics

You are visiting relatives. As you arrive you give little Abigail a present: some crayons and drawing paper. She takes them to a table, ignoring the chorus from her parents reminding her to say 'Thank you'. She is too busy for that. She starts drawing. A few minutes later she comes back to you and says 'Here, this is for you. It's a picture of you, sitting on the toilet.' You look at it. It isn't a work of art and it does you no favours. But it was drawn by her, and she did it for you. You give a broad smile, accept it graciously and say 'That's lovely! Thank you so much!'

This is a typical story. It happens in every society, in every family. It illustrates some important differences between secular and monotheist conceptions of reality. These differences will be the topic of this chapter, to parallel the differences between polytheism and monotheism described in Chapter 4.

The most fundamental is *relationship*. Characteristically the way religious individuals and communities relate to the divine is an important element of who they think they are and what their lives mean, adding a dimension to the richness of life. In theories of divine conflict our relationship to the divine may be limited or conditional: a god may have self-interested reasons for relating to you, or may impose conditions on the relationship. Monotheism abolishes the limits: the relationship is secure and designed as a blessing.

In secular theory humanity as a whole, although an important concept, does not relate to any personal agents outside itself. We happen to be here by accident, and what we will have for lunch happens to be there by accident except for the work done by other humans to prepare it. Humanity has not received any gifts and does not owe anything to anyone. It is more as though Abigail had found the crayons and paper on a rubbish tip. She might still have used them but they would never have meant so much because they would not have been from you.

It is a relationship of *trust*. You have thought about Abigail and what she might like. You could have given her a syringe and heroin, but you know the kind of thing a girl of her age will both enjoy and use to develop her skills and you had her best interests at heart. She does not have this overview of appropriate gifts; like all children, she accepts that there are many things she does not know and must accept on trust from adults. She trusts your judgement.

Similarly, monotheists have reason to trust that God provides what is good for us. For polytheists the trust may be limited. For secularists there is no act of trust at all: impersonal laws of nature do not have our interests at heart because they have no heart.

It is this lack of trust that produces the desire for knowledge and control. Our physical environment is like the paper and crayons brought home from the rubbish tip, just found there by accident and taken. If Abigail had indeed brought them from the rubbish tip her parents would have told her to wash her hands. Those things might be dirty. They might have germs. Because they had not been intentionally given by someone trustworthy, they could not be trusted. In the same way, if the resources we depend on just happen to be there as an accidental result of impersonal matter obeying impersonal laws of nature, we have no reason to trust them. Maybe a meteor is about to arrive from outer space and break up our planet into little bits. Maybe global warming was going to kill us all off anyway.

It is a relationship of *gratitude*. Abigail's actions have made it clear that the gift is appreciated. In religious traditions our lives and resources are gifts from the divine, so our relationship with the divine begins with gratitude. In some versions of polytheism the gratitude is relativised: the gods want something in exchange, or we'll be in trouble if we are not suitably grateful. In monotheism there is no relativising: we have been created for our own sakes, for our well-being, as an act of blessing. A relationship of gratitude is entirely appropriate.

Gratitude is infectious. When Abigail gives you the picture you respond by saying you are grateful. It is not really something you wanted, but you are still grateful. What you are grateful for is the delight in the gift, a delight which expresses and strengthens a warm relationship. You would not have been so pleased if the gift had not been welcomed so warmly. Thus gratitude for a physical gift generates gratitude for enthusiastic acceptance.

These interactions are the building blocks of strong loving relationships. Children and adults alike perform them spontaneously. Christian Communion services imitate it. Worshippers take wheat and grapes, use them to make bread and wine, and offer a proportion back to God as an expression of gratitude—while knowing that God does not need them.

It is possible that your generosity will rebound to your benefit. One day perhaps Abigail will visit you in your nursing home, take you out for a drive and push you round a park in your wheel chair. Nevertheless, if you calculate your giving with an eye to your own future benefit, the relationship will never be as strong. It is at its strongest when mutual love is the dominant motive, with no ulterior motives.

In secular theory there is nobody to thank. The world, environmental processes and human nature just happen to be there, the way things are. We learn not to be grateful that the sun shines, the rain falls, and bees pollinate flowers.

Secular theories of society express this absence of gratitude. Economic and technological programmes, both communist and capitalist, presuppose that the world, the living environment and human nature just happen to be there, accidental results of impersonal laws of nature. They have not been put there for any purpose. It is as though we have been dumped on an unknown island. As we explore it, we find other people similarly dumped.

We negotiate with them how to share the resources. So we create social contracts, rules about buying and selling and punishments for rule-breakers. Laws like that can never reflect truths about how we should live; instead they reflect the power relations between negotiators. The more we try to benefit ourselves the greater is the need to negotiate against others, and therefore the greater the need to measure resources. What matters most comes to be the measurements of the resources we buy and sell. Our theories of value, capitalist and socialist, take into account only what humans do. Valuing resources as they are comes to seem counter-intuitive. The rest, the unmeasured, slips into the background, taken for granted. In the story of Abigail, by contrast, the only thing that can be measured is the price paid for the crayons and paper. This price is of no interest to any of the characters; everything that matters is immeasurable. Thus secular value judgements and priorities develop a character very different from religious ones.

In these ways religious believers recognise dimensions to reality which secularism excludes. Ian Markham describes the difference:

> Those of us with a religious world-perspective… share the insights offered by scientists on the mechanics of the story, but see these mechanics as a part of a greater whole. The cause, the heart, and the hope of the universe are goodness and love. This is what a theist means by God. God is a being that causes all things to be, who has the characteristics of personhood in that s/he can decide, feel, act, and is good. It is an optimistic view of the universe. The universe on this account is not ultimately inanimate, but personal. It is in the nature of love that it needs to create more possibilities for personal relations whereby love can find expression and fruition. Thus it is in the nature of love to create. As the universe expanded, the drive was always towards the

emergence of life.[1]

These differences are expressed in our conceptions of the purpose of life. Polytheisms of divine conflict generally explain it in terms of meeting the needs of the gods; and since we are at the mercy of the gods we should do as they tell us, whether or not we like them. Monotheism tells us that God needs nothing and has created us for our own sakes, so the best way to live is to help each other towards fulfilment and happiness. Secularism takes its lead, on public matters, from atheism which tells us that we have not been created for any purpose at all. The question of how we should live then has no answer; ethics is either a misleading product of evolution or a method for manipulating each other.

Because these ethical conclusions are unpopular, in practice society continues to borrow and adapt moral judgements from its religious past. We have traced three. The environmental control project began with the hope of re-establishing the original perfection of the world that was destroyed when Adam and Eve ate the forbidden fruit. Secularising it had two opposite effects: by abolishing the original perfection it left us with the imperative of endless technological change, and by abolishing divine sanction it left us with no need to do it at all.

Much the same happened to the social control project. Calvinist reformers combined the monotheistic idea of moral progress with the dogmatic claim to be God's élite authorised to impose it. Once secularised, the project lost both the transcendent moral authority knowing how we should live and the permission to impose the new order on reluctant populations. Social engineers arrogated both to themselves by virtue of their scientific knowledge. In reality, of course, they never had anywhere near enough.

Liberal individualism has stronger roots in monotheism but also loses its justifications once it is secularised. The individual stops being a person-in-relation-to-God-and-society and instead becomes a free-floating owner of freedom and rights. Freedom stops being a God-given ability to choose between good and evil and becomes instead a power to be maximised for its own sake. Rights stop being divine permission to do what we have been created to do and become instead invisible possessions, socially imagined shields protecting us from abuse by others. Equality stops meaning that we are equally loved by God and means instead that we are equal in whatever manner the ruling classes choose to decree.

Confronting the practical issues

These adaptations of the ethical ideas inherited from Christianity mean that the issues described in the Introduction cannot be resolved within a secular framework of thought. Two reasons underlie them all. One is the absence of design. In monotheism the world order is set up so that fulfilment for one is consistent with fulfilment for all. In secularism there is no such presumption. Instead we find ourselves in an undesigned world with limited resources, so more for me probably means less for you. The other reason is that if the only values are the ones humans create, the most authoritative values are those of the ruling classes. Even if we left aside the roles of ambition and self-seeking, it would be an astonishing coincidence if the self-created values of all rulers were consistent with each other, let alone with the well-being of the powerless.

In the case of environmental destruction the control project is clearly the driving force. Environmentalists have pointed to many causes for the willingness of governments and large corporations to continue undermining the essential conditions for human life despite the overwhelming evidence for the harm being done. Behind them lies the idea that humanity can improve the conditions of life on earth by deliberately altering the natural environment. The drive to ever-greater artificialisation of life, such a dominant feature of western society's values, is now the greatest threat to our survival.

Monotheism offers a different route to a better future. The natural environment provides what we need. Some human effort is required to make adequate use of it, but nature provides us with adequate muscles and brains for the purpose. Shortage is the result of maldistribution, not the meanness of nature. Progress is a matter of caring for each other, using but not spoiling environmental resources. Sometimes there is a proper role for new technologies, but new technologies are not desirable for their own sakes.

The polarisation of wealth is largely part of the same story. The idea that experts can improve the conditions of life for everyone depends on a positivist belief that all the things making up a happy and fulfilled life are observable and measurable by a professional team of social engineers. In reality most of what makes us happy or unhappy cannot be measured. Those in positions of immense power, whatever their initial intentions, end up benefiting their own social class at the expense of others.

The main form of social engineering today is neo-liberal economic theory. Often it is counter-productive, as when governments, convinced that their success is to be judged by economic growth, and struggling to produce evidence of it, oblige employees to work longer hours with fewer resources but without reducing measurable output. Thus ordinary people's experience of life often deteriorates despite public statistics telling them they are better off. What keeps this system going is the myth of the economy, the *beliefs* that our well-being can be measured and that 'market forces' are real forces that restrict government options but can be manipulated by experts.

Monotheism by contrast tells us that God has provided enough for everyone, so an acceptable system is one that leaves nobody without. When one person has more than they need and another has less, the proper response is quite straightforward and needs no expertise or techniques: the one with more *gives* to the one with less—not as paternalistic charity but as justice, putting right the imbalance that had arisen. Whereas contracts like buying and selling, lending and borrowing, and all their elaborations like interest rates and mortgages, are social constructs characterising some societies but absent from others, free giving and receiving is foundational for all societies. All animals do it. Children love to feed ducks at the local lake. We would not have survived the first day of our lives if we had had to negotiate for our mother's milk. No system of contracts can replace giving and receiving. No amount of rules obediently kept can replace the relationship-building process of gift and gratitude. We know this instinctively; the difference between being given something and being sold it, for however low a price, is something we all understand.

This of course is anathema to capitalist theory. There is no shortage of economic experts insisting that redistributing wealth from rich to poor ruins the economy. However, as soon as we step outside the artificial constructs of economic theory, ordinary life tells a different story. Parents typically notice that one of their children is brighter, or more energetic, than another. They do not feed more or better food to their more able children, or demand child labour commensurate with the food and clothing provided. They accept that each child is different. Even parents who condemn welfare benefits to unemployed 'scroungers' will give whatever is needed to their own children, however inactive they may be. The reason for the difference is that they are motivated by love, not by a negotiated contract.

Most of the world's faith traditions recognise life in all its diversity as a gift. Society functions because at any one time enough of us are able to provide for the needs of others. We all begin life needing to take and unable to give in return. Most of us end life like this too. Some of us spend our whole lives like this. As long as there are enough people capable of providing for them, the existence of dependants is not a problem.

Social disapproval, therefore, should not be directed at those who need a lot and can only contribute little. It would be better directed at the over-rich who take more than their share of resources. If we made sure that everybody had the physical resources they needed and nobody had too much, we could all then focus on the more creative elements of life that transcend buying and selling.

Secularism has also contributed to militarisation, largely through the decline of an internationalist culture. We may contrast the internationalist mood at the end of the Second World War, that established United Nations and the Universal Declaration of Human Rights, with the endless superpower rivalries of today that generate military activity—especially in the area between Ukraine, Libya and Afghanistan, where the USA and Russia vie for influence. Increasingly the 'we' who are making progress in one way or another are conceived as the nation, or the ruling classes and their intellectual supporters, rather than humanity as a whole.

Like other monotheist principles, the unity of humanity survived secularisation for a while. Nineteenth century social engineers wrote histories of the world treating humanity as a unity making gradual progress. They knew that empires rise and fall. 'What was of infinitely greater importance to them', Nisbet summarises, 'was that, irrespective of what might happen to a single person on earth, the progress of mankind as a whole was ensured.'[2] Without this sense of humanity's unity progress could not have been something to get excited about. It would only ever be partial—a step forward here, a step back there.

After both world wars of the twentieth century the cry went up 'Never again!' It was still possible to appeal to the belief that humanity as a whole was capable of living together peacefully. However, although secularism inherited the idea of humanity as a unity, it discarded its theoretical underpinning. Our unity, no longer based on being equally created and loved by the same god, is based instead on a factual level from the evolution of the species and on a moral level from universal human rights. Neither of these is strong enough to support a vision of world peace. Although evolution has often been interpreted as progressive, it does not offer moral direction. 'There can be no such thing as the history of humanity, only the lives of particular humans,' John Gray argues. Looking for meaning in history 'is like looking for patterns in clouds'.[3] Humanity is a species, and species cannot control their fates. They are 'only assemblies of genes, interacting at random with each other and their shifting environments.'[4]

As for human rights, we have seen how the notion was developed by Europeans to give moral force to inherited Christian moral standards while removing all reference to the Christian God. Without its original justification it only survives as an ungrounded moral assertion. As such it is easily invoked by the powerful to bully others. Western governments criticise other governments for their poor human rights records while ignoring the rights of countless refugees looking for somewhere to live and being barred from one country after another. From a monotheist perspective, the concept of human rights is derived from the principle that nature's resources are provided for everyone, refugees included. An appropriate response would be an international programme to ensure that they all have somewhere to live and the resources to look after themselves. It is noteworthy how little influence this now has in public debate. Individuals may feel enough compassion to go to Lesbos or Calais to help, but the dominant discourse presupposes that the government of each state has no obligations to foreigners however desperate their circumstances. From this perspective, to help refugees would be an unnecessary act of generosity beyond the bounds of duty, especially if they pose threats to jobs. They are 'they' while the people who already live in our country are 'we'. The proclamation of the unity of humanity has now declined to a faint echo, barely audible behind the nationalist appeals that set us against outsiders.

Faced with foreign competition, secularism offers governments two ways to respond. One is the postmodern notion of incommensurability. This response parallels the ancient polytheism of divine conflict. The king of Assyria could claim that the true god of the whole world was Assur, Assyria's god. Assur had become the chief god by winning battles against other gods, and in the same way the king of Assyria ought to fight other kings for world supremacy. Meanwhile the king of Babylon made similar claims about his god Marduk. In their imperial propaganda neither accepted the existence of a higher authority competent to judge between the gods. As there was no court of appeal, the conflicting claims were incommensurable. The only resolution was by war. In the same way modern western governments, observing the different cultures of Russia, China and Islamic countries, interpret them as alien. We trade with them and are only too happy to make money out of them, but by thinking of them as different we limit our concern for their wellbeing. Because there are no overarching 'grand narratives', no right answers, disputes can only be settled by whoever has the biggest bombs. To suit the divisions Islam and Christianity get reinterpreted. Both began with visions of humanity as a unity, insisting that all humans are children of God, equally loved by God and deserving their due share of the earth's resources. Today, many people appeal to them as the exact opposite—as identifiers of difference, marking the enemy as aliens.

The other secular response is the blunt appeal to western supremacy. Of course every conqueror claims to be an enlightened liberator of the people they are oppressing, at least in their propaganda, but secularism has given western governments reasons to believe it. Science and technology are often taken as proofs of superiority. Western leaders often deride non-western societies for their backwardness, and adopt the social engineering stance that now comes so easily: 'we' know that the 'undeveloped' people of Papua New Guinea or the Amazon Basin would be better off if they became like us.

On its own the incommensurability theme claims that we are on an equal playing field with our opponents—so may the best team win. The supremacy theme goes further. It demands the extension of western culture throughout the world. The control project was from the start intended to apply universally. Needless to say the victims do not agree. So one conflict replaces another as the ongoing march of globalisation challenges the right of alternative societies to exist. As long as powerful forces consider themselves competent to determine the values other people should live by, such conflict will continue.

This gives modern western society the character of a control freak. Once its leadership became confident that 'we' will be able to understand how the world works and improve it, they convinced themselves that they knew what needed to be done. It then became difficult to understand why they should listen to others, let alone learn from them. To maintain this confidence reality is reduced to what can be measured. So the 'developed' western world, turning a blind eye to its own destructiveness, sees the rest of the world as 'undeveloped' and then corrects itself: no, that would be too unkind. The rest of the world is 'developing'—trying to become like us. It is a technological equivalent to the racist idea that black Africans have not evolved as far as white Europeans but one day will.

For those in positions of power the dangers of control freakery are magnified. Power characteristically brings over-confidence in one's own knowledge. A consequentialist approach to decision-making comes to seem natural. In everyday life there is a proper place for judging likely consequences before deciding what to do, but it can easily become a disguise for self-interest: we tell ourselves that on balance our plan will have the best outcome, while in reality caring more about the consequences for ourselves than for others. This weakness becomes all the more tempting when major international decisions are to be made and it is impossible to foresee all the consequences. Governments often feel pressure to ignore the interests of powerless people a long way away. So government ministers often judge that selling weapons to a war zone will create profits which might then be used to promote peace; or that reducing welfare benefits will help the economy to grow and eventually enable the poorest to get jobs; or that continuing to release pollutants and greenhouse gases into the air will make the country richer and enable it to tackle environmental issues sometime in the future. To those genuinely concerned for the issues these decisions are absurdly hypocritical, but they are often made. They characterise the self-deception so easily practised by those with too much power, imagining that they have a good enough overview of the future effects of their actions.

The rest of us, to the extent that we identify with ruling classes who behave in this kind of way, produce a kind of control freak society. When we are brought up with the idea that we (whoever 'we' are) understand the nature of reality, have progressed further than others and know what others need for their own good, it becomes easy to dismiss people who disagree as fundamentalists or as just ignorant. We believe too readily that the bombs our people drop on other countries are helping more than they are hindering. We imbibe too uncritically the values broadcast by the mass media of our own nation. When opponents fight to resist the onward march of western influence, we do not take the trouble to find out how their values differ from ours; we just denounce them as terrorists.

One of the reasons why this control freak tendency meets so little internal opposition is that, in the absence of a transcendent authority, secularism interprets values as rooted in whatever people want. It therefore lacks an adequate method for people to reflect on whether we want the right things or the wrong things.

Nevertheless, opposition is growing. Across the western democracies we are seeing a decline of the traditional left-right political divisions. New alliances are being formed. Environmentalists, poverty campaigners, anti-globalisation campaigners and peace activists are increasingly making common cause in opposition to institutions and industries that cause environmental destruction, war and poverty. We might think of these new alliances as opponents of the control project, seeking humbler, more democratic and celebratory ways of living. What they lack is a shared philosophy to justify and promote their preferred values. The moral concepts available to them are inadequate. They may appeal to a document like the Universal Declaration of Human Rights, or to statistics about how many people support or oppose something, or to an unanalysed belief that something is 'just plain wrong', or simply to their own feelings. What would strengthen their case is a philosophy which explains how there is a goodness better than the rules of the ruling classes, a truth truer than the dominant narratives, a set of values greater than what the most powerful want to do. The monotheism of divine harmony can provide it.

Moral truth

Monotheist ethics differs from secular ethics fundamentally because it believes in an intended design to our lives. On a godless account, where our values are what they are only because we have created them, each community and each generation will 'create' whatever values it chooses. This leaves us free to change them. It implies that whatever we believe today will have no authority when we are dead. In the long term, therefore, it leaves us with no reason to expect moral values to change in any particular direction, let alone to progress. Monotheism, by contrast, tells us there is a higher source of values than our own judgements. John Cottingham describes the difference. In a discussion of the meaning of life he asks whether, in the absence of God, we could see our lives as meaningful 'simply in virtue of their being directed towards the *flowering of our human nature?'* His answer is that if this flowering is to ground our morality,

> ...human nature in this context has to mean more than just a collection of contingent facts about the sort of creatures we humans have evolved to be: instead, it has to embody a normative ideal of what is noblest and best within us.[5]

This 'normative ideal' cannot be something we have created for ourselves. It must have a source from outside us. To believe that there is such a source

> ...encourages us with the hope that the pursuit of virtue, difficult and demanding though it often is, contributes however minutely to the establishment of a moral order that the cosmos was created to realise.[6]

In other words, to make sense of our moral beliefs—to keep open the possibility that some of them are true and matter—we need some sense of objectivity, some recognition of a moral authority that transcends the human mind. When we feel pleasure after a good meal or a good night's sleep, the pleasure can express the fact that they really are good for us. They help towards a fulfilling and constructive life. The pleasure an alcoholic receives in having another drink may, on the other hand, be equally pleasurable but objectively not so good. The same applies to negative judgements. When we react with horror at the news that a child has been raped or innocent people have been tortured, we do not just *feel* that the act was evil: we also *believe* it was evil, and would have been even if we had had no feelings about it. Thus our personal judgement is one thing, the truth of the matter another. When our judgements are correct, the two agree.

The mere existence of moral truths is insufficient on its own.

It leaves open the question: why should we pay any attention to them? Here lies a weakness in all the God-substitutes that function as moral authorities. I have argued that unbelievers who appeal to moral truths transcending the human are thereby betraying their unbelief: they are clinging to an act of faith in some transcendent authority. In practice, as we saw in Chapter 10, public debate about controversial issues characteristically appeals to objective moral truths even when debaters claim not to believe in them. Positively believing in them, however, is still not enough. If they exist, so what? What is it about them that gives us good reason to follow their advice? We would need reason to believe that their advice is for the greater good even when it does not seem to suit us.

Monotheism tells us that moral norms are built into the way life has been designed, by mental processes that understand how things work better than we do. Because the overall agenda for human life is given by God, it is not to be established by power struggles or interpreted to suit the ruling classes. We are created for fulfilment and we achieve it by reflecting in our own lives the creativity and benevolence of God.

So we need to believe not only that there are transcendent moral norms, but also that we have good reason to obey them. So how do we find out what they are?

In a realist account of morality public debate takes the form not of creating values but of trying to *discover* values which are already there. We might compare the process to scientific research, in the sense that scientists look for truths which would be true even if nobody believed them. Researchers inherit information from their traditions and build on them. At every stage there is a consensus that some theories are right and others wrong, while others again are topics of continuing research. Of the many questions that seem permanently settled some may be reopened when new information comes to light, but this does not stop scientists feeling confident that overall progress is possible.

Monotheistic ethical discourse is similar. Starting with the theory that a good god has created a universe sufficiently ordered for humans to understand how we can live at our best, we develop moral norms by reflecting on our experiences, relationships and environment. Some of our conclusions, like some scientific theories, will turn out to be wrong; but as communities reflect on their experiences of constructive and destructive lifestyles, gradual progress becomes possible. We make observations about what helps us live happy and fulfilled lives. We extrapolate from them to what helps other people around us live happy and fulfilled lives. We can then extrapolate further to communities, nations and people at the other side of the world whom we are never likely to meet.

Unbelievers can do most of this too, but for those who believe we create our own values there are no right answers so there cannot be any progress towards them. For monotheists there can. When the values of different individuals conflict, therefore, the task is not to balance them against each other by a political voting system or by an economic system of fluctuating prices and wages, but by shared public reflection and debate about which values enable us all to flourish and experience life as a blessing, and which do not.

How then do we go about judging between right and wrong? Here too there is an important difference between secular and monotheist approaches. One way to appreciate it is to focus on the role of moral rules. In Chapter 10 we saw how communitarian secular approaches to seeking moral consensus, such as the one offered by John Rawls, take as a starting-point the moral norms that seem right—in the sense that the community has inherited them and accepts them—and set about devising a philosophical system that explains why they are right. Indeed, it is difficult to imagine what alternative procedure there could be in a world where we create our own values. This order of procedure has the effect that the moral norms—the rules—take pride of place.

Secular society accepts, for example, that murder and rape are morally wrong. It forgets that the wrongness of these acts has a history; they were once explained in terms of God's will, and before that their wrongness was not necessarily accepted. Instead it treats their wrongness as a socially agreed response to experience. So the rules are accepted first, and the moral theories later turn them into a system. This makes the rules prior to the system.

Religious traditions do not need to focus on rules in the same way. Some do, especially those appealing to biblical texts or church authorities. More open, less dogmatic religious traditions derive moral judgements from their overall theory of who made us and for what purpose. We can spend time meditating on who made us and why. We can reflect on who we are, who we are responsible for and what we can do, and ask ourselves which acts, in our situation, our creator might recommend. From this perspective the reason for living a moral life is not the rules themselves. The rules are just guidelines which work most of the time. More important is the fact that our lives have been given a purpose to which we can respond. To be a good person, responding to moral truth, will mean something different to each of us, something different every day; but if we care about who made us, and for what purpose, we are more likely to get it right. Moral theories in tune with this approach are situation ethics and virtue ethics.

The major world faiths usually produce moral recommendations along these lines. An apt summary is a text attributed to Jesus:

> You shall love the Lord your God with all your heart, and with all your soul, and with all your strength, and with all your mind; and your neighbour as yourself.[7]

Unlike the theories characteristic of secular ethicists this is not an appeal to rules, or to any system of rationality. It appeals to an emotion. Secularists may ask why this is an appropriate procedure at all: how will adopting an emotion solve anything?

When secularism reduces values to whatever we choose to create, and thereby treats our wants as foundational, what remains to be done is to *calculate* how to achieve as many wants as possible. From a religious perspective the calculations are secondary; what matters most is to make sure we want what we ought to want. Our wants are best directed when we care about what God cares about. So what matters most is to direct our desires accordingly.

Thus the conscience replaces positivist calculations. There remains an important place for calculations, but when we do not limit our judgements to what can be measured a much wider range of considerations becomes available. We can tell from our own experience what a particular person in a particular situation must be feeling. To take into account the immeasurables that we become aware of in local situations is to do what no class of experts can do for us. Morality is thus democratised. Each of us in our own situation has access to relevant information which cannot be measured and often cannot be put into words at all, let alone acquired and assessed by a class of experts. What we do with the information will depend on the state of our consciences, the degree to which we exercise love in practice.

Consciences are not just instinctive responses. Biological studies tell us that what we want comes from a mixture of nature and nurture: self-interested instincts, altruistic instincts, learned selfishness and learned altruism. Consciences can be educated, well or badly, as virtue ethicists argue. Every religious tradition offers methods. Sometimes what we want is what needs to be done, sometimes it is not. When we appreciate that the moral task is to align our wants with the highest values, it becomes clear that the methods we need are not of technical control, but of reflecting on our own hopes and ambitions and directing them towards the highest values. The day before Theresa May became Prime Minister of the UK, Archbishop Rowan Williams was asked what advice he would give her. His advice was 'Pray, so that you do not lie to yourself'.[8]

At this point I am echoing traditional religious teaching as it is directed to individuals. I include it here because we also need to apply it to societies. The process of secularisation has allowed this kind of discourse to continue, but has reduced its application to individuals who choose to accept it and apply it to their personal lives. We need to revive it on a public level. It is part of the moral task of *communities* and *nations* to check whether they are lying to themselves and to see themselves as others see them, so as to spot their own weaknesses and seek to overcome them. The policies of governments should be guided not just by calculating how to maximise national wealth and power, but by a moral hope of working towards a more harmonious and peaceful world.

In these ways monotheistic morality operates with methods very different from secularism. How, then, does the content differ?

The dominant agenda of secularism was described in Chapters 7 and 8. Only humans have intelligent minds. Nobody else has the capacity to be in charge of the world, so we must be in charge. We therefore need to gather information, and on that basis work out what to do. When we have established what we are going to achieve we make it happen. Hence the search for humanity's omnipotence and omniscience. As for humanity's benevolence, we all think our intentions are for the best. Those who identify with the ruling classes forgive their failings; others condemn them. This secular agenda puts unlimited demands on us: we need to know more and more, and do more and more.

By contrast monotheism tells us that we are not, and cannot be, in charge. We cannot know enough about how the world works. We cannot know the final objective of progress. Our motives are always mixed—with good intentions, but limited by personal concerns. We find it easy to find fault with others; when it comes to ourselves, we need help to see what is wrong. Unless we check our intentions and actions against the highest standards we end up deceiving ourselves.

From a monotheistic perspective, therefore, it is a good thing that we are not in charge. God is in charge. God does not have our limitations. The moral agenda is to celebrate and value what we have been given, and care for each other. We do not need to organise the world, so we do not need to be anywhere near so busy. Whereas secularists often treat hard work as one of the highest virtues, for monotheists there are limits to what needs to be done. Instead our task is to pay attention to each other's needs. The information we need, therefore, is not so much scientific as moral and spiritual.

Collaboration

So far this chapter has focused on the differences between monotheist and secular accounts of public morality. However there are similarities which need to be clarified.

Some religious believers feel the need to justify their ethical concerns and actions in an exclusively religious way, for example by appealing to biblical quotations. To do so is to imply that the reasons for their concerns are different from other people's reasons. If for example they claim that it is biblical texts that persuade them to campaign against climate change or for development aid, their reasons cannot be shared by secular fellow-campaigners.

It is a popular misconception that this kind of dogmatic approach to current issues is characteristic of religious believers. In fact the reverse is the case. Many religious leaders do expect members to believe what they are told, and some believers do uphold anti-establishment beliefs simply because religious leaders or texts tell them to. This often happens in debates on abortion, evolution and sexuality. However recent social research by Linda Woodhead and others has shown that they are only a small minority. Most believers reflect on their moral concerns in an open-minded manner similar to the way unbelievers do.[9]

This makes a difference to how we understand the practical relationship between believers and unbelievers. If we imagine that believers make their moral judgements, and do their campaigning, for reasons that are completely different from the reasons unbelievers do, then the two groups can only support each other on a superficial level, as a pragmatic alliance. The underlying motives, being completely different, may tear the alliance apart whenever a controversy takes a new turn. When we recognise that the overwhelming majority of believers hold their ethical stances *for the same practical reasons* as unbelievers, this tension does not arise. A current example would be the debate about fracking ('hydraulic fracturing'). The argument in favour of it is that it a source of energy. It is very much part of the environmental control project, an attempt to extract gases deep underground to meet the requirements of technological and economic development. The main arguments against it are that it contaminates local water supplies and adds greenhouse gases to the atmosphere. There are believers and unbelievers on both sides, appealing to the same practical arguments. Similarly, for believers and unbelievers alike, concern about climate change is generated by the scientific evidence and animal rights campaigners feel compassion for suffering animals.

Because believers and unbelievers can support the same objectives for the same practical reasons, they can co-operate with each other and agree how to go about their tasks. There is still a difference between the two groups, but it is on the more philosophical level I have been describing in this chapter: believers can *justify* their values more adequately by appealing to an authority that transcends the ruling classes. Unbelievers, on the other hand, must choose between the idea that 'we create our own values' and some kind of transcendent God-substitute. Brian Hebblethwaite described the situation:

> Where an ethical ideal is held to be a purely human… product of creation, it is bound to possess a certain arbitrariness. However noble, it can only be offered and commended as one possibility among others… But where an ethical ideal is held to reflect the ultimate nature and purpose of things… it is seen to be objective and compelling—compelling not in a way that overrides freedom and responsibility but morally compelling as the ideal behind the whole creation and the law of our life whereby alone we find our own true good.[10]

We all presuppose at least some of this when we disapprove of what other people have done. Thus believers, even while agreeing with unbelievers about moral truths, can explain them better than unbelievers can. There is nothing unusual about this. The difference characterises all social projects that are not driven by a positivist philosophy. We know that the world goes round the sun, but only some of us know that the sun is near the edge of one of many galaxies. We all eat, but only some of us understand the digestion system. None of our actions are based on complete knowledge because we never have complete knowledge. What matters is that we have *enough* knowledge to know what to do. In the same way, first we learn about right and wrong, then later we ask questions about the meaning of right and wrong. Somebody who has only a hazy idea of what they mean by right and wrong may still feel confident that refugees should not be left to drown in the Mediterranean. A Christian or Muslim with an elaborately worked out belief about moral authority can co-operate with such a person, and affirm the belief as far as it goes, while holding additional beliefs about how to make sense of the moral claim.

Summary

To summarise this chapter, the essential differences between secular and monotheistic ethics are derived from the question of how we relate to the forces producing the world and our lives. According to secularism, life was not intended. The forces creating us and the world are impersonal. We cannot have a personal relationship with them, let alone trust them or thank them. Therefore it is up to us to make what we can of this accidental life. Because we cannot trust the forces, the dominant inference is that we need to take control. This means acquiring scientific knowledge for new technologies. It has turned out, though, that however much science and technology we develop, it is never enough for the control we seek. Therefore we need to work harder and harder in the hope of achieving it. The people who work hardest and contribute most come to be seen as the most valuable, while the people who do little work but need a lot of help are judged a drain on society. Although the ghost of Nazism still reminds us not to say so, the inevitable conclusion is that we would be better off without the people who are more of a hindrance than a help to the communal agenda.

Monotheism turns all this upside down. The forces creating us and the world are personal. They provide us with all we need for a fulfilled life. We can relate to them. The relationship is one of trust and gratitude. We accept what we are given with confidence that it is provided for our benefit. We do not need to alter it. All we need to do is to use it for its intended purposes, valuing the richness of our environment and caring for each other. Progress is not technological or economic, but moral. The proper response to what we have been given is not to replace it with something else, but to enjoy it, celebrate it and include everybody in the celebrations.

Chapter 13. Evil's causes

A defence of monotheism would not be complete without a response to the most common criticism of it: that a good god would not create a world like ours with so much suffering and evil. This complaint has been recorded since ancient times. Since the eighteenth century the debate on it has been extensive and has been given a name, theodicy.

In Chapter 14 I shall offer my own defence, drawing on the work of other theodicists. My position is similar to John Hick's in his *Evil and the God of Love,* though there are differences. First, however, this chapter addresses a prior question. The literature usually assumes that the problem of evil arises only for monotheism, not for alternatives like polytheism or atheism. I believe this is not the case; if anything, the problem is solved more easily by monotheism. However, to survey the whole range of responses to evil would be far too big a task for this one chapter. I shall therefore limit myself to describing the *types* of response, and focus on the two questions most relevant to this book. One is about origins: how does each theory explain why there is any evil in the first place? The other is about the ethical implications: in any one theory, what if anything can we do about it?

Discussions of theodicy are often designed to help believers in distress—the bereaved, or people watching a loved one endure great suffering. Pastoral books of this type often make claims which are not really monotheistic. One type of discourse is whether we should expect God to intervene in the world order to stop suffering, perhaps in response to prayer. This idea contains an element of divine conflict: if God created the world as it is but then intervenes to correct its worst features, it looks as if the original creation was flawed—so one action by God corrects an error made by an earlier action. A similar idea is that God suffered in Jesus on the cross, usually for reasons along the lines of the atonement theories described in Chapter 5. Surprisingly, Hick was sympathetic to this idea and even went so far as to claim that the death of Jesus was 'an evil than which no greater can be conceived'[1] for which, of course, we have no evidence. At best, appeals to the suffering of Jesus set up a divine dualism. It is as though you meet in court the man who burgled your house, and he tells you that he was burgled too. You would be even less impressed if it turned out that he himself had planned the burglary of his own house.

My aim here is not the pastoral one of defending God's goodness against the question 'Why is God making my husband suffer?', but the more general one of defending monotheism against the question 'How can you believe in a good god in the light of all the world's evils?'

The literature usually distinguishes between two types of evil. One is 'non-moral' or 'natural' evil, harm caused to people by the environment. The most frequently cited are earthquakes and cancer. The question here is why a good god would create a world in which these things cause suffering; why not create a world without them?

The other type is moral evil. People suffer because of the morally evil acts committed by others.[2] If human action is determined, there is no difference between the two types as a creator god will be just as responsible for human acts as for environmental events. If, on the other hand, we have free will, we are responsible for what we do. This means God is not directly responsible for evil human acts but is still responsible for enabling us to perform them. We can still ask why God allows this much freedom.[3]

Monotheism and evil

Monotheists have usually appealed to the 'free will defence'. This argument is that God's gift of freedom to humans is a positive good as it allows us to become morally good by our own free choices. Evil is what happens when we fail. Without the possibility of freely choosing evil we would not have the option of freely choosing good.

The most influential modern defence of this position is John Hick's *Evil and the God of Love*. Hick distinguished between two Christian explanations of evil, which he attributes to Irenaeus and Augustine respectively. Both attribute evil to God's gift of free will to humans, but in different ways. The distinction has been widely accepted and I agree with him in preferring Irenaeus' account.

Although Augustine's dominated most of Christian history, it conflicts with modern understandings of reality. The most obvious issue is the staged account of history. According to Augustine God first created a perfect world, complete with morally perfect humans, Adam and Eve. The Fall, and later the crucifixion and resurrection of Jesus, in his view caused significant changes to the nature of human life. This raises the question of why Adam and Eve, in their perfect state, freely chose to sin. Augustine believed that the serpent in the Garden of Eden was the devil in disguise, but this did not solve the problem: as noted in Chapter 5, if a perfect god would only create perfect beings, where did the devil come from? Modern understandings of history describe it more in terms of gradual change, without any original perfection.[4]

Augustine also argued that the world as it is is perfect. All evils, natural and moral alike, were in his view the direct result either of human actions or of God punishing them.

> Since there is happiness for those who do not sin, the universe is perfect; and it is no less perfect because there is misery for sinners… the penalty of sin corrects the dishonour of sin.[5]

Few today would be happy with the idea that plagues and floods, let alone punishment after death, re-establish the perfection of the created order.

What Hick calls the 'Irenaean' theodicy predates Augustine. Irenaeus, writing in the second century, argued that humanity was in a process of development. When God created humans they were in their infancy and, like children, did not always do the right thing. As we use our freedom we learn from experience to choose good and reject evil.[6] In the Garden of Eden, 'the man was a little one, and his discretion still undeveloped'.[7] Humanity is

> ...making progress day by day, and ascending towards the perfect, that is approximating to the uncreated One... Now it was necessary that man should in the first instance be created; and having been created, should receive growth; and having received growth, should be strengthened; and having been strengthened, should abound; and having abounded, should recover [from sin]; and having recovered, should be glorified; and being glorified, should see his Lord.[8]

There are limits to the quality of this early Christian account. Irenaeus was not as skilled a theologian as Augustine and could be inconsistent.[9] Nevertheless we can see here a theodicy consistent both with Hebrew monotheism and with modern understandings of history and evolution. In accordance with it, Hick described the world as a 'vale of soul-making', an environment in which finite persons may develop the qualities of moral personality.[10] We need not take this to exclude any other motives God may have, either for humans or for other parts of the created order.

This developmental theodicy was revived in the nineteenth century by Schleiermacher. In the meantime Augustine's had triumphed, but by the nineteenth century Augustine's staged account of history was no longer credible. The idea of long-term gradual progress fitted the ideas of the time.

Like Irenaeus, Schleiermacher believed that humanity had initially been created imperfect but capable of being brought to perfection. Our present imperfection therefore belongs to our God-given nature.[11] He saw evil as punishment for human sin but not directed to the sinner; people suffer as a result of other people's sins.[12]

After Schleiermacher, and before 1914, a variety of theologians developed this approach. Characteristic themes were that God permits evil to allow human freedom; that nature is a suitable environment for moral development; that the future will bring good out of evil; and that there is little or no punishment after death.[13] To Henry Drummond,

> Evolution is... a light revealing in the chaos of the past a perfect and growing order, giving meaning even to the confusions of the present, discovering through all the deviousness around us the paths of progress, and flashing its rays upon a coming goal. Men begin to see an undeviating ethical purpose in this material world, a tide, that from eternity has never turned, making for perfectness.[14]

These themes drew on characteristic ideas of the time. One was evolution, with the idea that over time animals, humans, consciousness and freedom of choice have developed out of earlier life forms. Another was progress. Within a staged view of history progress, if envisaged at all, is expected to take place only when one era replaces another—so most of the time the efforts of ordinary humans have no part to play. Within a linear view of time it is possible for progress to be gradual, and therefore for each person to play a part.

Among the popular nineteenth century theories of progress were the ideas that it was inevitable, that it could be achieved by control of nature as discussed in Chapter 7—the Industrial

Revolution seemed to be achieving it—and that it could be achieved by social engineering, as discussed in Chapter 8. These themes became a hostage to fortune when the optimism was shattered by the First World War. People wondered whether there was in reality any historical progress at all. Some theologians reverted to variations on the Augustinian tradition. Since then developmental theodicy has still been defended, most notably by F R Tennant early in the twentieth century and later by John Hick. However, it has come under persistent attack. Atheism was on the rise until the 1970s and overwhelmingly retained belief in progress. Within Protestant Christianity, meanwhile, the most influential theologian was Karl Barth, who rejected rational attempts to make sense of Christianity. The main movements, therefore, were not to replace one theodicy with another but to reject theodicy, either in the name of atheism or in the name of a Christianity which cannot be rationally explained. Paradoxically the idea of progress, the product of monotheism, is retained within secularism and atheism but is often treated with suspicion by Christian theologians.

Objective accounts of evil

It is this 'Irenaean', developmental theodicy that I shall defend. What is distinctive about it is that it combines two assertions: that evil is objectively real, more than just a subjective human evaluation; and that humanity has power to overcome it. Non-monotheistic accounts of evil either retain its objectivity while leaving us helpless to overcome it, or deny its objectivity altogether.

Ancient polytheisms varied. In some evil might be understood more or less subjectively, in others it was more objective. I shall focus on the objective systems first. At one extreme is an undetermined chaos where anything might happen. The polytheism of Homer's gods approximates to it. We are free, but we have no security. We are left to fend for ourselves in an unpredictable world so we have no idea what to do. This predicament, far from being right and proper in the overall scheme of things, is the unplanned result of unpredictable actions of gods. Less chaotic are accounts where the gods establish a certain amount of order while allowing for some disorder and tragedy, or punishing humans for disobedience. When, for example, ancient Mesopotamians suffered from illness, drought or military defeat, they experienced them as real evils and attributed them to divine actions. They then needed to explain why the gods were angry, and the characteristic answers were cultic—usually failure to provide adequate sacrifices.

Dualistic theologies, with a good god and an evil god, are in a sense a simplification of the same worldview. In theory it might be possible to believe that all the gods are evil, but in practice this does not happen. The thought of it is just too depressing. Wherever there are evil gods there is always some higher god who is good, even if powerless. Even the ancient Gnostics believed that above the evil creators of the world there was a benign god.

In theological dualisms, then, the evil god may be more powerful than the good god but the good god is the supreme moral authority. In some traditions the evil one is not described as a god, but what we call it is less important than its function. Divine conflict is still there, but without the range of independent agents. This dualism characterised Zoroastrians, Manichaeans, Bogomils and Cathars. As noted in Chapter 5 it is still common in Christianity. The sociologist Rodney Stark, denying that thoroughgoing monotheism is possible at all, argues that

> Judaism, Christianity, and Islam are *dualistic* monotheisms—each teaches that, in addition to the existence of a supreme divine being, *there also exists at least one evil, if less powerful, supernatural being.*[15]

These dualisms clarify a problem which is shared by all polytheisms of divine conflict: why would a powerful god be evil at all? Believers naturally expect the creator of the universe to have knowledge and power far exceeding ours. For such a powerful god, a benign stance towards humanity is easier to understand; any deity who creates us can be expected to have positive reasons for doing so. By contrast, if a divine being, so powerful and clever as to create this universe, has a gratuitous desire to make us suffer, we are left with a puzzle. Why create us then? There must be something deeply wrong, some flaw. What caused it? This was the agenda of many ancient myths. Gnostics asked: if this evil world is to be explained by evil gods, how do we explain evil gods? Their answers characteristically produced ever more complex theories of divine relationships. A common pattern is a sequence of emanations or creations. If p is perfectly good and the world has been created by an evil or stupid x, it would not make sense to believe that p deliberately created x like that. However, if p created q who created r and so on until w created x, it begins to appear a more credible account of the origin of evil. In reality, of course, the sequence does not solve the problem at all; it simply complicates the picture.[16]

If there are one or more evil deities, another question is the heavenly power relations. Dualist theologies often explore it. Are the good and evil gods both equally powerful, eternally struggling against each other? Will the battle between good and evil continue eternally? Or can we expect that one day the good god will triumph, as Zoroastrianism taught? If so, what are we waiting for? Why not now? Thus the idea of one or more evil deities does not solve the problem of evil at all. It simply transfers it to the heavens. As Hick remarks,

> The puzzles attending human imperfection, free will, and sin are reiterated, but not further illumined, by transferring them to a superhuman plane.[17]

While transferring them to a superhuman plane fails to solve the theoretical puzzles, it makes the practical situation worse. If evil is caused by gods, overcoming it is something only gods can do. This makes dualism fatalistic. It tells us that we humans are dumped in a situation where evil is part of the world's character by divine decree. Even if the decree comes from an inferior god, there is nothing we can do about it. We may hope that one day the evil god will be overcome by other gods, but this is nothing more than a hope. All we can do is wait. There is no point in trying to make the world a better place.

Thus dualism presents us with two problems, the motives of the evil god and our own helplessness. No dualist tradition has found a satisfactory solution to either. A third problem is that it leads to a polarised view of humanity. Since it treats everything as the creation of either a good god or an evil god, it encourages black and white judgements. Jeffrey Russell explains:

By insisting upon the struggle of two hostile principles warring for the mind, and by calling for war upon the evil principle, dualism abets repression... This encourages the growth of the psychic shadow, the projection of hostilities, and the increase of destructive behavior. Dualism may arise from, or at least reinforce, a paranoid schizophrenic experience of the world as divided into good guys (or spirits) and bad guys (or spirits).[18]

A different type of dualism contrasts a good god with an impersonal evil force. Plato's divine creator is an example. Rejecting Homer's account of Zeus as the creator of evil as well as good, Plato described the universe as created by a good god who was restricted to using two pre-existent elements. One was chaotic, unformed matter. The other was the 'forms', which we might think of as a set of ideal blueprints for every created thing. Evil is the result of matter's limitations. However if neither matter nor a limited god are ultimate and self-existent, we still have to ask what created *them*: another divine being or an impersonal process? The problem is pushed back rather than solved.[19]

Hick argued that Leibniz's *Theodicy,* with its claim that this is the best possible world, is of the same type. In the early eighteenth century Leibniz described God as able to consider every possible universe and choose the best. It would have been better if God had had more options, but they were limited. Hick added that Leibniz's intention to proclaim the supreme goodness of this world backfires. If evil is caused by Satan we may hope that one day Satan will be defeated; but if it is caused by logical necessity there is no such possibility.[20] As the saying puts it, 'the optimist thinks this is the best possible world; the pessimist fears that the optimist is right'.

I therefore propose to generalise that polytheist and dualist accounts of objective evil suffer from two weaknesses. One is that explanations of evil are not really given at all. If illnesses and floods are caused by angry gods, what makes them angry? The explanations are merely pushed out of sight into the divine world which humans cannot expect to understand. Thus evil is explained by the unexplained: we just have to accept that this is what the gods are like. From a human perspective, therefore, misfortunes are true tragedy. There is absolutely nothing good about them, no redeeming feature.

The second weakness is that resolution of tragedy lies outside our powers. Apart from performing our cultic duties there is absolutely nothing we can do to stop our misfortunes happening again. Evil becomes inescapable, built into the nature of reality. There is no hope of a better life in the future.

Subjective accounts of evil

Subjective theories argue that what we count as evil is only evil in the sense that humans judge it as such; otherwise it is not really evil at all. I shall describe three ways the illusion of evil is described. They overlap.

The first is determinism. According to this theory everything happens in accordance with the laws of nature and could not have been otherwise. Normally, when we make moral judgements about an action we imply that the agent could have acted otherwise. If this is not the case an action may still have results which please or displease us, but it becomes meaningless to praise or blame anyone for their actions. Similarly, to describe a specific event as good or evil is to do no more than to express how we feel about it.

It remains possible for determinists to believe the whole universal order has objective value. This is the characteristic position of monist traditions. Monism proposes that all things are one, or derived from one source. There is an underlying unity a bit like the god underlying the gods as described in Chapter 2. In some ways monotheism can be interpreted as a variant of monism. However, monism in its characteristic form in Indian philosophy states that only the limits of human understanding make us believe in evil; what we experience as evil would be recognised as good if only we could see it in its full cosmic context.

In western thought monism usually takes the form of pantheism, which identifies God with the universe, or nature. It first appeared in Heraclitus' statement that 'all things are beautiful, good, and right; men, on the other hand, deem some things right and others wrong'.[21] More influential was Plotinus, the founder of Neoplatonism in the third century CE, with his account of emanation. Plotinus referred to the source of the universe as 'the One', which is also both 'Being' and 'the Good'. It radiates its nature, unconsciously and inevitably, to create the universe. Emanations further from the One are less good and less real. The last stage of emanation is therefore the least good and the least real. So evil exists necessarily, but merely as a lack of good. Critics have claimed that on this point Plotinus is not consistent. It is as though, by identifying the One with both Being and Goodness, he treated existence and goodness as inseparable—so that the non-existence of evil would be an inevitable conclusion from the initial account of the One.[22]

Monism was revived in early modern times by Spinoza. To Spinoza, reality forms a determined and perfect whole, with everything following by logical necessity from the divine nature. Nothing is contingent: the world necessarily expresses the perfection of God, or Nature. Our desires and wills are also determined, and we erroneously conceive of evil from our finite perspective. Again, the things we normally consider evil only seem evil because of our lack of real knowledge: 'If the human mind possessed only adequate ideas, it would form no conception of evil'.[23]

Characteristically, then, monism makes two claims about evil: that it is illusory, and that what we experience as evil is determined. In western thought the idea that all evil is illusion is usually considered unsatisfactory. If you are in great pain, or have just suffered a tragic bereavement, the consistent monist will tell you that what you are going through is good really; it is only the limits to human understanding that make it seem evil. This is unlikely to help. Telling us that our sufferings would be revealed as good, if only we understood more, does not alter the fact that we experience them as evil. The only practical advice the consistent monist can give is to think of it differently. No doubt this is true of some suffering, and there are those who believe that all suffering can be relieved to some extent when a person has been trained in appropriate thought patterns; but to treat this as an adequate response to all suffering does not do justice to the evils we experience. On a practical level it makes things worse, by insisting that we just have to put up with it and implying that we are to blame for our own suffering.

Critics therefore complain that monists often seem to be judging from the perspective of an affluent comfortable life without appreciating the intensity of the suffering many people endure. If we persuade ourselves that suffering is illusory we become uncaring. To tell a sufferer that, seen from a universal perspective, there is nothing wrong, is to abandon any hope for a world with less suffering. On the contrary, Russell argues,

> The evils of the world are so many, so great, and so piercingly immediate that they demand not mystical acceptance, but the will to take arms against them.[24]

Meanwhile it is much harder to treat our own suffering as illusory because we experience it ourselves. This raises the danger of taking our own suffering more seriously than that of others, and thus increasing the tendency to self-centredness. Western critics therefore sometimes blame monism for features of Indian society, like the caste system, which encourage the poor and disadvantaged to accept their lot without seeking improvement.

Atheism is the position usually believed to avoid the problem of evil altogether. It tells us there is nothing to explain: the world and human life have come into existence without any plan or purpose, so what we experience as evil is whatever the laws of nature throw at us. Since they have no consciences, we just get what we get.

This is true, but only for atheists who consistently adhere to the reduction of values described in Chapters 10 and 11. In the absence of any thinking, evaluating beings with greater authority than humans, it follows that only the human mind can declare anything good or evil, and any such declaration means no more than whatever people choose to mean by it. From a consistent atheist perspective, therefore—that is, if there is no moral authority higher than the human—it is up to each of us to decide for ourselves what to count as good and evil, or indeed whether to have a concept of evil at all.

Here, then, is a third way of accounting for the illusory nature of evil. For monists what appears evil is good really. For determinists to call an event evil is merely to describe a human reaction to the inevitable. For atheists, whether or not they are determinists, we 'create our own values' when we call some things evil just as we do when we call other things good. Even if the evil events that upset us were freely chosen in order to spite us, calling them evil is just our own subjective response.

At this point we need to clarify what we are describing as evil. If we apply the subjective theory to pain it seems too absurd to be credible. Atheists experience it in the same way that believers do; they do not *decide* to feel pain. However it is not pain that generates the problem of evil. Pain and suffering relate to each other, but in a complex way. Nineteenth century philosophers like Jeremy Bentham used to think of pain and pleasure as opposite ends of a spectrum. Now scientists take a different view. Pain is a physical sensation with its own nerve structure. As a mode of sensation it has no opposite. Pleasure, on the other hand, is a mental condition. The opposite of pleasure is called by various names like displeasure, suffering and discomfort.

Pain has an essential warning function. It operates according to regular laws which ensure that it is usually strong enough for the purpose. Sometimes it causes suffering, but not always. Many people voluntarily put themselves in painful situations, to sail round the world or climb high mountains, accepting it as part of a valued experience.

It is suffering that generates the problem of theodicy. Here there is real distress, sometimes caused by pain but sometimes by other causes. Among other animals pain is a common feature of life but suffering is more restricted. When a bird's wing is damaged and it can no longer fly, it may be in pain but it does not as far as we know worry about how to care for its chicks or whether it will survive. Humans do have such worries. Suffering depends on a range of faculties which characterise self-awareness: the ability to think about the past and speculate on the future, to regret, wish, hope, and imagine what life would have been like in different circumstances.

Thus for those who believe we create our own values it is possible to distinguish between our pain, which is not our own creation, and our suffering which is. Still, this remains a very reductionist account. It tells us that, apart from the values we ourselves create, all we get are experiences, some of which are painful or generate unpleasant feelings. To go beyond these factual statements of feeling and call an event evil is to create (or more realistically, inherit) a concept of evil, which we then apply to the experience.

This means that, from the perspective of someone who thinks we create our own values, nothing is evil except when we choose to count it as evil, and we could always have chosen otherwise. So when our house is burgled, when our life partner dies an agonising death, when the bombs drop on our home town, we experience it as evil *only because of the values we have created*. Pain may be there, but not evil. The problem of evil disappears not because there is no god to blame, but because evil itself disappears—unless we choose to invent it. We could dispense with it, along with the idea of goodness. Evil becomes the negative counterpart of Stevenson's emotivism: 'I disapprove of this: do so as well'.

Few people really believe this, and even fewer live as though it is true. Atheists have the same unpleasant experiences as believers, and feel angry and resentful just like everybody else. In practice they do not treat their own misfortunes in the relativist way demanded by the theory. Instead they borrow a realist account of evil from their culture. Every culture, of course, can provide one; but the borrowing is inconsistent with the atheism.

Summary of alternatives

To summarise my argument, evil is either a real feature of human experience or it is a creation of the human mind. Theories of divine conflict describe it as a real feature caused by divine beings whose evil nature cannot be adequately explained, and leave us helpless in the face of tragedy. For monists everything that happens is good really, and it is only our ignorance that makes us interpret it as evil. For determinists and consistent atheists it is an invention of the human mind in the same way that good is.

These interpretations are not ethically helpful. In each case we are left helpless: whether our fate is determined by our stars or our genes, we are stuck with it. They tell us to abandon hope.

A more ethically constructive interpretation will need to have two features. The first is that it takes evil seriously. It is not an illusion: it is real to us, with our human minds, even if it is not real to other forms of life. The second is that we are not trapped in it. We can do something about it.

This is what monotheism offers: creation by a god who deliberately designs us for well-being and provides us with an appropriate balance between order and freedom. Metaphysically we might think of monotheism as a midway point between an ordered, determinist monism and a chaotic polytheism. When we compare the ethical implications, however, the positions are changed. Monism, atheism and polytheism have much in common. Monotheism stands apart by stressing both the reality of evil and human potential to overcome it. Terence Penelhum describes how

> ...the theist, in believing in God, believes *both* that God created the world *and* that much that is in the world is deeply deficient in the light of the very standards God himself embodies. The inconsistency seems to result from two distinguishable functions which the idea of God has. It is an ultimate source of explanations of why things are as they are; it is also the embodiment of the very standards by which many of them are found to be wanting.

Therefore believing in such a god leads to emphasising evil rather than arguing it away:

> The existence of evil is not something the facts of life force the theist to admit, in the way in which the facts of the fossil evidence forced some nineteenth century theists to admit the antiquity of the world. The existence of evil is something the theist emphasises. Theists do not see fewer evils in the world than atheists; they see more.[25]

To live constructive lives, we need to believe two things. One is that some states of affairs really are better than others. Evil, like good, is a real dimension of life. Without this, we are back in the world of Nagel's 'irony' where nothing at all matters, and Nagel himself acknowledged that we cannot really live like this. The other is that life is not essentially tragic. Faced with evil, we need to believe we can do something about it. We need hope. We need to believe that somehow, even if long after we are dead, what is wrong can be put right. Monotheism shows how both can be true at once.

Chapter 14. Evil in God's good world

This chapter offers my main defence of monotheism against the most common criticism, that a good god would not create a world containing so much evil. My overall position is the one John Hick described as 'Irenaean' theodicy. This is the theory that God created a good world, but part of the goodness is the freedom granted to humans. Our freedom enables us to develop moral goodness, but also moral evil. Thus there is real evil, it is caused by humans, and it can be corrected.

General excess of evil

To begin with the general criticisms: many opponents argue that an omnipotent god could have achieved this objective with less evil or none at all. Thus Frederick Sontag writes:

> I can easily conceive of better worlds than the one we occupy, and I find it quite clear that our present system is wasteful in achieving good results for everyone (if we accept this as God's intent).[1]

Defenders of God reply that important features of life would be lost. Thomas Aquinas argued in the thirteenth century that God designed life to be good for us, and on the whole it is, but a world with no suffering at all would have to exclude many features we value:

> A lion would cease to live, if there were no slaying of animals; and there would be no patience of martyrs if there were no tyrannical persecutions.[2]

We may prefer to do without the tyrannical persecutions but we can sympathise with Aquinas' point.[3] Recent defenders of God have often accused critics of assuming that a loving god should be aiming for a 'hedonistic paradise'. Instead Hick suggested we should be asking whether this is the kind of world

> ...in which moral beings may be fashioned, through their own free insights and responses, into 'children of God'?[4]

Puccetti replies that the world could have been arranged in a different way, preserving the basic aim but with less suffering:

> The Humane Veterinarian need not give his pets LSD or heroin, but he should at least shorten their suffering... True, we often sacrifice our children's pleasure for their moral gain: but we also try to spare them pain when it is not necessary for that purpose, and it is just this which Hick's postulated "Father of us all" does not seem concerned to do.

For example, God could have provided a world without carnivores; it could still have constituted a 'vale of soul-making'.[5]

Hick replied, rightly in my view, that evils are exceptional only in relation to other evils. Hitler is often invoked as an extreme monster whom God should have eliminated. If he had not existed, we would now be describing somebody else as an exceptional monster who should have been obliterated.[6] Each of us from our own vantage point 'may indeed cry out to God to revoke his gift of freedom, or to overrule it by some secret or open intervention', but

> ...if we take with full seriousness the value of human freedom and responsibility, as essential to the eventual creation of perfected children of God, then we cannot consistently want God to revoke that freedom when its wrong exercise becomes intolerable to us.

This 'can be of no comfort to those who are now in the midst of that suffering', but it may be true nevertheless.[7] When we suffer intensely we cannot imagine anything worse, but our imaginations are attuned to the realistic possibilities.

Some critics assume that to believe in God is to believe in the constant possibility of divine intervention. On this basis one can ask why God did not intervene in specific cases. Puccetti argues of an unsupervised toddler drowning:

> If it became subsequently known that a *man* witnessed the child's falling into the pool and could have saved her, yet did nothing at all about it, we should certainly not consider him benevolent. Yet we are expected to believe, or at least not hold it an irrational belief, that God did just that.[8]

Although it is a common complaint, divine intervention of this type would of course produce a completely different world. It is the regularity and predictability of pain and loss that makes our actions morally significant. Evolution normally selects against excessive pain because it is counterproductive[9] but it is not fine-tuned to each individual situation.

Natural evil

Most criticisms of theodicy are more specific. Some relate to natural evil, suffering caused by natural events. Others relate to moral evil, the suffering of some people caused by the actions of others.

The debate on natural evil usually focuses on either environmental destruction or illness. Environmental destruction includes earthquakes, volcanic eruptions and tsunamis. Earthquakes are the most commonly cited. They do not necessarily cause suffering. Somebody has to be at the site, unprepared. Earthquake zones are well known. Human deaths in them usually result from inadequately reinforced buildings; to treat them as an argument against God would be like living at the North Pole and blaming God for the hypothermia.

However I think there is more to the issue. Modern secular society, with its expectation of control, is more inclined to find fault with the environment than other societies have traditionally done. Once the finger of blame is pointed at the environment, it becomes part of the case against God.

To illustrate the issues I shall draw on reports of the 2004 Boxing Day Tsunami in the Indian Ocean. This tsunami was exceptionally destructive over an area from Indonesia to India. It was also well reported and researched. The popular western media described it as a conflict between humanity on the one hand and a hostile nature on the other. The concept of humanity-as-a-whole battling against recalcitrant matter is so firmly embedded in western culture's worldview that it could be taken for granted. Every destroyed hotel, every death witnessed to this image of our place in the world.

Environmental researchers and indigenous populations told a different story. It was available in the western media, but not so widely broadcast. Most westerners would have been unaware of it. They offer two main challenges to the dominant narrative. One is that indigenous populations were better equipped to handle tsunamis. Modern western 'development' has largely ignored their traditional knowledge.

> In the Town of Gunung Sitoli on Nias Island, Indonesia, the local traditional house which was built nearly a century ago survived without any damage, while a house next door, a six-year-old brick and cement-made home was destroyed without a trace.[10]

They knew how to build houses resistant to the local weather. More generally the destruction or weakening of mangrove trees removed an essential line of defence:

> In the 2004 tsunami in the Indian Ocean, healthy mangroves, the leading edge of the forest, took the brunt of the great wave's energy when it hit—yet few trees were uprooted... However, where mangroves had been weakened, even relatively slightly, by ecological harm caused by humans—like pollutants from inland development and agriculture—they were much less able to protect the inner coastline, even if they had not been thinned by strong storm winds.[11]

In some places destruction of mangroves was combined with other effects:

> Along the Eastern coast of India, for example, miles of coastal mangrove forests had been cleared to make way for the rapid expansion of commercial shrimp farms... The effluent from those intensive farms had also polluted many miles of the coast, destroying stretches of coral reef that, to make matters even worse, had also been mined extensively. Again, these submarine barriers would once upon a time have helped reduce the power of a tsunami, but with such natural barriers so diminished, the wave was able to strike with full force.[12]

The other main challenge comes from the responses of local people. Indigenous people who were least influenced by western lifestyles survived much better. In closer touch with nature, they knew the tsunami was coming and knew how to respond. This was the case on many islands. An American reporter interviewed a Moken man who explained how they did it. The Mokens are nomads who move between islands in the Andaman Sea.

> The Moken believe that ocean waves are created by the spirits of the sea... In response to why the tsunami came, he said, "The big wave had not eaten anyone for a long time, and it wanted to taste them again." The Moken has a legend that is

> passed from generation to generation about the Laboon, the "wave that eats people." It is believed that the angry spirits of the ancestors brought the tsunami. The myth tells that, before the giant wave comes, the sea recedes. Then the waters flood the earth, destroy it and make it clean again. On these islands the cicadas are usually loud, but suddenly went silent before the tsunami hit. Saleh Kalathalay noticed the silence and warned everyone about the tsunami. The Moken started to flee toward higher ground long before the first wave struck and were saved.[13]

The same was true of animals. The Yala National Park in Sri Lanka was badly affected by the tsunami. Park workers and tourists died as the flood waters surged through it. Much to the surprise of the wildlife officials, however, the animals survived. They had sensed the danger and retreated in time.[14]

We cannot of course examine every known natural disaster to assess whether it is consistent with creation by a good god. However, I think these reports illustrate a blind spot in modern secular culture. Because of the presumption of human control of nature, we respond to the unexpected in inappropriate ways. From major events like a tsunami or earthquake to minor irritants like snow blocking the roads, we draw on our narrative of humanity-as-a-whole-pitted-against-nature, and instead of learning to respect the environment we call for more research and technology so as to control it. What the Andaman Islanders and the Sri Lankan animals did was the opposite: they became aware of what nature was doing and adapted their behaviour so as to live in harmony with it. Whatever the advantages and disadvantages of their lifestyles, their response to the tsunami makes it clear that the finger of blame for the massive suffering cannot be used as an argument against God. It is, rather, an argument against modern attempts to control nature.

Apart from natural disasters most of the discussion of natural evils has focused on illness. According to the oldest records from Mesopotamia and Egypt, illnesses were caused by demons. The Hebrew scriptures denied the power of demons and attributed illness to God's punishment of sin. The Ten Commandments, an early text, describe Yahweh as 'a jealous God, punishing children for the iniquity of parents, to the third and fourth generation of those who reject me'.[15] Later, Ezekiel expected that in the future being planned by God only individuals would be punished for their own bad actions.[16] After Ezekiel some Jews seem to have believed that this was the case in their day.[17] The fact that life is not so simple is the chief topic of the biblical book of Job. It is a question to which the Hebrews did not find a satisfactory answer.

Unlike the ancients, we today attribute many illnesses to physical processes too small for the eye to see. This does not exonerate God, of course; we can still ask why God allows them. Theodicists usually argue that illness and the accompanying pain are warning systems. Typically we are doing too much or too little of something, or our living or working conditions are unhealthy. Many self-help and alternative therapies are based on these claims.

Some causes are cultural. We do what our society considers normal, and for four hundred years western society has conceived of progress in terms of turning away from nature and creating artificial lifestyles. Immense amounts of investment and innovation are devoted to making our lives more and more artificial. In our living and working conditions, our eating habits and leisure activities we often prefer, or are forced into, patterns of behaviour for which our biology has not prepared us. Much suffering, therefore, is caused by refusing to accept the limits to what constitutes a healthy environment and what our bodies can do. Environmentalists can list hundreds of examples. An obvious one is cancer. It is frequently cited as a reason why there cannot be a good god. Often it comes for no apparent reason to one individual but not another. Yet it ill behoves a society that pumps ever-increasing amounts of carcinogens into the air to blame God for the result.[18]

Pain in late childbirth illustrates how unplanned social processes can cause suffering. Having one's first baby is a major physical challenge. Biologically the best time for most women is the teenage years. Whereas the authors of the Bible took for granted that women had their first babies at this stage, teenage pregnancies are now frowned on. Society imposes social disadvantages on teenage mothers. While on the one hand medical technology eases the pain of later pregnancies, the benefits are offset by social and economic pressure to delay parenting. Characteristically, modern society congratulates itself on its achievements in making life easier, without noticing the ways it is making life harder. It thereby makes its artificial technologies essential and reinforces the narrative of humanity-pitted-against-nature.

These are only examples. Each of us has a different body and responds in different ways to the pressures. Air pollution is a factor in one person's cancer, but the next door neighbour is free of it. One 35-year-old has a trouble-free pregnancy, another needs medical intervention. It is all too easy to ignore the external factors and attribute the misfortunes to nothing but illness. Even when we do not know of any artificial causes of an illness, most of us now live in an environment so heavily altered by modern industry that we can never be sure we are not being affected in some way.

Critics of modern medicine have often argued that its character is too individualistic and reductionist. It isolates the individual with the illness, treats the body as a system of interacting physical elements, and looks for physical causes within the body. This contrasts with most of the older understandings of health and illness which focused on treating the whole person rather than the parts, and paid more attention to the patient's social context.[19]

Pain and suffering are also caused by individual lifestyle choices. Today doctors often begin appointments by asking three questions: Do you smoke? Do you drink alcohol? Are there signs of diabetes? We spend more on making ourselves ill with tobacco, alcohol and sugar than we spend on our health services.

Another common social cause of suffering is excessive expectations. We differ in our skills and needs. We need help from others, and most of us can provide some help in turn. Some of us are capable of doing most things in the usual range of human activities. Others have severe limitations, either from birth or after an accident or illness. Why does God allow, for example, genetic diseases?

In a society which is relatively content to live in the environment it has, there are plenty of human resources available to care for those with greater needs. Unfortunately modern society is constantly trying to maximise the resources it invests in its pet projects, like the ones described in Chapters 7 and 8. As a result it often resents having to divert resources to caring for the neediest people, who will not in any case contribute to these projects. There is a tendency to treat the disabled as hindrances to society, and provide insufficient resources for them. As a result their suffering increases.

Added to this is the cult of competitiveness, a trait regarded much too highly in capitalist society. We often put our bodies under excessive stress to keep up with other people and match their achievements.

Mental issues add another dimension. We know that many illnesses have a mental element. However we know very little about the cause-and-effect relationship between psychological states and physical illness. It may well be that physical illnesses have mental illnesses as contributory causes more often than we know. If so, it may be that many physical illnesses are partly caused by inadequate social conditions.

One of secularism's distinctive features is the default assumption that there is no life after death. The main medical institutions are expected to operate on the basis that death is the complete end for the dying individual, so that he or she will never experience anything at all ever again. The result is a tendency to keep the dying alive as long as possible. Sometimes there is an additional motive in the possibility of a new cure. The obvious fact that we are all going to die tends to be camouflaged by hospital activism, treating every death as a medical failure. Unfortunately, those subjected to the activism do not write posthumous newspaper articles telling us what their last dying days were like, but there is no doubt that a great deal of pain and suffering is caused by our cultural refusal to assess with due compassion the best time for each person to die, and let them die then.

In these ways modern western society causes a great deal of suffering which could be avoided if we learned to live more in harmony with the way our bodies have evolved. Much of what seems like natural evil turns out to be caused by poor lifestyles, either chosen or imposed.

This is not to say that if we avoided all these harmful actions we could abolish all suffering caused by illness. However I do think we can make a more modest claim: that if we made a priority of living in harmony with our bodies and our environment, we would be in a far better position to understand the remaining suffering and judge what to do about it.

Animal suffering

The question of animal suffering is complicated by the fact that we do not know what it is like for any given species to suffer. What philosophers call 'the problem of other minds' refers to the fact that, even in the case of other humans, we have no way of checking whether their suffering is anything like our own. We simply cannot get inside their minds to feel what they feel. To believe that other humans suffer as we do is a basic principle of morality which children learn at an early stage. In the case of other species our ignorance is magnified: we cannot know what it feels like for a tiger or an eagle to suffer.

In general we might think in terms of a spectrum of views. At one extreme is Descartes' theory, now discredited but still influential in some circles, that animals do not have souls and therefore do not suffer at all. After Descartes vivisection became a common practice. His view dominated the world of animal experimentation until the second half of the twentieth century. At the other extreme many people extend their natural sense of sympathy for other people as though other forms of life suffer in the same way. A classic case is Charles Darwin's:

> I cannot see as plainly as others do, and as I should wish to do, evidence of design and beneficence on all sides of us. There seems to me too much misery in the world. I cannot persuade myself that a beneficent and omnipotent God would have designedly created the Ichneumonidae with the express intention of their feeding within the living bodies of Caterpillars, or that a cat should play with mice.[20]

That caterpillars can suffer in any meaningful way is almost certainly false. Whether mice can is uncertain. Since suffering depends on a wide range of faculties, the type and intensity of possible suffering is likely to vary from one species to another. There are certain kinds of continuity between humans and other forms of life. Our consciousness differs in degree, not in kind. Higher mammals behave as we would when they are in situations where we would feel pain. The sensory and nervous systems of other vertebrates are similar to ours. Higher vertebrates can be taught through administering pain and pleasure.[21] In general, therefore, we have good reason to believe that some forms of life suffer in ways similar to our own suffering, and there is growing understanding of animal consciousness and therefore their ability to suffer. This has implications for human treatment of animals. Given the way pain has developed as a warning system, we can expect that animals have developed appropriate instincts for coping with being caught and eaten by their traditional predators. However unpleasant it may seem to us so see a fox catching and eating a hen, hens have evolved to cope with it. It is a different matter altogether when human cruelty is involved. Hens have evolved to cope with being eaten by foxes, but not to being kept in a cage all their lives. If they suffer from this treatment, it is a moral evil rather than a natural one.

Moral evil

We now turn to moral evil, human actions which cause suffering. Why does God allow them?

In the middle of the twentieth century a number of atheist philosophers argued that it should have been possible for an omnipotent god to create people who were free but who always freely did the morally right thing. I find this unconvincing. As Hick argued, it would only be freedom in a limited sense:

> ...one who has attained to goodness by meeting and eventually mastering temptations... is good in a richer and more valuable sense than would be one created *ab initio* in a state either of innocence or of virtue.[22]

Much suffering that seems natural is in fact moral. In political and military affairs, for example, government decisions cause wars and, in turn, starvation and disease. Political and economic policies often lead to alliances and threats that produce poverty and exploitation. Whenever the effect is indirect the victims are often unaware of the human causes and may instead blame God or refuse to believe in God. Similarly, we are characteristically quicker to blame others for their evil actions than to notice the evils we commit ourselves. This leads us to place the blame elsewhere.

Why do the innocent suffer at all? Granted that we have been given freedom to do good or evil, why should innocent people suffer the effects of other people's evil acts? This question was much discussed in the Hebrew scriptures but never satisfactorily answered there. People have asked it ever since. Some schools of thought argue that we get what we deserve. Some eastern traditions teach that our condition in life is our due dessert for previous incarnations. Some western self-help movements take the view that we bring our troubles upon ourselves. At the time of writing there is an increasing trend, encouraged by some of the media, to blame the poor for their poverty. It is a common temptation for those living comfortable lives to convince themselves that the less fortunate have only themselves to blame.

It does not take much imagination to appreciate how different things would be if the evil suffered and the good did not. When we saw someone suffering the obvious response would be to judge them morally inferior. Those in need of help would be, almost by definition, undeserving. We would therefore become unforgiving. Conversely, it would be impossible to perform a 'good' action without also being aware that one was helping oneself as well. It would become virtually impossible to do the right thing simply because it was right and without expectation of reward.

In Christian ethics, following the passion and crucifixion of Jesus, there is a strong tradition of emphasising the role of self-sacrifice for the common good. If we only ever got what we deserved this would become pointless. If true altruism is to be possible, Hick argued, 'suffering must fall upon mankind with something of the haphazardness and inequity that we now experience'.[23]

Another challenge to theodicy is the extremity of immoral

acts. If it is necessary for people to suffer from other people's immoral actions, why did God allow evils to be as great as they sometimes are? The most common illustration in recent times is the Holocaust where millions of Jews were killed in gas chambers. Why would a good god allow this? The question has generated a huge literature. In my view Hick's response, as given above, is the right one: suffering is comparative.

However a passage from Dostoyevsky's *The Brothers Karamazov* has been cited so often that it deserves attention. Ivan Karamazov describes a five-year-old girl being deliberately tortured by her parents. He addresses his brother:

> Do you understand why this infamy must be and is permitted? Without it, I am told, man could not have existed on earth, for he could not have known good and evil. Why should he know that diabolical good and evil when it costs so much? Why, the whole world of knowledge is not worth that child's prayer to 'dear, kind God'!

In some versions of Christian theodicy the time will come when we all do turn away from evil and become perfect—either in this life or a future one. Some theologians argue that this future harmony will justify, or compensate for, the sufferings people endure now. Ivan Karamazov replies:

> Too high a price is asked for harmony; it's beyond our means to pay so much to enter on it. And so I hasten to give back my entrance ticket... It's not God that I don't accept, Alyosha, only I most respectfully return Him the ticket... Imagine that you are creating a fabric of human destiny with the object of making men happy in the end, giving them peace and rest at last, but that it was essential and inevitable to torture to death only one tiny creature—that baby beating its breast with its fist, for instance—and to found that edifice on its unavenged

tears, would you consent to be the architect on those conditions?

Thus Ivan argues that the torture of just one child is too high a price to justify humanity's ability to distinguish between good and evil. However the ability to make this distinction is presupposed in the narrative. If he himself, and we the readers, did not distinguish between good and evil, we would not be troubled by these acts or consider them cruel. Animal life is full of actions which we can interpret as cruel, performed as far as we know without any moral qualms. When humans perform acts of great cruelty without showing remorse, popular discourse often condemns them as 'animals'. We expect humans to distinguish between good and evil and act accordingly. When people fail to make this distinction the acts of cruelty become more, not less, likely. What disappears is not the cruelty but the perpetrator's moral awareness.

One of the commonest criticisms of theodicy is that life is not fair. All through history people have lamented that good people suffer and evil people live successful and happy lives. Moreover some are born with healthy bodies while others are born with physical disabilities. Some live short and painful lives. Some are still-born. As Christopher Southgate puts it, 'The heart of the problem is that the experience of many individual living creatures seems to be all suffering and no richness'.[24]

Theodicists often argue that these injustices will be redressed in the next life. Among them was Hick.[25] One possibility would be what he called a 'book-keeping view', that God allots rewards and punishments to redress the balance for each individual. In practice this is widely believed; many people positively want their enemies to be punished. Hick preferred to believe in an unending 'enjoyment of a common good' which 'would render worthwhile *any* finite suffering endured in the course of attaining to it'.[26] However he did not think people could go straight to it after this life, because 'it is far from clear that an individual who had been instantaneously perfected would be in any morally significant sense the same person as the frail, erring mortal who had lived and died.' There must therefore be an intermediate state of continuing sanctification.[27]

The view has had many critics. Puccetti, for example, distinguishes between the 'bookkeeping view' which

> ...would be like a human parent letting his children get sick or injured unnecessarily, then giving them Christmas presents each year in accordance with how much each suffered[28]

and what he calls 'the Divine Provident Fund idea', Hick's position, where

> ...disproportionate individual suffering leads ultimately to everyone sharing in an infinite pool of heavenly rewards'.[29]

Personally I find this debate somewhat unsatisfactory. It is as though both sides are committed to a strong individualism. Although I do believe in life after death I would prefer to believe that, rather than settling old scores, it enables us to put our quarrels behind us. It is a good thing that we do not know what it is like; when religious leaders claim to know what will happen after death we usually end up with oppressive doctrines like the Christian Hell described in Chapter 5.

To my mind a more helpful approach would be an analogy with family life. Some children are better behaved than others. Some are more helpful than others. As they grow to maturity some become self-reliant while others continue to depend on their parents for help or money. Good parents do not keep accounts. They provide whatever each child needs, accepting the diversity as part of life's richness. Part of our growth in spiritual maturity will be letting go of our individualism, with its demands for equal treatment and its complaints when others receive more than we do.

Limits to understanding

In this chapter I have offered some reasons why the evil we experience is consistent with a good god. When people are suffering intensely, rational explanations are not what they need; more important are sympathetic friends who will be with them and share the pain. The reasoning performs a different function: to defend belief in God against those who think the world's sufferings refute it.

However, reasoning can never be sufficient on its own because of the nature of the topic. It is telling that the question of theodicy has seemed most troubling at two points in history. The first was in the second and third centuries, when early Christians debated whether the world had been created by the god of Jewish monotheism or by the evil gods of some Gnostic theories. At this point monotheism was being deliberately challenged in the name of very different theologies. The second is the modern era, as European intellectuals from the eighteenth century onwards convinced themselves that humanity should be able to establish a complete understanding of reality and pass judgement on God's actions. Charles Taylor, for example, describes how the sense of being detached observers with an overall picture of how the universe works led people to think they should be able to question God's goodness and find the answers.[30]

An essential part of the case for theodicy is therefore to recognise the necessary limits of human understanding. What we can believe about God should be consistent with reason—not self-contradictory—but humble enough to acknowledge that God is beyond human understanding. Defenders of an omnipotent god, for example, do not argue that God could have made any imaginable world. Even the most determined monotheist does not claim that God can make a triangle with four sides; the apparent inability is only because we define 'triangle' as a shape with only three sides. The same applies to questions like 'Can God make a stone so heavy that God cannot lift it?' Far from being a limitation of God's power, it just expresses the power of human imagination. To argue that a good god could have created a better world in the first place is similar. Sontag's confidence, cited above, that a world with less evil would be compatible with human freedom, presupposes that we know how to create worlds and plant them with free and moral humans. For all the excitement about robotics in some quarters, we are nowhere near being able to do any such thing. It is pure fantasy, generated by the control culture at its most arrogant. There are far too many limits to our knowledge.

Moreover self-interest gives us all incentives to distort moral judgements. G R Evans writes that Augustine's pronouncements on evil

> …must be read in the light of one central principle: that the effect of evil upon the world is to make it impossible for the sinner to think clearly, and especially to understand higher, spiritual truths and ideas.[31]

On this point Augustine was surely right. Elderly people forget what it is like to be a teenager and denounce the young for doing what they themselves once did. Powerful governments 'defend their country's interests' by undermining the interests of other countries. Multinational companies 'develop' 'undeveloped' regions of the world by chopping down forests and growing cash crops, thereby ruining ecosystems. Characteristically, our self-centredness tempts us to mistake our own interests for the greater good.

The socially immature often divide people into two simple categories, the good ones and the bad ones. Of course they count themselves among the good ones. There is no shortage of cheap novels and television programmes encouraging this view. Dualist theology encourages it too. Those with greater maturity recognise that we are all shades of grey, not black or white; but even then we can probably think of evil actions performed by others which, we think, we would never stoop so low as to commit. Yet studies have shown that the worst atrocities get committed by pretty normal people. The pilots who dropped the nuclear bombs on Japan and the German officers who took Jews to the gas chambers were, by and large, ordinary people trusting their superiors and obeying orders. Hannah Arendt's *Eichmann in Jerusalem*[32] is a classic illustration. Eichmann had no personal malice towards Jews. He even had Jews in his family. What makes him frightening, Arendt says, is his banality.

> He merely, to put the matter colloquially, never realized what he was doing... It was sheer thoughtlessness—something by no means identical with stupidity—that predisposed him to become one of the greatest criminals of the period... With the best will in the world one cannot extract any diabolical or demonic profundity from Eichmann.[33]

In other words, the trouble with Eichmann

> ...was precisely that so many were like him, and that the many were neither perverted nor sadistic, that they were, and still are, terribly and terrifyingly normal... this normality was much more terrifying than all the atrocities put together.[34]

When we imagine that we would never have done such things we may well be fooling ourselves. We use moral judgements for two purposes: to guide us in our own lives, and to condemn others. We tend to judge ourselves by our motives but others by their actions. As a result we see more evil in others and less in ourselves; yet it is our own behaviour that we can most easily alter.

Our mental pictures of the world's evils depend on our sympathies. We know what it is like for ourselves to experience what we have already experienced. We can comparatively easily imagine that other humans respond in much the same way.[35] It is harder to know what it must be like for other people to have experiences we ourselves have never had, and harder again to know what the experiences of animals must be like.

This ignorance about the inner experiences of others leaves plenty of scope for misjudged sympathies. We have not evolved to cope with the huge amounts of bad news from the mass media, so we become selective. Some crises or tragedies engage us; others we ignore. In times of war we are horrified by the destruction caused by our enemies but more forgiving of the side we support.

Thus our sympathies, and the extent of our awareness, limit our conceptions of the world's evils. However much analysis we do, some people think the world is a pretty good place and are grateful to be alive; others find it tragic; others again commit suicide in despair. None of us has a God's-eye-view of all the good and bad aspects of life on Earth.

Summary of theodicy

Reflecting on the literature it seems to me that we can draw out a rough generalisation. Comparing Sontag with Hick, or the Holocaust with a peaceful and happy community, I suspect that, the more moral evil there is, the harder it is to believe in a good god. Since believing in a good god continues to be the most convincing ground for believing in the possibility of social progress, a feedback loop opens up. The two world wars and the Holocaust led many to abandon hope in progress or God or both. There followed a mood of international determination to ensure that the same tragedies did not get repeated, but it had also become clear how cruel and destructive ordinary people could become. Large-scale intense cruelty had produced evidence against progress, thereby in the longer term encouraging the view that humanity is incapable of anything better.

Conversely, when communities experience life as pleasant and fulfilling they are more likely to believe the world has been made by benign forces. This in turn will encourage a response of gratitude and an expectation that others, in poorer conditions, should also be enabled to share life's goodness. Evil suppresses the hope of a better world, good promotes it. The feedback loop can work either way.

If there is some truth in this, it partly explains why monotheism is unpopular today. In a society that believes that we, or rather our ruling classes, know how the world works and are successfully improving the conditions of human life, every human-induced disaster becomes a motive for more interventions, more artificiality, more humanity-against-nature. The more we blame the environment for our own failures, the harder it becomes to believe the environment was designed for our well-being. When, instead, we accept and celebrate our community and its environment, it becomes easier to believe it is given to us as a blessing.

In Chapter 13 I argued that the problem of evil is not unique to monotheism. It also applies to polytheism where the problem, far from being solved, is transferred to the heavens; and to monism and atheism, which simply urge us to re-imagine it as not really evil at all. In another sense, though, monotheism *is* unique. Both atheism and the polytheism of divine conflict tell us to accept misfortune, tragedy, pain and suffering as inevitable features of life. In their accounts good and bad health, love and hatred, helping and manipulating, are equally normal. In monotheism they are not equal. We have been designed capable of either, but are also invited to let go of the worse and aspire to the better. Monotheism explains the existence of evil as a feature of reality caused not by gods but by humans. The bad news is that we, collectively, are responsible for it. The good news is that we can do something to overcome it. There are good reasons for hope.

Chapter 15. What is God playing at?

In this book I have argued that beliefs about gods set the context for ethical norms. Different kinds of gods sanction different kinds of morality. The emphasis has been on distinguishing three models: divine conflict produces one kind, divine harmony another, divine absence another again.

In Chapters 4 and 12 we saw how monotheism differed in its ethical implications from polytheism and secularism respectively. In this chapter I develop further the ethical implications of monotheism: if monotheism is true, how should we live?

The outlines have already been established. We have been created by a good and omnipotent god who gets things right and does not make mistakes. We have been created as a blessing, so that we may flourish and enjoy life. We have been put in a world also designed to be a blessing, both to us and to other forms of life. What are we to do with it?

Among recent analyses I find Linda Zagzebski's account helpful. God did not need to create us. There was no self-interest involved. It is love that motivates God to create us. The relationship is similar to the way parents treat their children.

> A good parent loves her child and wants him to develop into a full person. She also knows that her child's personhood has to be cultivated by giving him the space to grow, and that that means gradually giving the child autonomy. The motivation for treating the child in this way need not be that doing so makes the child morally better, nor that autonomy is good, nor that the loving relationship she wants to have with her child is good. Still less need she do it because the overall amount of good in the world will increase if she does so. She does this simply because to love her child is to love a person, and that necessarily requires accepting the necessary

> condition for personhood, her child's autonomy. The parent might want this for her child even if the child did not use his autonomy to do good or to be better off, and even if much less good were produced in the world overall. Her treatment of her child is fully explained by the fact that she loves her child, and that is the way loving parents' act.[1]

Thus God creates us and loves us as persons in our own right. 'To be a person is to have value in addition to whatever value a person has because of her nature.'[2] This, in Zagzebski's view, is why God permits evil. It means that

> ...even a perfect being might love in such a way that he would be willing to permit any amount of evil, not for the sake of some good, but out of love for persons... God does not weigh the evil He is permitting against something else... Allowing persons to develop their personhood is justified, not because the existence of persons or free persons is good... but simply because loving persons is something good persons do and because loving persons in such a radical way that any evil is permitted for the sake of their personhood is something a perfectly good being would do.[3]

Acting in this way, God is the supreme source of value and exemplar of moral goodness.[4] Our response at its best is to follow God's example.

> In imitation of God, we try to love as he loves, not for the sake of something else, not even for the sake of the love itself, but just because the love of God has the power to attract us, to make us want to imitate God. To learn to love like God is to learn to love just because we want to, and that means learning to become the kind of persons who love just because they want to.[5]

If Zagzebski's account is akin to anything so far described in this book, it is the *blessing* of the first chapter of Genesis. We have not been created for any external purpose—neither to burn sacrifices nor to help the economy grow nor to produce new technologies. We have been created for our own fulfilment: to celebrate and love. We can enjoy life *now*.

Nevertheless, even this account of humanity has an objective built into it. There are better and worse ways of living. If, as Zagzebski claims, 'the love of God has the power to attract us, to make us want to imitate God', then our celebrating, our acceptance of the blessing, gives us a direction of travel. There is the possibility of *progress* in the way we respond to God's goodness.

I therefore propose to combine Zagzebski's analysis with the older theological tradition of 'deification'. This is very different from the deification that the control project, described in Chapter 7, claimed for humanity. There, the absence of God led to humanity arrogating to itself the omnipotence and omniscience of God, and therefore seeking to acquire them. In the theological tradition humanity's deification is a matter of accepting our limitations but becoming more like God through moral and spiritual development. An example is Irenaeus' description of humanity, as noted in Chapter 13, 'making progress day by day, and ascending towards the perfect, that is approximating to the uncreated One'. Although suppressed in the West this concept of humanity's vocation remained popular in eastern Orthodoxy[6] and has been revived from time to time in western Christianity.[7]

On this account we are now somewhere along a long historical process, neither at the beginning nor at the end. How God makes it possible is to be explained scientifically. From the initial creative act—presumably the Big Bang—came gases and an expanding universe. Gases formed stars and planets, and life developed on our planet. Most of this history does not need describing here. One important stage, however, does, and this is the story of our development of self-awareness and free choices.

It is the point at which we cease to be links in a fixed causal chain and instead become able to do things which were not predetermined, either by God or by unbreakable laws of nature. I shall offer two accounts of it. The first draws on evolutionary theory to describe how our freedom developed, the second on a biblical text expressing its ethical significance.

The evolution of freedom

Evolutionary theory has been interpreted in many different ways, some of which conflict with the position I am defending here. Before turning to its positive contribution, therefore, we need to be clear what evolution is not.

Evolution is not a force. The word means gradual change over time. It does not cause anything; it only describes. The causes of the changes are a myriad different things.

Evolution is not determinist. It does not explain all our features. It is true that some of our characteristics exist because, if our ancestors had not had them, the population would have died out; what is not true is that all our characteristics or actions have to be the way they are.

Unfortunately Darwin was over-influenced by Malthus' population theories and exaggerated the role of competition. We are not constantly competing against each other to have more children. Contrary to his expectation the rich usually have fewer children than the poor. What evolutionary theory shows is more limited; that the sexual libido and the desire to produce and nurture children have to be strong *enough* in every generation to maintain the population. The point can be easily understood by comparing the present human population with our ancestors of, say, a hundred thousand years ago. Like us they had diverse characteristics. Through natural selection we are descended from some of those people. Others had no children, and others again had children whose descendants died out some time between then and now. Thus evolution by natural selection presupposes that, at any given time in the past, some individuals produced lines of fertile offspring which still survive, and others did not. Some were gay or celibate, but every species alive today exists because its ancestors produced *enough* offspring. If this is true of our ancestors a hundred thousand years ago, it is equally true of us today. There is no evidence that natural selection is reducing the proportion of gays and celibates, either in humans or in any other species. The theory of evolution does not, therefore, show that all our characteristics have evolutionary causes; all it shows is the rather obvious fact that our ancestors did enough to ensure the survival of the species.

Evolution is not a model for ethics. It has often been treated as such. This is an adaptation of an older idea that roots ethics in the order of nature. The medieval philosopher Thomas Aquinas thought we could rationally derive moral precepts from the laws of biological nature. For example, children ought to be nurtured by their parents and humans ought to live peacefully together. This presupposed that the ways of nature were designed by God to be consistent with our well-being.[8] Four centuries later Spinoza disagreed, arguing that the laws of biological nature are completely indifferent to ethics; in nature the big fish eat the little fish, and it is just as natural for people to use force and fraud to attain their ends.[9] The publication of Darwin's *Origin of Species* in 1859 revived the question but within a very different culture, largely committed to the idea of inevitable progress. Herbert Spencer interpreted evolution as 'the survival of the fittest' and took it as an ethical model for human societies. Believing that the 'fittest' pass on their superior traits to their children, he saw it as a moral duty to encourage them to flourish and reproduce at the expense of the 'unfit'.[10] Capitalist economic theory has been heavily influenced by the idea.[11]

Most evolutionary scientists today argue that the story of humanity's evolution does not in itself give us any ethical models at all. It merely describes the long process by which we have become the kinds of animals we are. If we are to imbue this process with any kind of moral significance, positive or negative, we shall have to derive it from elsewhere.[12]

Evolution is not progressive. The idea of evolution as progress played an important part in its popularity during the nineteenth century. As a law of nature it seemed to be guaranteeing long-term improvement. Today, however, evolutionary scientists deny that any such improvement can be inferred from evolution. Although it describes gradual change over long periods of time, the change is not in any particular direction. Natural selection produces changes in response to environmental changes, so there are no overall trends. The one exception is increasing complexity. To claim that evolution constitutes progress, therefore, is a value judgement that the evolutionary story itself does not justify.

This may seem rather odd; of course we want to believe that humanity's arrival in the world was progress! However the scientific account of evolution, like all the sciences, is based on observed data. Moral values like progress are not observed in the same way. If we want to believe in progress we must look to another source. Monotheism is one. It can accept the scientific account of evolution and set it within a wider story of an intended, purposeful and progressive creation. The evolutionary sciences describe how we have turned out the way we are; divine intention describes the purpose behind it. Unlike the scientific account on its own, therefore, monotheism can extrapolate to future progress.

Granted these limitations to the meaning of evolution, it is still possible to see in it the story of how the human brain developed the ability to make free, undetermined, choices between alternative courses of action. First we inherited instincts, some of which are for self-defence and some for co-operation. Later we developed awareness of choice between 'selfish' and 'altruistic' actions. In the abstract, if we had no self-interest, perhaps we would always choose altruistic actions. We could then acquire perfection at no personal cost. What makes the moral task significant is that we do have selfish motives. Characteristically, moral tensions arise when self-interest conflicts with the common good.

Evolutionary biologists distinguish between 'selfish', 'co-operative' and 'altruistic' behaviour. The words are borrowed from descriptions of present day human behaviour and stripped of their moral implications when applied to other animals. Species which still survive do so because past generations produced fertile offspring. This is 'natural selection'. Within this process, 'selfish' behaviour is where individuals protect their own lives or maximise their chances of fertile offspring. Most natural selection is of this type. 'Co-operation' is where an individual provides help to another individual, expecting help in return. This 'tit for tat' pattern has been studied in other animals, especially chimpanzees. It becomes possible when individuals can distinguish other individuals and remember who has done what in the past. They can then co-operate with past co-operators while discriminating against free-riders who have accepted help but have not returned it.[13]

Animal 'altruism' extends co-operation to a wider group. An example is the dominant male in troops of Chacma baboons. He places himself in an exposed location as a lookout while the other troop members forage. This provides a benefit to other troop members but puts him at risk: predators will see him first and he is not getting anything to eat. Some troop members will be his relatives, but not all, and he is not receiving any benefit in return. Sociobiologists who believe all behaviour can be explained in terms of selfishness argue that, because selfishness includes the fertility of one's offspring, the benefits to the baboon's offspring exceed the danger to the baboon himself.[14]

All this selfish, co-operative and altruistic behaviour can be performed instinctively, without thinking about it. An additional element is when an individual attributes mental processes, like beliefs and intentions, to other individuals. Those who can do this then become able to respond not just to actions, but to the intentions they attribute to the actions. Studies have shown that chimpanzees can do this. If one chimpanzee hurts another, there is a benefit to the victim if he or she can judge whether the action was deliberate.[15]

The next stage is to attribute mental processes to oneself. This may have happened to our ancestors way back in the mists of prehistory, though there is some evidence that it is more recent. Julian Jaynes argues that in Homer's Iliad, probably written in the 8th century BCE, the characters never plan what to do. There is no introspection. They blame each other for misdeeds but consider their own deeds to have been determined by the gods. When King Agamemnon robs Achilles of his mistress, it is a god that grasps Achilles' hair and warns him not to strike Agamemnon. Later on Agamemnon explains himself: the action was not his decision. It was the god Zeus, and the Fates, who made him do it: 'So what could I do? Gods always have their way'. It seems bizarre to us today, but Achilles fully accepts the explanation.[16] Jaynes' theory is disputed; perhaps the development took place much earlier. In any case it remains the case that most of us find it easier to pass judgement on other people's actions than on our own.

Once individuals can reflect on their own mental intentions they become able to choose between actions. This is a major development. Patricia Williams notes three essential criteria. The first is a sense of self: they must be capable of asking themselves 'Why am I doing this?' The second is the ability to generate problems, solve them and thereby decide what to do. The third is the ability to follow through these deliberations in action.[17] According to Ernst Mayr,

> ...the shift from an instinctive altruism based on inclusive fitness to an ethics based on decision making was perhaps the

most important step in humanization.[18]

The historical sequence, as revealed in these studies, is generally accepted. What is debated is how much has changed. As we saw in Chapter 10, some reductionists argue that human morality is nothing but these processes: altruism and freedom, far from having the meanings we normally attribute to them, are simply continuations of evolved patterns of behaviour, albeit supported by erroneous beliefs about freedom and morality.

Others believe that new processes have developed out of the old ones: that proto-altruism develops into real altruism and awareness of choices into real freedom. Scientists describe the change as 'emergence': just as organic matter emerged out of inorganic matter, defenders of free will argue that it emerged out of instinctive behaviours. Whereas reductionist theory argues that complex entities and processes can be understood by breaking them down into their constituent parts, emergence theory argues that new processes 'emerge' at more complex levels. Philosophers usually describe the 'hierarchy' of sciences with physics at the bottom and the 'higher' sciences each depending on the entities and processes at 'lower' levels; for example biology depends on physics and chemistry. If complete reductionism is in principle possible, this means the laws of all the sciences can be reduced to the laws of physics. If not, free will can be explained as a property of the human mind that can emerge when the necessary conditions are in place.

If this is the case a major change has taken place at this point. Before it the agent has no awareness of free choice. Similarly, before the victim has developed a similar awareness he or she does not blame the agent and instead 'suffers' in a limited sense, perhaps akin to some other animals. Once the change has happened people become aware that they can reflect on the likely outcomes of their future actions and choose between them accordingly. Their actions can then become moral or immoral, and it becomes meaningful to praise and blame. Praising and blaming make it possible to develop much richer relationships. Suffering becomes far richer and more nuanced than mere pain. It also becomes possible to speculate not only about the effects of our actions on other people, but also about whether the conditions of human life could become better than they are.

Instinct comes first. The rational ability to reflect on choices and the freedom to choose one action rather than another only arise long after our various instinctive desires have been established—desires for self-defence, for competitive advantage, for co-operation, for altruism. Rational reflection and freedom of action are built upon these instincts and are given their meaning by them. Thomas Hardy's poem 'Before Life and After' describes the significance:

A time there was—as one may guess
And as, indeed, earth's testimonies tell –
Before the birth of consciousness,
When all went well.

None suffered sickness, love or loss,
None knew regret, starved hope, or heart-burnings;
None cared whatever crash or cross
Brought wrack to things.

If something ceased, no tongue bewailed,
If something winced and waned, no heart was wrung;
If brightness dimmed, and dark prevailed,
No sense was stung.

But the disease of feeling germed
And primal rightness took the tinct of wrong;
Ere nescience shall be reaffirmed
How long, how long?[19]

By drawing attention to the changes the poem challenges us to face the moral significance of our ability to remember, foresee, regret and hope. If we were to give these up we would not suffer the way we do. Some versions of monism and fatalism still encourage people to 'go with the flow', accept whatever happens and abandon any attempt to change their circumstances. My personal experience of living with socio-economically very different communities leads me to suspect that fatalism is attractive at the extremes. It comforts individuals in extreme pain and communities in conditions of extreme powerlessness by telling them their circumstances are inevitable or 'meant to be'. It also occasionally helps people with immense wealth and power by exonerating them from moral responsibility. Nevertheless, the overwhelming majority of us would rather accept the added suffering for the sake of a richer and more meaningful life. It is only in extreme conditions that we think it is not worthwhile.

Developmental psychologists study the process. Abraham Maslow's 'hierarchy of needs' is a helpful analysis. Our most basic needs are physiological. The other levels are, in ascending order, safety and security; love and relationships; esteem; and self-actualisation.[20] The lower levels need to be met first. When they are met we naturally turn our attention to the higher ones. One of the criticisms of Maslow's original theory was the individualistic nature of his concept of self-actualisation. Accepting the criticism, in his later work he suggested that the self only finds actualisation in giving itself to a higher goal outside itself, through altruism or spirituality.[21]

So we have developed with both selfish and altruistic instincts. Both were well established in us before we developed the self-consciousness and free will that made it possible to choose between them. When we are threatened selfishness usually takes priority, and by being selfish we threaten others in turn. When we are successful and unthreatened it becomes easier to be altruistic, and altruistic acts help others to be altruistic too.

The ethical task is to develop the altruistic at the expense of the selfish, to benefit the common good and sometimes freely sacrifice our own interests for the purpose.

Freedom in Genesis

I now propose to read the second and third chapters of the biblical book of Genesis as a different description of the same development. I have already referred to the first chapter of Genesis as one of the classic texts of monotheism. It emphasises that a god of supreme power and goodness designed the world to be a blessing, declared it good and invited humanity to 'be fruitful and multiply'. Reading it as an account of how the world was created, two questions naturally arise from it. First, if God is so omnipotent, this implies that God determines everything. We have no freedom. Secondly, if everything God has created is good, why is there any evil or suffering?

Since monotheism raises these questions today, it will have raised them even more acutely at a time when most people attributed evil to different gods with different personalities. We should not therefore be surprised if the text immediately proceeds to tackle them. The following interpretation draws on other scholarship[22] but is my own.

I follow the consensus of scholars in denying that Genesis 3 contains a story of a primeval Fall, or that the serpent was the devil in disguise. The 'myths' of Genesis 2-11, rather than being histories, are descriptions of what life is normally like, put into the form of stories a bit like a novel or a children's story book. Understood like this they have been analysed by many scholars and a wide array of meanings has been found in them. Here I focus only on the way it accounts for free will and evil. Genesis 2 notes four gifts to humanity which, between them, enable us to do evil. The first is freedom:

> The Lord God commanded the man, 'You may freely eat of

> every tree in the garden...' (Genesis 2:16).

I am using the NRSV translation. The word 'freely' translates a Hebrew idiom, literally 'eating you may eat'. Perhaps what is granted is not freedom as such but permission to use it. In any case, free will is indicated; the story would be meaningless on a determinist account of humanity.

Here we find a response to one of the central dilemmas of theology: divine control. If the creator of the universe is not in complete control things can go wrong, contrary to God's intentions, for no good reason. If this is the case life is essentially tragic: misfortune is inevitable and there is nothing we can do about it. If, on the other hand, God is in complete control, we are left with no freedom of our own. We are puppets on a string. Genesis resolves the dilemma by asserting first that God is in complete control (the claim of Genesis 1) and then that God withdraws from control sufficiently to give us freedom.

The second gift is law:

> ...but of the tree of the knowledge of good and evil you shall not eat (Genesis 2:17).

The freedom God gives us enables us to do good things, but also evil things. Moral law distinguishes between the two. God wants the best for us and advises accordingly.

Unfortunately a great deal of Christian rhetoric has distorted the constructive role of moral law. Some have contrasted a law-bound Judaism with a Christianity based on freedom, faith or grace. In practice Christians, like everyone else, find rules are needed for good practice. Some go to the other extreme and treat obedience to God as 'walking in the narrow way', constantly suppressing our freedom in order to please God. In Genesis, though, it is not that the garden is full of forbidden trees and just one from which Adam may eat; rather, all the trees except one are permitted. The world is full of possibilities, but our options exceed the ones that enable us to live at our best.

The third gift is creativity:

> Out of the ground the Lord God formed every animal of the field and every bird of the air, and brought them to the man to see what he would call them; and whatever the man called every living creature, that was its name (Genesis 2:19).

Like any parent of a young child, God takes a lump of mud, makes it into the shape of an animal and asks 'What shall we call this one?' When Adam offers a suggestion, that is its name. Good parents withhold their own ideas and encourage their children's creativity. Similarly God does more than just enable us to choose between one thing and another. We are given power to think of something new. Some of our new ideas are good, some are not.

The fourth gift is desire:

> The rib that the Lord God had taken from the man he made into a woman and brought her to the man. Then the man said, 'This at last is bone of my bones and flesh of my flesh; this one shall be called Woman, for out of Man this one was taken' (Genesis 2:22f).

The Hebrew text uses words of intense excitement. The strength of delight in the opposite sex, the bonds of passion, the joy of sexual activity and the shameless enjoyment of the other person's naked body are all parts of the good creation.

Freedom, law and creativity make it possible for us to disobey the moral laws. It is our desires which give us a motivation. Typically evil arises when our desires conflict with the common good.

The text then moves to the temptation and the commission of the first sinful act. The characters egg each other on, eat the forbidden fruit, feel guilty and blame each other. Thereafter one sin leads to another until society is dissolved, first in the Flood and later at the Tower of Babel. It is worth noting that at the point when this spiral of deterioration begins—when Eve commits herself to eating the forbidden fruit and the first sin is committed—the narrative slows down. The hearer is invited to pay close attention and sympathise:

> So when the woman saw
> that the tree was good for food,
> and that it was a delight to the eyes,
> and that the tree was to be desired to make one wise,
> she took of its fruit and ate (Genesis 3:6).

We are all torn between two responses to wrongdoing. Our own misdeeds, and those of our friends, we understand and excuse. When it comes to other people's misdeeds we notice the dreadful results which follow and build up feelings of indignation. It takes maturity to recognize that an act can be both very understandable and very harmful. This is what the text does.

In these texts God withdraws. By creating the universe God ceases to be everything; there is other reality. In the Platonist and Aristotelian traditions this creates a problem: to say that it is in God's character to create seems to undermine divine self-sufficiency.[23] Divine harmony puts more emphasis on God's love: relationship is more important than self-sufficiency.

By giving us free will God also withdraws from complete power.[24] The freedom we have is not the freedom we would have in a polytheist system, where different gods permit and prevent different activities for different reasons. Nor is it the same as the freedom we would have in an atheist system, where both our freedoms and our limitations are completely unplanned. Instead our freedom has parameters designed by God for our benefit. There are limits to what we can do. We can choose between good and evil to the extent that God sees fit.

In a sense perhaps God also withdraws from complete knowledge. In Christian theology those who argue for predestination have often pointed out that a God who can foresee the future must have created us knowing exactly what we would do and can therefore be said to have predetermined our every action. An alternative is that God, in giving us freedom, chooses to withdraw not only from being everything and causing everything, but also from knowing everything.

The ethical agenda

Progress, therefore, is ethical. In Chapter 12 I referred to Jesus' 'summary of the law', the commands to love God and one's neighbour. In the context of social ethics loving God means something like this. Whether we admit it or not we generally adopt an attitude of *trust* towards the processes maintaining the universe and our environment. Just as we normally trust the forces of nature by assuming that they will carry on providing for us even though we only know a tiny proportion of what they are doing, we also trust our general intuitions that murder and rape are to be avoided and children are to be fed and cared for. In practice we invest a huge amount of trust in these values. We are pleased about them. Only very rarely, in exceptional circumstances, would we wish them to be otherwise.

The appeal to love our neighbours is linked to it. Other people are loved by God before we attempt to echo God's love. God's love for us, and them, is the supreme model for the best way we can relate to other people. Taking our lead from God's love empowers us to direct our actions towards their well-being. The emphasis is not on lists of rules but on adopting a stance which reflects God's love for them. Of course a sentimental feeling towards others does little on its own; the point is that if our desires are directed towards their well-being, our consciences will lead us to do caring things.

So for monotheists the Golden Rule applies: we should treat others as we would wish to be treated ourselves. Using our own experience of what life is like, our pleasure and happiness, our pain and unhappiness, helps us appreciate the kinds of things that enable a fulfilled life, and how in turn a fulfilled life can enable us to engage in other constructive activities. These other activities characteristically include helping other people to achieve fulfilment in turn. They may even include willing endurance of suffering for the sake of others.

Spiritual traditions offer practices of prayer, meditation, self-examination and confession to help us make these kinds of progress. We know at first-hand what we want, and we can generally extrapolate to other people's wants. By reflecting on them we can ask ourselves whether we are wanting the things that are most constructive, or whether we need to redirect our desires. Used well, they can help us reflect on where we are in the great scheme of things and where we might go next.

The final objective of progress is beyond our vision. We may believe there is one to look forward to, but we cannot see what it will be like. Our hopes are envisioned partially, in stages on the way: the rule of law, the abolition of slavery, health care for all, an end to wars. Different people and nations have different hopes for progress.

These stages on the way are provisional. The further we try to look into the future, the hazier our vision becomes. Those who research cures for illnesses do not anticipate that when all current research programmes are successful there will be no more need for research. Those who support charities to feed the hungry may look forward to the day when all the hungry are fed, but do not anticipate that all charitable giving will then cease. What we care about now is not for the sake of a future when our descendants will have nothing to care about; instead, like parents who try to give their children a better education than they themselves had, we expect that our efforts, if successful, will enable our descendants to care about things we have not yet thought of.

So at any one stage we can foresee some improvements and work towards them, but we do this on the understanding that they are stages on the way to something beyond what we know about.[25]

To be meaningful, progress must be universal. It is comparatively easy to observe progress for an individual or even a nation state. These, however, are not necessarily contributors to overall progress. We all understand our own interests better than the interests of foreigners, so individual and national visions of progress are always in danger of benefiting some at the expense of others. One person's wage increase may be at the expense of another. Improved environmental conditions in one country may be caused by exporting toxic chemicals to another. Our hopes for the future therefore need to be checked against the highest hopes for humanity as a whole—and indeed for life as a whole. The Enlightenment commitment to universal progress was such an aim, a search for something better than a zero sum game. Such universal progress, to be credible at all, must appeal to a vision that transcends all individual and national interests. Tolstoy's self-doubts, described in Chapter 11, were to the point: if his achievements were contributions only to his own wealth and fame they would be meaningless once he was dead, but if they were positive contributions to a wider society they could outlive him.

So just as a meaningful commitment to progress needs an act of trust in a future we cannot envisage, it also needs an act of trust in a universal well-being that we cannot envisage. Progress must mean progress for humanity as a whole—or better, perhaps, for life on earth as a whole.

We therefore have to accept a lot on trust. This is inevitable on any non-positivist account of reality, but especially if reality stems from a divine sphere that by its nature transcends human knowledge. Religious traditions often describe this as mystery. Thus the theologian Reinhold Niebuhr argued that the physical facts of our experience reveal that there is more to life than physical facts:

> The dramas of man's history can be explained by discerning various patterns in history, but they are too multifarious to fit into any of these patterns. They can be fitted into a framework of meaning only if the meaning has a penumbra of mystery. The mystery consists of a power and a love beyond our comprehension which overrules these various historical dramas.[26]

Atheists often reject the appeal to mystery as special pleading. There is good reason for this, since many religious believers appeal to mystery when trying to defend nonsense. However atheists just as much as believers make acts of trust in what they do not know. For example, it is a common procedure in scientific research. When scientists find something they cannot explain, the standard response is to propose an explanatory theory and test it by looking for data which might support or refute it. Whenever the most successful theory implies the existence of something never yet observed, far from refusing to believe in it they give it a name, ask questions about what it must be like and look for more explanatory theories. This is not so different from the history of religious speculation. In effect it was happening in a haphazard way over the course of millennia, as one theology after another speculated about what kinds of divine forces must exist to explain the world as they experienced it. At the edges of what we know there is always mystery.

In this way our knowledge is always limited. Atheism has a habit of tending towards one of two extremes. It does not imply positivism—positivism is a later justification—but it does imply that, apart from the more limited knowledge of other animals with smaller brains, what humanity does not know is not known. In this sense humanity's knowledge is supreme. At the other extreme the reductionist evolutionary theories of the mind described in Chapter 10 are a bit like a modern equivalent of ancient Gnosticism: they tell us that the forces producing our minds have designed them for very limited purposes, including self-deception.[27]

Most religious traditions avoid the extremes by offering an account of who made us and for what purposes. Monotheism gives us reason to expect that our minds can understand enough to live constructively in harmony with each other, if we want to, but not enough to know everything or to be in complete control of our affairs. We depend on our natural environment and other people in many ways, some of which we know about; but we also depend on them in countless ways we do not know about. Our ignorance is no problem at all, as long as we are confident that we can trust the forces maintaining the universe. Our security lies not in our own achievements, but in the generosity of the powers that make our lives possible.

Chapter 16. Conclusion

Why do progressives need God?

Because progress means change for the better: better for everyone, not some at the expense of others; better for always, not now at the expense of future generations. Mixed in with the battles, the elections, the winning and losing, the enslaving and liberating, the legislating and repealing, there is a process of genuinely seeking different ways of living that will bring about a better future.

As long as our ideas about a better future are nothing more than personal preferences we are not being progressive, just self-centred. To be a progressive is to believe in truths about a better society that are more than just personal preferences. Whether or not we think it through, when we adopt progressive values we presuppose higher standards, standards that transcend the interests of individuals, nations and generations. In other words, we believe in moral truths which are true whatever any one individual thinks, whatever the policies of the ruling establishment, whatever the ideas of the age.

It is not enough to believe these standards just happen to exist. To co-operate in working towards them we also need to believe they are achievable. We need good reason to believe that the possibility is built into the way the world functions.

So progressives make two acts of trust: that a better society is theoretically possible, and that by working together we can achieve it. We maintain these acts of trust despite the evidence to the contrary. We cannot know everything. Most of what goes on around us is unknown to humanity, let alone to us personally. At each stage in our history, in every field of research, we have unanswered questions. Sometimes our ignorance prevents action. When it does we look for new explanations. Just as Newtonian physics seemed to explain most of the known universe until Einstein provided a wider setting and explained some of its errors, so also modern society understands its values well enough for many purposes but not for all. In order to resolve the practical crises facing western society today we need a wider ethical framework, a sort of Einsteinian revolution in our understanding of morality which will release us from our current impasse and show us how to make real progress.

We cannot know, so we trust: that a better state of affairs, better for everyone, is achievable and would work. It must fit the way the world works better than our present systems. The simplest, most common way of describing this act of trust is to say that the transcendent standards *know* how we can live better.

Modern society usually prefers not to examine its values this far. To do so is to break the taboo on religion. Alarm bells ring. While this is understandable in view of Europe's history, to appeal to values while refusing to think about what we mean by them is like eating bacon while denying the existence of pigs.

This book has described how we got this blind spot. Our hunter-gatherer ancestors experienced life as a combination of gift and threats. Their agenda, at its broadest, was to minimise the threats by maintaining positive relationships with the forces maintaining the universe. They therefore conceived of them as personal, as gods. As time went on different societies understood the gods in different ways. Rulers often believed that their nation would suffer if the correct forms of worship were not maintained. Even if they did not believe it, they found it a useful idea since control of the people's beliefs was a powerful tool of government.

Medieval Europe inherited this tradition. Dissident worship was seen as a threat to the stability of nations. However there also developed negative attitudes to life and terrifying theories about everlasting punishments in Hell. Those who believed in them quite logically judged that they should not let their eternal destiny be determined by the commands of rulers. For some, being burnt at the stake would be worth the price. For others the cruel Christian god became incredible. A succession of wars was eventually brought to an end by a radical innovation, a secular system of government. Beliefs about God and the afterlife were henceforth to be a private matter for individuals. This-worldly public matters were to be the business of governments unconstrained by religious doctrines.

Thus the ruling classes and intellectuals distanced themselves from Christianity, pleased to dispense with its divisive doctrines while taking for granted its moral values. The result, unforeseen at first but now celebrated, is to refuse to recognise any transcendent authorities telling us what we ought to do. Instead we tell ourselves that we create our own values. We think this has proved successful because of our advances in science, even though scientific advances are compatible with religious belief.[1] The real reason for expelling God from public discourse was the cultural trauma of pessimistic Christianity.

Once it abandoned the role of Christianity in its public life, secularism could no longer justify its values. The unity of humanity, the sanctity of life, progress, compassion, rights, freedom and equality were all inherited from monotheism, mainly through Christianity. Secularism inherited them, abandoned their theological justifications, and thereby weakened them. They still survive, but filtered through the mesh of secularism. At best they mean less than they once did; for some they mean nothing at all. They survive because secularism, by refusing to recognise transcendent moral authorities, cannot replace them. When government policies seem moral or progressive it is because we are still applying to them value judgements inherited from our Christian past.

The older conception was often abused. Rulers could present their vested interests as the will of God, thus discrediting God in the eyes of their opponents. However, refusing to acknowledge any moral authority higher than humanity, far from preventing this abuse, accentuates it. As long as we believe there are right answers it remains possible to work together to find them and work for them. When we believe there are no right answers there is nothing to find; all that remains is to promote our own interests. This means that the most powerful no longer need to appeal to God; they only need to appeal to their own decrees. When we have power we easily convince ourselves that we know what is best for everybody. We imagine that our own intentions are so benign that there is no need for a moral authority above us. It is the oppressed and exploited who can most easily see the faults of the ruling classes. When they complain that the actions of their governments are wrong they are presupposing higher standards, moral truths that transcend human authorities and pass judgement on them.

With or without God, the appearance of progress is often a disguise for power struggles. The difference is that, as long as we share a belief in God's transcendent standards, we have reason to believe progress is possible: that there is a truth about how we can live better, and that it is achievable. Without God, there are no transcendent truths—only the preferences of individuals, and we know only too well that they conflict with each other.

So secularism tells us that we create our own values, while actually giving us a mixture of watered-down Christian values and the preferences of the ruling classes. It works well enough to maintain the hierarchical structure, but the fault lines are obvious enough. When the behaviour of the ruling classes is publicly seen to favour the rich and powerful at the expense of the poor and powerless, or democratic governments like Britain sell military weapons to very different governments like Saudi Arabia, or nothing significant is done to reduce global warming, the cry goes up that their values are wrong. The cry would be a lot louder and more credible if the people voicing it could explain what they mean by calling them wrong, but we lost the language to do so when we privatised religion.

The growing numbers of people who describe themselves as

'spiritual but not religious' witness to the intellectual vacuum. Characteristically, such people are still determined to avoid the dogmas of each particular religious tradition but find it impossible to believe there are no moral truths transcending the values we make up for ourselves. Some things, they feel sure, are just plain wrong even when governments decide to do them. Somewhere in that vacuum they expect there is moral truth; but to examine what it means is to run the risk of ending up with religion. Until we acknowledge the existence of higher standards openly enough to talk about them, examine what we mean by them and apply them to our own society, we shall continue on our destructive paths.

We might summarise the differences between polytheist, monotheist and secular attitudes to life something like this. For Christmas, Aunt Janet gave each of three children a DVD with a computer game. One of the children installed it, started playing, found she could not win, and in her exasperation wrote a review complaining that there was a bug in the program. The second installed it, started playing, found she could not win, and decided that it was a really good game which would occupy her for months. The third broke it into bits, looked at under a microscope, dissolved a fragment in some acids and listed the components.

We can respond in any of these ways to the life we have. We can conceive of it as full of value and meaning, either negative or positive. A vale of tears, or a blessing from someone who loves us. Alternatively we can tell ourselves there is nothing to it except what modern science can measure; and modern science, based as it is on observation data, does not discover values.

I have argued for the second of these. It is the only one that can sustain hope in progress. With a positive attitude to the forces creating us we are helped to perceive true values by recognising that we are designed to be blessed—and so is the rest of creation. In this way the monotheism of divine harmony helps us to affirm the meaning, value and purpose of our own lives, and at the same time to overcome our instinctive self-centredness for the sake of the common good. The things we need are given by God to the community so that the community may flourish. It flourishes when its individuals have positive relationships with each other, their environment and God. Just over 1800 years ago the Christian bishop Irenaeus described the purpose of our lives:

> If, then, thou art God's workmanship, await the hand of thy Maker which creates everything in due time; in due time as far as thou art concerned, whose creation is being carried out. Offer to Him thy heart in a soft and tractable state, and preserve the form in which the Creator has fashioned thee, having moisture in thyself, lest, by becoming hardened, thou lose the impressions of His finger. But by preserving the framework thou shalt ascend to that which is perfect, for the moist clay which is in thee is hidden there by the workmanship of God. He will cover thee over within and without with pure gold and silver.[2]

Notes

Chapter 1

1 http://climate.nasa.gov/scientific-consensus/, accessed 19 April 2016. In 2014 Naomi Klein wrote: 'Preliminary data shows that in 2013, global carbon dioxide emissions were 61 percent higher than they were in 1990, when negotiations toward a climate treaty began in earnest'. Since then there have been no significant initiatives to reverse the trend. Klein, *Everything*, p. 11.

2 It is true that more energy sources have been found than were anticipated in the 1960s and 1970s. An influential publication *The Limits to Growth* (Donella Meadows et al, 1972) was based on a computer simulation of the use of resources at an expanding rate. It attracted both positive and negative responses from the start, and regular updates have been published since then. Recently James Dyke has argued that it underestimated the ability of technology to make new resources available, but this has been at the cost of ever-increasing pollution. http://www.theguardian.com/environment/blog/2016/apr/19/why-limits-to-growths-forecasts-are-still-relevant-today, accessed 19 April 2016.

3 See, for example, the Trussell Trust's figures: https://www.trusselltrust.org/2016/04/15/foodbank-use-remains-record-high/, accessed 20 April 2016.

4 Wilkinson, *Spirit Level*.

5 The term is associated with USA President Woodrow Wilson, but originated with H G Wells.

6 Feiveson, *Unmaking the Bomb*, p. 4.

7 http://johnpilger.com/articles/a-world-war-has-begun-break-the-silence-, accessed 18 April 2016.

8 *The Better Angels of Our Nature*, London: Penguin, 2012.

9 Klein, *Everything*, p. 21.

10 G K Chesterton, *The Illustrated London News*, August 29, 1931, quoted in http://docslide.us/documents/chesterton-aphorisms.html, accessed 9 August 2016.

11 Clatworthy, *Faith*.

12 Vidal, *Monotheism*, pp. 410-11. This essay was the Harvard University Lowell Lecture in 1992.

13 *The Redemption of God: A Theology of Mutual Relation* (Washington, DC: University Press of America, 1982), p. 156. See also Ruether, *Sexism*, p. 1.

14 Welch, *Risk*, p. 112.

15 Gnuse, *No Other Gods*, p. 148.

16 Gnuse, *No Other Gods*, p. 149.

Chapter 2

1 Eliade, *Patterns*.

2 Gnuse, *No Other Gods*, p. 215.

3 Burkert, *Creation*, p. 150.

4 Burkert, *Creation*, pp. 129-137.

5 Burkert, *Creation*, pp. 34-39.

6 Burkert, *Creation*, pp. 150-152.

7 Bottéro, *Mesopotamia*, p. 130.

8 Eliade, *Patterns*, p. 38.

9 Eliade, *Patterns*, pp. 38-39.

10 Eliade, *Patterns*, pp. 40-52.

11 Burkert, *Greek Religion*, p. 119.

12 Uffenheimer, 'Myth', pp. 141-142; Lambert, 'History', p. 171.

13 Bottéro, *Mesopotamia*, pp. 63-4, 186-196.

14 Hick, *Interpretation*, p. 30; Schwartz, 'Transcendence', pp. 1-4; Weil, 'Breakthrough', p. 33.

15 Raeburn, *Agamemnon*, pp. xxxiii-xxv.

16 Bottéro, *Mesopotamia*, pp. 44-48.

17 E Hornung has argued that apart from this, Egyptian religion was thoroughly polytheistic, while J Assman has argued that the crisis over Akhenaten's regime produced

more complex beliefs, adding to the traditional gods a higher ultimate deity who was not directly revealed. Baines, 'Egyptian Deities', pp. 53—57.

18 Baines, 'Egyptian Deities', pp. 56-57.

19 Baines, 'Egyptian Deities', pp. 32-3.

20 Porter, *One God*, p. 245.

21 Versnel, 'Thrice', p. 88. Versnel suggests that Xenophanes 'was unable to escape from his cultural universe... While *experimenting* with one he was *living* with a second' (p. 101).

22 J-P Vernant has argued that the Greek pantheon constitutes a hierarchical divine society, with each god having specific attributes although the relationships are complex. Versnel, 'Thrice', pp. 82-83. Walter Burkert on the other hand considers the world of Greek gods 'potentially chaotic'. Burkert, *Greek Religion*, p. 119.

23 Versnel, 'Thrice', pp. 104-105.

24 Versnel, 'Thrice', pp. 115-119.

25 On Mesopotamian texts see Porter, *One God*, p. 228 and Bottéro, *Mesopotamia*, pp. 42 & 91. On Greek texts, Versnel, 'Thrice', pp. 112-130.

26 Albrektson, *History*, pp. 42-52; Janzen, 'Moral Nature', p. 461.

27 Burkert, *Creation*, p. 31, 93-95.

28 Van De Mieroop, *History*, p. 243.

29 Bottéro, *Mesopotamia*, pp. 91-92.

30 Porter, *Anxiety*, pp. 214-5, 235-237; Parpola, 'Monotheism', pp. 165-80.

31 Janzen, 'Moral Nature', p. 461; Assmann, *Gods*, p. 30.

32 Burkert, *Creation*, p. 31, 93-95.

33 Gnuse, *No Other Gods*, p. 22.

34 Burkert, *Greek Religion*, p. 57.

35 Frevel, 'Beyond', p. 2.

Chapter 3

1 I have not taken account of scholars who take the Bible to have been composed by God, either through direct dictation or some kind of unique inspiration. To include their views would introduce a much wider range of possibilities, and anyway I find their theories unconvincing. I have described my reasons in Clatworthy, *Liberal Faith*. On this matter I have depended heavily on the writings of John Barton.

2 Gnuse, *No Other Gods*, pp. 63-69; Brueggemann, *Theology*, pp. 159-164.

3 Gnuse, *No Other Gods*, pp. 12-15.

4 Archaeologists have found a great deal of continuity between the Canaanite culture of the lowlands and the Israelite culture of the highlands, especially in pottery, farming techniques, tools and the construction of buildings. In the case of pottery even the collar-rimmed jar, once considered specifically Israelite, now appears to have Canaanite prototypes. Even the early stages of farming in the highlands show well developed techniques, implying that those who first farmed there had already been farmers elsewhere. Examples are terrace building to hold run-off water and the construction of lime-coated cisterns. However there is some evidence of non-Canaanite influence, such as the elliptical village, a defensive technique characteristic of nomads. Some may have come from Egypt with the memory of an exodus and the god Yahweh, while some may have come from Syria with the practice of circumcision, rejection of pork and stories of the patriarchs (Gnuse, *No Other Gods*, pp. 32-53).

5 For example Israelite villages usually had no defensive walls. Gnuse, *No Other Gods*, pp. 32-3 & 44.

6 Gnuse, *No Other Gods*, pp. 34-36 and 199.

7 Gnuse, *No Other Gods*, pp. 34-51.

8 Gnuse, *No Other Gods*, pp. 74-75 & 196; Albertz, *History 1*, p.

60.

9 Albertz, *History 2*, p. 415. The Isaiah texts are 5:19, 25ff; 6:11; 8:10, 17-18; 10; 14:24-27; 29:15; 30:1. See also Saggs, *Encounter*, pp. 49-52.

10 Barton, *Understanding*, pp. 136-140. Barton adds: 'Of course, what we have in Isaiah is a theological form of natural law, as were most natural-law theories before the Enlightenment.'

11 Albertz, *History 1*, p. 148.

12 Smith, *Palestinian Parties*.

13 The evidence is limited; it is not until the reign of Jehoshaphat (860 BCE) that it became common for parents to give their children Yahweh-based names. Conflict arose earlier, at the time of Elijah, when Jezebel killed prophets of Yahweh (850-840 BCE). Since she gave her own children Yahweh-based names, she cannot have been totally opposed to his worship. The most likely explanation is that her victims opposed the worship of gods other than Yahweh (Gnuse, *No Other Gods*, pp. 75-76).

14 Gnuse, *No Other Gods*, pp. 74-75, 87; Albertz, *History 1*, p. 60.

15 Deuteronomy 14-17 and 23-24. Albertz, *History 1*, pp. 199-201, 216, 225.

16 Gnuse, *No Other Gods*, p. 105.

17 Crossan, *Jesus*, 222, 266, 270ff, 341.

18 Gnuse, *No Other Gods*, passim; Albertz, *History 2*, pp. 414-426; Nikiprowetzky, 'Ethical Monotheism'; Lind, 'Monotheism'; Janzen, 'Moral Nature'. 'Second Isaiah' or 'Deutero-Isaiah' are names given to the author(s) by modern scholars since authorship is unknown.

19 Isaiah 40:22-23.

20 Isaiah 41:21-24; 43:11; 44:8-17.

21 Gnuse, *No Other Gods*, pp. 74 & 131-132.

22 Gnuse, *No Other Gods*, p. 22.

23 Albertz, *History 2*, p. 425. So also Gerd Theissen: 'The Jewish

monotheism which came into being in the situation of a defeated people ravaged by war, embraced the unique vision of an overcoming of war.' This is because 'When everyone recognizes the one and only God, there can be no more wars; this is a logical notion, if wars are wars between different gods.' Realistically, he adds that 'this logic does not govern the behavior of Jews, Christians, and Moslems'. Theissen, *Biblical Faith*, p. 71

24 Lynch, 'Mapping', pp. 48-55. Frevel lists Deuteronomy 4:39, 4:35, 10:17; Isaiah 43:10, 44:8, 45:18; 46:9; and Psalm 96:4-5 ('Beyond', p. 5). On subordinate divinities, Lynch notes that Nehemiah 9:6 asserts Yahweh's sole divinity while simultaneously marvelling that all heavenly divinities worship him.

25 Smith, *Origins*, pp. 9-10, 153 & 193.

26 Römer, 'Yhwh', pp. 2-3; Albertz, *History 2*, p. 419.

27 Olyan, 'Isaiah'.

28 Assmann, *Gods*, p. 138.

29 Isaiah 49:6-7.

30 E.g. Stark, *One True God*, pp. 52 & 111.

31 Isaiah 44:5.

32 Isaiah 43:14-17.

33 Isaiah 2:4.

34 Isaiah 40:9-11; 41:21; 43:15; 44:6; 52:7-12.

35 Smith, *Palestinian Parties*, pp. 98-99.

36 How could a high-ranking official in the imperial capital have held such egalitarian views? We do not know, but my guess is to do with his expatriate status. We want the place where we live to be improved and provide the best services; we want the place where we lived as children to stay the same so that we can visit it and feel moved by the memories—especially if we think of it as a holy place with a distinctive lifestyle. Over time the memory can idealise it, and a return visit may disappoint. Whatever Nehemiah's own lifestyle, Jerusalem should obey Deuteronomy.

37 Smith, *Palestinian Parties*, pp. 102-103.

38 Smith, *Palestinian Parties*, pp. 110.

39 Albertz, *History 2*, p. 375.

40 A Jew was still a Judean; English translations use both words to translate the same Greek word. Judea was the name of the Roman province, so a Judean, or Jew, was someone from that province. Just as today we may refer to someone as French because they used to live in France or their parents were French, the ancients would refer to people being Jews because of their national connections. The point is described in greater detail in Chapter 6.

41 Lynch, 'Mapping', pp. 49-50.

42 Garr, *Image*, analyses the question at length. Smith, *Priestly*, argues that 'with the singular verb following, clearly this context implicitly asserts that what other texts commonly view as plurality is, as far as Genesis is concened, a divine singularity' (p. 48).

43 Smith, *Priestly*, pp. 60 & 69.

44 Smith, *Priestly*, p. 104.

45 Psalm 104:26. God defeated Rahab in Psalm 89:9-11 and Leviathan in Psalm 74:12-17. The only possible exception is 1 Chronicles 21:1, for which see Day's comments below. Janzen, 'Moral nature', pp. 464-465.

46 1 Samuel 29, 2 Samuel 19, 1 Kings 5 and 11 and Psalm 109; Day, *Adversary*, pp. 25-32.

47 *Adversary*, pp. 69-104.

48 Day, *Adversary*, pp. 107-124.

49 Day, *Adversary*, pp. 127-145. In this instance it could be *a* satan, or *the* satan, or the proper name Satan. Day thinks it could be any adversary, human or divine, possibly a military commander, but other scholars disagree. The story is also told in 2 Samuel 24, an earlier text, where however it is Yahweh who incites David to hold the census.

50 Day, *Adversary*, p. 128. The texts are *Jubilees* 23:29 and

Assumption of Moses 10:1.

51 Day, *Adversary*, p. 63. This is the traditional account of Zoroastrianism, but the evidence is slight and some scholars disagree.

52 An evil spirit attacked King Saul in 1 Samuel 16: 14-23, 18:10, 19:9. In 1 Kings 22:19-23 the prophet Micaiah describes a vision of Yahweh giving permission to an evil spirit to misinform prophets so that they would advise the king to go into battle.

53 Tobit 6:1-8:3. A Jewish woman of Ecbatana, south of the Caspian Sea, was plagued by a demon called Asmodeus. She married seven men, but each time Asmodeus killed her bridegroom before they slept together. On the eighth occasion the angel Raphael advised Tobias to burn the heart and liver of a fish. The smell was so foul that Asmodeus fled all the way to Egypt . It had become possible for at least some literate Jews to believe this.

54 Lynch, 'Mapping', pp. 66-67.

55 Hurtado, *One God*, pp. 42-67 & 83; McGrath, *Only*, pp. 14, 30 & 59-60.

56 Brevard Childs, for example, argued that monotheism is 'theologically inert'. Barr, *Concept*, p. 138.

57 Barton, *Understanding*, pp. 168-169.

Chapter 4

1 Anthony Herbert, *Theology in Green*, No. 4, October 1992, p. 39, quoting C N Cochrane's *Christianity and Classical Culture*, OUP, 1944, p. 166.

2 There is a good discussion of the contrast between these approaches to history in Hick, *Interpretation*, pp. 61-64.

3 Lambert, *Destiny*, p. 65.

4 Helm, *Understanding*, pp. 27-28 quotes a few texts from Augustine, citing *On Christian Doctrine*, trans. D W Robertson Jr, Indianapolis, Bobbs-Merrill, 1958, p.45.

5 Hyman, *Atheism*, pp. 20-22.

6 Barton, *Understanding*, p. 1.

7 Janzen, 'Moral nature', p. 464. See also Lynch, 'Mapping', p. 61.

8 Genesis 1:22 & 28.

9 Psalms 33, 104 and 146. Brueggemann, *Theology*, pp. 154-158.

10 Clayton, *Predicament*, p. 40.

11 Barton, *Understanding*, p. 8.

12 Goodman, 'Monotheism and ethics', p. 21.

13 *Moses* 2.48, translated by F. H. Colson in *Philo* (Loeb Classical Library; Cambridge: Harvard University Press, 1935) 6:471-73, quoted in Brown, *Ethos*, pp. 12-13.

14 Gnuse, *No Other Gods*, p. 153.

15 Bury, *Progress*, p. 7; Nisbet, *Progress*, pp. 59-60.

16 Bury, *Progress*, pp. 21-22 & 73.

17 Nisbet, *Progress*, p. 141.

18 Bury, *Progress*, p. 21.

19 Bury, *Progress*, p. 22.

20 Nisbet, *Progress*, pp. 60-61. The quotation is from Augustine's *City of God*, Book 12, Chapter 22.

21 Nisbet, *Progress*, pp. 59-60.

22 Nisbet, *Progress*, p. 44.

23 Gray, *Straw Dogs*, p. 47.

24 Hume, *Natural History of Religion*, 9,20.

25 Stark, *One True God* and Glory.

26 Stark, *Glory*, p. 32, italics in original.

27 Stark, *One True God*, p. 116, italics in original.

28 Stark, *One True God*, pp. 22-26, 34, 171 & 176.

29 Stark, *One True God*, p. 35. See also p. 233.

30 Gray, 'Humanism', p. 41.

31 Assmann, *Price*, p. 18.

32 Assmann, *Price*, p. 13.

Chapter 5

1 Acts 17:16-34. See also Mark. 10:6 = Matthew. 19:4; Mark. 13:19 = Matthew. 24:21; Matthew. 25:34; Luke 11:50; Jn. 17:24; Acts 10:9-16, 28; 11:5-10; 14:15-17; Romans. 1:20, 4:17; 2 Corinthians 4:6; Eph. 1:4; Hebrews. 4:3; 9:26; 11:3; 1 Timothy 4:1-4; 1 Peter. 1:20; 2 Peter. 3:4; Revelation. 4:11; 10:6; 13:8; 17:8.

2 Matthew. 6:26 = Luke. 12:24; Matthew. 10:29; Luke. 14:6; Matthew. 6:28f.

3 Luke. 13:15; 15:4; Matthew. 12:11 = Luke. 14:5.

4 E.g. Matthew. 13:1-43.

5 Irenaeus, *Against the Heresies,* 2.2.4.

6 Irenaeus, *Against the Heresies,* 2.5.4.

7 Thus J N D Kelly, noting the lack of discussion about redemption in the sub-apostolic age, writes: 'It must be admitted that, as compared with the New Testament, the Apostolic Fathers as a whole are not greatly preoccupied with sin, and that their writings exhibit a marked weakening of the atonement idea... What looms much larger in their imagination is the picture of Christ as the lawgiver, the bestower of knowledge, immortality and fellowship with God (Kelly, *Doctrines,* p. 165). Scholars now recognise that the idea took much longer to develop.

8 Crossan, *Birth,* pp. 282-287.

9 E.g. 1 Tim 1:4, 7; 4:7; 6:20; Titus 1:14f; 3:9; Jude 4,7. Dunn, *Unity,* pp. 275-283.

10 Fisher, 'Mark'. Of the other exorcisms, most first appear in Mark. Rousseau, *World,* p. 88, lists: Matthew 4:11, 23, 25; 7:28-29; 8:14-16, 28-34; 10:1-8; 12:15-16, 22-50; 15:21-28; 17:14-20; Mark 1:12-13, 21-34; 3:7-15, 20-35; 5:1-20; 6:7, 13; 7:24-30; 9:14-19, 38; 16:9, 17; Luke 4:1-13, 31-41; 6:17-19; 8:2, 26-39; 9:1-6, 37-43, 49; 10:17-20; 11:14-21; 13:32; John 7:19-20; 8:39-52; 10:21; 12:31; 14:30; Acts 13:6, 8; 16:16-18; 19:13-16, 19. Meanwhile the Sadducees considered most exorcistic beliefs

heretical. Rousseau, *World*, p. 90; Kee, *Medicine*, pp. 128-9; Twelftree, *Exorcist*, pp. 170-171.

11 Ephesians 6:11-13, 1 John 3:8-10 and Revelation 12. Kelly (*Satan*, p. 159) summarises the role of Satan in Revelation as still the official accuser of humans, but an accuser who will go too far. He still has some time to operate on earth but will be imprisoned in the Abyss for a thousand years. There will then be a short release, before he is punished for ever in the Lake of Fire, with wicked humans, Death, Hades, the Beast from the Sea and the Beast from the Earth.

12 Meeks, *Origins*, p. 115.

13 The text that affirms this most clearly is Psalm 37.

14 He incorporated them into his Christianity by saying they have been created by God and implied that they work for God (1 Corinthians 10:26; 2 Corinthians 4:6, 7:7; Galatians 4:3; Romans 1:20, 4:17, 8:38-39; Colossians 1:16, 2:8, 20-21). Sometimes he claimed that they had been overcome (Galatians 1:3-4; 4:3-4; Colossians 1:13, 2:15); or that they would be overcome in the future (1 Corinthians 15:24f; Romans 16:20; 1 Corinthians 6:3; Philippians 2:10); or that Christians should have grown out of subservience to them (Galatians 4:8f; Colossians 2:20).

15 When he speaks of them he says the idols worshipped by pagans are lifeless (I Cor 10:14-21, 12:2). Kelly, *Satan*, p. 56.

16 One text, Matthew 12:27-28, implies that Jesus did *not* have a greater power over them than other exorcists had. Sanders, *Jesus*, p. 135.

17 J P Meier, *A Marginal Jew. Rethinking the Historical Jesus* Vol. II, Anchor, Doubleday, 1994, p. 661, quoted in Geert van Oyen, 'Demons and exorcisms in the Gospel of Mark', Vos, *Demons*, p. 101. One of the Dead Sea Scrolls, 11 QPs Apa, contains three incantations against Belial which contain only prayers, imposition of hands and a simple declaration in the name of God, without any devices or magical terms.

Rousseau, *World*, p. 91.

18 The Nicene Creed is so called after the Council of Nicaea in 325 CE. It was revised in 381. Since then it has remained unchanged except that the western church has added that the Holy Spirit proceeds from the Son as well as the Father.

19 Fowden, *Empire*, p. 3. Eusebius, the fourth-century biographer of Constantine, described him as the earthly counterpart of the divine Word, just as monarchy was the earthly counterpart of monotheism. Momigliano, 'Monotheism', argues that this was an innovation. Esler disagrees: 'The emperors of Rome had always acted as guarantors of the happy relationships between the Romans and their gods', even it it meant persecuting Christians. *World I*, p. 273.

20 Young, 'Insight', pp. 113-126. The quotation is from p. 124.

21 The Second Book of Maccabees describes these events. It contains a story of a mother and her seven sons all being tortured because they refused to eat pork. We are told the last dying statement of each one. They all looked forward to being rewarded in the next life. For example, the third son 'quickly put out his tongue and courageously stretched forth his hand, and said nobly, "I got these from Heaven, and because of his laws I disdain them, and from him I hope to get them back again"'. 2 Maccabees 7:10-11.

22 1 Peter 2:19-21. See also Hebrews 2:10: 'It was fitting that God, for whom and through whom all things exist, in bringing many children to glory, should make the pioneer of their salvation perfect through sufferings'.

23 For Irenaeus, Christ 'became what we are in order to enable us to become what he is'. *Against the Heresies* 5, preface. Cf. 2 Clement 1.2f. Kelly, *Doctrines*, pp. 163-188, 377-379.

24 'Every man is also made juster, that is to say, becomes more loving to the Lord after the passion of Christ than he was before, because a benefit actually received kindles the soul

into love more than one merely hoped for. Our redemption, therefore, is that supreme love of Christ shown to us by His passion, which not only frees us from slavery to sin, but acquires for us the true liberty of the sons of God, so that we fulfil all things not so much from fear as from love of Him who exhibited so great favour towards us, that favour than which, as He Himself attests, none greater can be found: "Greater love," He says, "hath no man than this, that he lay down his life for his friends"'. *In Epist. ad Rom;, Opera,* ed. Cousin, ii. p. 207, quoted in Rashdall, *Atonement,* pp. 358-9.

25 Rashdall, *Atonement,* p. 443.

26 Wright, *Jesus,* p. 273.

27 Young, 'Insight', p. 113.

28 Romans 6:17,18; 7:14; 1 Corinthians 6:20; 7:23.

29 In the New Testament the word for 'ransom' is used only here and in the equivalent text in Matthew 20:28. Elsewhere it was used for freeing a slave, buying back prisoners of war, giving compensation for damages, buying back ancestral land and propitiating angry gods. The text can mean that Jesus was offering himself to God as compensation or propitiation on behalf of others, or it could mean God's act performed with Jesus' cooperation. Collins, *Mark,* pp. 68-70.

30 According to Gregory of Nyssa Adam's sin put humanity into the power of the devil. To rescue us God offered Jesus to the devil as a ransom. It was a trick. The devil knew Jesus was born of a virgin and renowned as a miracle-worker, so he agreed. He did not realise that Jesus, behind his human appearance, was also divine. Jesus could escape. The devil was 'caught like a fish by the bait'. Others, including his contemporary Gregory of Nazianzus, argued that this would have been an unjust act by God, and anyway disliked the idea that the devil had any rights at all. Gregory of Nyssa replied that the devil was only getting his deserts, and in any case he would benefit in the long run because at the final

restoration of all things even he would be saved. Kelly, *Doctrines*, pp. 380-386.

31 Romans 5:12-14 and 8:18-23. It is possible that a Christian reference to a Fall in *1 Enoch* is a little earlier, but the dating is uncertain. *1 Enoch* is not in the Bible but was treated as scriptural by the early Christians.

32 Satan's fall was described in many different ways. It was a moral lapse, a loss of status or a physical departure from heaven to the lower air, the earth or the underworld. It took place either before the creation of humanity, or at the time of Adam and Eve or with the Watcher angels in Genesis 6. Satan's first sin was either pride or envy or lust. His punishment took place, or would take place, at one of these times or at the advent of Christ, or his passion or second coming, or a thousand years after the second coming. Theologians were equally unsure whether he had a physical body, how he related to other demons and whether he could ever be saved. Russell, *Satan*, p. 31.

33 Augustine believed demons were fallen angels, living eternally, endowed with supernatural powers of perception, enemies of the happiness of humans. They operated psychologically, not physically. They could interfere with the physical basis of the mind to create illusions (Brown, *Augustine*, p. 311). Augustine's logic is that angels who are saved must surely know they are saved—after all, saved humans know as much. On the other hand the angels who were destined to fall must have either not known whether they would fall, or known that they would fall, or been in error. None of these possibilities is compatible with perfect bliss. Therefore there must have been a distinction between the two types of angels right from the time of their initial creation. God must have *predestined* the Fall (*City of God* 11.11, 12.9).

34 *City of God* 11.20.

35 Hick, *Evil*, p. 70.

36 Wright, *Meaning*, pp. 105-6.

37 In the final paragraph of his *Christus Victor* Aulén wrote: 'I am persuaded that no form of Christian teaching has any future before it except such as can keep steadily in view the reality of the evil in the world, and go to meet the evil with a battle-song of triumph.' Aulén, *Christus Victor*, p. 176.

38 Romans 4:25. See also Romans 5:8-9 and Hebrews 9:6-15.

39 Anselm's position is summarised in Stott, *Cross*, pp. 118-9.

40 George, *Reformers*, pp. 219-223.

41 https://www.uccf.org.uk/about/doctrinal-basis.htm, accessed 18 July 2016.

42 Brunner's language emphasises the offence caused to God: 'Sin against God is an attack on God's honour. Sin is rebellion against the Lord. But God cannot permit His honour to be attacked; for His honour is His Godhead, His sovereign majesty. God would cease to be God if He could permit His honour to be attacked. The law of His Divine Being, on which all the law and order in the world is based, the fundamental order of the world, the logical and reliable character of all that happens, the validity of all standards, of all intellectual, legal, and moral order, the Law itself, in its most profound meaning, demands the divine reaction, the divine concern about sin, the divine resistance to this rebellion and this breach of order. The holiness of God requires the annihilation of the will which resists God. God is not mocked. If this were not true, then there would be no seriousness in the world at all; there would be no meaning in anything, no order, no stability, the world order would fall into ruins; chaos and desolation would be supreme. All order in the world depends upon the inviolability of His honour, upon the certitude that those who rebel against Him will be punished.' Brunner, *Mediator*, pp. 444-5, cf. p. 462. Similarly Stott writes that what sent Christ to the cross 'was

neither the greed of Judas, nor the envy of the priests, nor the vacillating cowardice of Pilate, but our own greed, envy, cowardice and other sins, and Christ's resolve in love and mercy to bear their judgment and so put them away. It is impossible for us to face Christ's cross with integrity and not to feel ashamed of ourselves.' Stott, *Cross*, p. 83, cf. p. 89.

43 Brunner argued that whereas the laws of nature are the laws of divine creation, 'external laws', the law of penalty expresses 'Divine Holiness itself'. Forgiveness 'would be the declaration of the non-validity of the unconditioned order of righteousness which requires penalty'. Brunner, *Mediator*, p. 447. Stott agrees: 'The crucial question we should ask, therefore, is... not why God finds it *difficult* to forgive, but how he finds it *possible* to do so at all.' Stott, *Cross*, p. 88. To Packer 'The heart of the justice which expresses God's nature is *retribution*, the rendering to men what they have deserved; for this is the essence of the judge's task. To reward good with good, and evil with evil, is natural to God... Retribution is the inescapable moral law of creation; God will see that each man sooner or later receives what he deserves – if not here, then hereafter. This is one of the basic facts of life. And, being made in God's image, we all know in our hearts that this is *right*.' Packer, *Knowing God*, p. 158. So also Brunner, *Mediator*, p. 464.

44 Stott, *Cross*, p. 89.

45 *Church Times*, 27 April 2007 p.12. See also Stott, *Cross*, p. 123.

46 Brunner accepted the tension and insisted on a 'two-fold nature of holiness and love'.Brunner, *Mediator*, pp. 467 & 519. Stott, characteristically, agrees: *Cross*, p. 130.

47 The need for retribution is not as obvious to others as it is to substitutionists. In modern legal systems retribution is one type of justification for punishment, but it usually needs to be balanced against others such as deterrence and reform. Furthermore, since retribution itself is intended to redress

the moral balance, it presupposes an end point when the balance is restored. Eternal punishment offers no such end point. Equally problematic is the idea of imposing the punishment on somebody other than the offender. In the ancient world this was considered more acceptable; today it is considered a crime in itself.

48 Mark 2:16.

49 They are accessible via www.earlychristianwritings.com.

50 Ernst Fehr and Urs Fischbacher, 'The nature of human altruism', *Nature*, Vol. 425, 23 Oct 2003, pp. 785-791. www.nature.com/nature.

51 Augustine, *City of God* 21,11-12.

52 *City of God* 21, 12.

53 Taylor, *Secular*, p. 138.

54 Ariès, *Hour*, pp. 190-91.

55 Muchembled describes the period from 1550 to 1650: 'The image of a terrible God, concerned by every act a human being committed, was echoed by that of a demon of extraordinary power relentlessly stalking his prey, from the cradle to the grave. This personalization and internalizing of sin was the foundation stone of the modernization of the West. A period of extreme unease, in a world perceived as calamitous and under the eye of a stern God, set in around the middle of the sixteenth century. Both Catholics and Protestants believed they could see the internal abyss opening up before their eyes and the devil seizing every opportunity to invade their being. This sense of personal guilt impelled people to engage in a desperate search for proof that the creator had not abandoned humankind. Christian heroism, foreign missions, the evangelization of other peoples and the destruction of the internal enemy represented by witches were all part of this same universe.' Muchembled, *Devil*, pp. 109-110.

56 Delumeau, *Sin and Fear*, p. 107.

57 Bonner, *Hell*, p. 132.

58 Delumeau, *Sin and Fear*, p. 14.

59 Delumeau, *Sin and Fear*, pp. 2-23. The acts of mortification will no doubt have helped suppress the libido.

60 Brown, *Body*, p. 84.

61 Augustine, *City of God*, 14,16.

62 Augustine, *Op. imperf. c. Jul.* 2,42; *de nupt. et concup.* 2,36; *de pecc. mer. et remiss.* 2,11., quoted in Kelly, Early Christian Doctrines p. 363.

63 *Against Jovinianus*, 1.16, cf. 1.49. The Latin is *nuptiae terram replent, uirginitas autem paradisum.* O'Loughlin, Thomas, *Celtic Theology: Humanity, World and God in Early Irish Writings*, A & C Black, 2000, p. 114.

64 Delumeau, *Sin and Fear*, pp. 14-17.

65 Bullough, *Sexual Variance*, pp. 357-82; Richards, *Sex*, Chapter 2.

66 C. Plummer, quoted in Bullough, *Sexual Variance*, p. 357.

67 Chadwick, *Bossuet*, p. 34.

68 Knaacke, J C F et al, *The Righteousness of God: Luther Studies*, 1883, 1.226.14ff & 26ff, quoted in Reardon, *Reformation*, pp. 80-81.

69 *Institutes*, 1.6.2. Reardon, *Reformation*, pp. 183-186.

70 Reardon, *Reformation*, pp. 76, 93, 130-131, 170. See also Voak, *Hooker*, p. 155.

71 Richardson, *New Dictionary*, art. 'dogma'. I have described these developments at greater length in Clatworthy, *Liberal Faith*.

72 Hunsinger, *Barth*, pp. 32-39

73 Barth, *Church Dogmatics*, Edinburgh: T & T Clark, 1956, Vol I, Part 2, p. 774, quoted in Markham, *Engagement*, p. 8.

74 *The Church and Liberal Catholicism: A Joint Pastoral Letter by the Cardinal Archbishop and the Bishops of the Province of Westminster*. Jodock, *Modernity*, pp. 264-5.

75 The Rationalist Association, for example, was founded at this

time, naming itself in contradistinction to Christian dogma. https://newhumanist.org.uk/history, accessed 19 July 2016.

Chapter 6

1 Veyne, *Private Life*, p. 59.
2 Locke, *A Letter Concerning Toleration* 7, 9-10. Nongbri, *Before Religion*, pp. 101-102.
3 John Locke, *A Letter Concerning Toleration*, 6.
4 Locke, *A Letter Concerning Toleration*, 12-13. Nongbri, *Before Religion*, p. 102.
5 E.g. Clark, SRL, 'Atheism considered as a Christian sect', *Philosophy*, April 2015, pp. 277-303.
6 Bremmer, 'Atheism', p. 12.
7 Buckley, *Origins*, p. 9.
8 Wootton, 'Histories', especially pp. 25-26.
9 Wootton, 'Histories', p. 33. Wootton describes the period from 1680 to 1715 as 'a take-off point for irreligious speculation' (p. 49).
10 Kors, 'D'Holbach', p. 276.
11 Beiser, *Sovereignty*, pp. 143-6.
12 Smith, *Meaning*, p. 43.
13 Nongbri, *Before Religion*, p. 86.
14 Nongbri, *Before Religion*, p. 2.
15 Nongbri, *Before Religion*, p. 6.
16 Nongbri, *Before Religion*, pp. 77-84.
17 There remains scholarly debate about whether certain earlier religious leaders would have seen themselves as creating a new tradition rather than reforming or modifying what they had inherited. The most likely examples are Mani and Mohammed. Nongbri discusses whether certain words, mainly 'Judaism' and 'Islam', denoted a movement whose members thought of it as 'a religion' in the modern sense before the modern era. The Greek word for 'Judaism' first appears in 2 Maccabees, a history of the Jewish war of liber-

ation in the second century BCE. Similarly, the Gospel of John often refers critically to 'the Jews'. By comparison with equivalent words for Greekness and Persianness, Nongbri argues that 'Judaism' has a more general connotation (pp. 49-50). Perhaps a modern British equivalent would be the word 'French'. A French person might be someone who lives in France, or comes from France. There are British stereotypes about French food and French lifestyles. Among the stereotypes is being a Catholic. For the writer of John's Gospel, in the first century CE, a Jew would have had a similar range of meanings: someone who lives in, or comes from, or holds beliefs characteristic of, the Roman province of Judea.

Islam has a different story. In the Qur'an the word means submission, surrender or obedience. This allows for alternative translations. One text (Sura 3:52) describes a short conversation between Jesus and his disciples. What the Christians say, after affirming their belief in God, is in some translations 'We are Muslims', but in others 'We submit to him' (i.e. to God, p. 59). Although it seems odd to us, familiar as we are with the idea of Islam as one religion and Christianity as another, it appears that in the early days anyone who submitted to God would count as a submitter and therefore a Muslim; indeed there is evidence that some Jews and Christians were part of Mohammed's movement and were considered Muslims in his day (p. 62). Smith, *Meaning*, p. 114 argues that it is impossible to translate 'I am not a Muslim' into Arabic. *Lastu bi-muslimin* would mean 'I do not submit to God'.

Christianity was similar. Eusebius of Caesarea, writing in the 4th century CE, described Christians as an *ethnos*, a nation, like Jews and Greeks (pp. 54-55).

18 I discuss these developments in greater detail in my *Liberal Faith*. There was much anxiety that modern knowledge might disprove the existence of God. They therefore liked the

idea that religious belief was separate from modern secular knowledge and therefore beyond disproof.

19 In 1760 De Brosses proposed that 'savages' were like children, living in an uninterrupted state of childhood and never passing the level of the four-year-old (Baal, *Symbols,* p. 11; in the early 20th century Jung's account of the human psyche included the idea that 'primitives' are in a lower phase of evolution with less developed consciousness. Baal, *Symbols,* pp. 154-156. Later Evans-Pritchard described the result as 'a flavour of smugness which one may find either irritating or risible' (Evans-Pritchard, *Primitive Religion,* p. 15). When a generation of researchers were willing to travel all over the world to study radically different societies in order to explain religion, while hardly ever checking their findings against the beliefs and practices of churches in their own home towns—a discretion which might have saved them from many an error—it is tempting to look for a motive. Perhaps it is the natural human reluctance to believe that one's next door neighbour is at a lower stage of evolution than oneself. It is easier to believe it of distant foreigners.

20 Tylor's 'the belief in spiritual beings' was too restrictive for those who wanted to emphasise ritual rather than belief. For Marett the object of religion is 'whatever is perceived as a mystery and treated accordingly'. More recently Baal has proposed 'all explicit and implicit notions and ideas, accepted as true, which relate to a reality which cannot be verified empirically'. Baal, *Symbols,* pp. 35, 68 & 3 respectively.

21 'Chinese religion: an overview', Jones, Lindsay, Ed, *Encyclopedia of Religion,* Detroit: Macmillan, 2005. Nongbri, *Before Religion,* p. 25.

22 Pharo, Lars Kirkhusmo, 'The concept of "religion" in Mesoamerican languages', *Numen* 54 (2007), pp. 28-70.

Nongbri, *Before Religion*, p. 26.
23 Graham, *Rock*, p. 14.
24 Graham, *Rock*, p. 25.
25 'Everyone has the right to freedom of thought, conscience and religion; this right includes freedom to change his religion or belief and freedom, either alone or in community with others and in public or private, to manifest his religion or belief, in worship, teaching, practice and observance.' Article 9.
26 https://www.churchofengland.org/renewal-reform/about-rr.aspx, accessed 9 September 2016.

Chapter 7

1 'The historical roots of our ecologic crisis', *Science*, 10 March 1967, pp. 1203-7.
2 Preface to *The Great Instauration*, 1620. Full text on http://www.constitution.org/bacon/instauration.htm, accessed 22 September 2016.
3 Genesis 1:26-28. Bacon's interpretation of the text is not supported by Hebrew scholars today.
4 Sheldrake, *Rebirth*, pp. 29-32, provides a list of such quotations, arguing that nature should be tortured as witches were, and recommending such procedures as very masculine. See also Merchant, *Nature*, pp. 168-169.
5 Ecotheologians sometimes draw attention to the one biblical text describing the state of nature as needing alteration: 'For the creation waits with eager longing for the revealing of the children of God; for the creation was subjected to futility, not of its own will but by the will of the one who subjected it, in hope that the creation itself will be set free from its bondage to decay and will obtain the freedom of the glory of the children of God. We know that the whole creation has been groaning in labour pains until now' (Romans 8:19-22). E.g. Southgate, *Groaning*, p. 2.

6 Merchant, *Nature*. See also Capra, *Turning Point*

7 Erdozain, *Soul*, p. 50.

8 Descartes, *Discourse*, Chapter 4, p. 53.

9 To make matters worse the force acted on matter at a distance, which contradicted the dominant idea of a clock-like universe with the different parts impacting on each other directly. Dunn, *Empiricists*, p. 98. For debates about unobservables see O'Hear, *Science*, pp. 82-105.

10 Kors, 'D'Holbach', pp. 277-279.

11 *Philosophie*, ii. 397-411, quoted in Kors, 'D'Holbach', pp. 285-286.

12 Pierre Simon Laplace, *A Philosophical Essay on Probabilities*, 6th ed., trans. F. W. Truscott and F L Emory, New York: Dover, 1961, p. 4, quoted in Barbour, *Issues*, p. 59.

13 Barbour, *Issues*, pp. 58-59.

14 Quoted in Black, John, *The Dominion of Man*, Edinburgh: Edinburgh UP, 1970, p. 30.

15 O'Hear, *Science*, pp. 107-8.

16 O'Hear, *Science*, pp. 106-110.

17 Mandelbaum, *Reason*, pp. 11-12.

18 Mandelbaum, *Reason*, p. 18.

19 Hanfling, *Logical Positivism*, pp. 1-8.

20 Hanfling, *Logical Positivism*, p. 111.

21 http://www.theguardian.com/uk/commentisfree, accessed 22 September 2016.

22 Pickstock, *After Writing*, p. 123; Taylor, *Secular*, p. 271; Hyman, *Atheism*, p. 77.

23 In effect God is domesticated, created in the image of humanity. Placher, *Domestication*; Hyman, *Atheism*, pp. 20-22; Dupré, *Religion*, p. 15.

24 The sequence is still reflected in those popular defences of atheism which combine angry condemnations of religious belief with claims that science's failure to find evidence for gods should be reason enough to disbelieve in them. I have

in mind the works of the leading 'new atheists' Richard Dawkins, Sam Harris and Christopher Hitchens.

25 Nisbet, *Progress*, p. 172.

26 Mandelbaum, *Reason*, pp. 87-88.

27 Fichte, *The Vocation of Man*, quoted in Nisbet, *Progress*, p. 275.

28 Stepelevich, Lawrence, 'Feuerbach and the Young Hegelians', Critchley, *Companion*, p. 114.

29 http://www.theecologist.org/blogs_and_comments/commentators/2986552/camerons_real_climate_policy_promise_the_sky_frack_the_earth.html, accessed 19 April 2016.

30 http://www.independent.co.uk/news/uk/politics/david-cameron-accused-of-breaking-promise-over-britains-beauty-spots-with-raft-of-fracking-licences-a6777306.html, accessed 19 April 2016.

31 Another recent example is the British Government's 'Cutting Red Tape programme'. https://cutting-red-tape.cabinet office.gov.uk/ and https://www.gov.uk/government/uploads/system/uploads/attachment_data/file/69598/pb13819-red-tape-environment.pdf, accessed 19 April 2016. Much 'red tape' consists of environmental protection. Despite Government assurances, many environmentalists have argued that environmental protection will be significantly weakened. See http://www.theguardian.com/environment/blog/2012/mar/20/red-tape-challenge-environmental-regulations, accessed 19 April 2016.

32 Abian, Alexander, 'Hate Winter? Here's One Man's Solution: Blow up the Moon', *Wall Street Journal*, 1991, quoted in Northcott, Michael, *The Environment and Christian Ethics*, Cambridge: CUP, 1996, pp 59-60.

33 *The Gay Science*, 1880, p. 95, quoted in Hyman, *Atheism*, p. 170.

34 Ward, Keith, *Divine Action*, London: Collins Flame, 1990, p. 83, quoted in Markham, *Against Atheism*, p. 66.

35 Gray, *Straw Dogs*, p. xiv.

36 *Straw Dogs*, p. xiv.
37 O. Stern in *The New York Times*, 14 January 1917, quoted in Jaki, *Purpose*, p. 18.

Chapter 8

1 Bottéro, *Mesopotamia*, p. 129.
2 The Bible makes two references to this practice: 1 Samuel 2:12-17 and Bel and the Dragon, a Greek addition to the book of Daniel included in the Apocrypha.
3 There is extensive literature about this. See for example Honderich, *How Free*.
4 *Summa Theologica* 1.88.a2.
5 Bullock, *Dictionary*, art. 'Social engineering'.
6 Bury described three stages in the development of the idea of progress. In the first, before the French Revolution, it was taken for granted and not examined closely. In the second a search began for a general law that would define it. The study of sociology was founded. Socialists appealed to it. The third was after 1859, with evolutionary theory. Bury, *Progress*, pp. 334-5.
7 Kincaid, 'Positivism'; Nisbet, *Progress*, pp. 235, 252-257.
8 Taylor, *Secular*, pp. 80-84, 119-124.
9 Taylor, *Secular*, pp. 119-120.
10 Taylor, *Secular*, pp. 121-122.
11 Nisbet, *Progress*, p. 246.
12 Spencer, *Social Statics*, New York: Appleton, 1865 [1850], p. 32, quoted in Mandelbaum, *Reason*, p. 234.
13 Walker, *Sentencing*, p. 36.
14 Nisbet, History of the Idea of Progress, p. 150.
15 Nisbet, *Progress*, pp. 287-289.
16 Chesterton, *What's Wrong with the World*, p. 248, http://www.theguardian.com/books/booksblog/2010/jan/08/gk-chesterton-world-whats-wrong, accessed 9 January 2016.
17 Illich, Ivan, *Deschooling Society*, Middlesex: Penguin, 1971.

18 Government's response to the Ninth Report from the Education and Skills Committee, Session 2006-07, http://www.publications.parliament.uk/pa/cm200607/cmselect/cmeduski/1101/110104.htm, accesssed 29 March 2016.

19 Klein, *Everything*, p. 60.

20 http://www.theguardian.com/politics/video/2012/oct/08/george-osborne-tory-conference-video, accessed 25 March 2016.

21 I say 'seventy years' because comparisons with the time of the Second World War are difficult to make. Leaving that aside the closest comparison would be with the 1930s Depression.

Chapter 9

1 *Leviathan*, Chapter 13. The 'war of all against all' is a quotation from his *De Cive*.

2 Locke, *Second Treatise*, §4.

3 Locke, *Second Treatise*, §6.

4 Locke, *Second Treatise*, §§14-15.

5 Locke, *Second Treatise*, especially Chapters 7-9.

6 Ramsay, *Liberalism*, p. 7.

7 Both these beliefs conflict with the theological trends described in Chapter 5, the first with the doctrine of Hell and the second with the exaltation of dogma. They continue to play subordinate roles in western Christianity today. It cannot get rid of them altogether because this would undermine its claim to be monotheistic; but today, while Locke is often read as a philosopher, he is rarely read as a theologian. In his day there would not have been such a sharp distinction between the two; indeed he remained one of the best-read theological writers throughout the eighteenth century.

8 Locke, *Second Treatise*, §4.

9 Finnis, *Natural Law*, pp. 206-210.

10 Varkemaa, 'Summenhart', p. 188.

11 Locke, *Second Treatise*, §6. His argument for the right to own property (§§26-43) is no longer convincing. It depended both on God and on an analogy with common land, which still existed in his time. God had given the world to humanity in general, but individuals came to own parts of it by 'mixing' their labour with resources taken out of the state of nature, thus making it their own property. He then applied the argument to the ownership of land, claiming that it did not deprive others because there was such a plentiful supply. Anyway, appropriating land and putting it to good use increased its value. In support of these points he compared the condition of land in England with America, where in his day there was much less cultivation.

12 http://www.ushistory.org/declaration/document/, accessed 3 June 2016. Bramsted, *Western Liberalism*, p. 149, discusses the role of theological appeal on that occasion.

13 Bentham, J, *Introduction to the Principles of Morality and Legislation*, ed. W. Harrison, Oxford: Blackwell, 1967, p. 125. Ramsay, *Liberalism*, pp. 12 & 144.

14 Berlin, *Four Essays*.

15 Ramsay, *Liberalism*, pp. 13, 18 & 35.

16 Berlin, *Four Essays*, p. 122. Similarly Friedrich Hayek argued that without this restriction on its meaning, freedom would mean satisfying whatever desires we had, such as flying like a bird. Miller, D., Ed, *Liberty*, Oxford University Press, 1991, p. 83, quoted by Ramsay, *Liberalism*, p. 41.

17 J P Day, 'On liberty and the real will', *Philosophy*, 1970, 95, p. 260 and H Steiner, 'Individual liberty', *Proceedings of the Arisotelian Society*, 1974, 75, p. 43, quoted by Ramsay, *Liberalism*, pp. 46-47.

18 Berlin, *Four Essays*, pp. 122-123.

19 Coates, K and Silburn, R, *St Anne's: Poverty, Deprivation and Morale*, Nottingham: Nottingham University Department of

Adult Education, 1967, quoted by Ramsay, *Liberalism*, pp. 233-235.

20 See for example http://www.filmsforaction.org/articles/the-likely-cause-of-addiction-has-been-discovered-and-it-is-not-what-you-think/, accessed 26 August 2016.

21 Ramsay, *Liberalism*, pp. 54-66. Ramsay notes that some oppose the distinction between negative and positive freedom on the ground that any kind of liberty can be expressed in terms of both freedom from and freedom to.

22 Bramsted, *Western Liberalism*, pp. 682 & 714.

23 E.g. Berlin, pp. 145-154.

24 Ramsay, *Liberalism*, pp. 48-49. Apart from Berlin, Ramsay quotes Dyer, D P, 'Freedom', *Canadian Journal of Economics and Political Science*, 1964, 30.

25 E.g. Nozick, *Anarchy*, p. 214.

26 Ramsay, *Liberalism*, pp. 69-74.

27 Ramsay, *Liberalism*, p. 145.

28 MacIntyre, *After Virtue*, p. 69. He is mistaken on a minor point: in fact there are a great many people who practice witchcraft and call themselves witches.

29 Ramsay, *Liberalism*, pp. 20-30.

30 Bentham, J, *Introduction to the Principles of Morality and Legislation*, Ed. W. Harrison, Oxford: Blackwell, 1967, Chapter 1, §10.

31 Hayek, F, *The Counter-Revolution of Science*, London: Collier-Macmillan, 1955, pp. 37-38; Popper, K, *The Poverty of Historicism*, London: RKP, 1961, p. 135. Ramsay, *Liberalism*, pp. 8-14 & 103.

32 This makes it possible to read him as a social engineer, only committed to individual liberty and minimal government as a means to the 'progress of opulence'. So argues Nisbet, *Progress*, p. 191. See also Ramsay, *Liberalism*, p. 15.

33 Others argued that people are by nature only partly egoistic. Thus John Stuart Mill argued on a utilitarian basis that we

should act in the interests of general happiness, not just our own happiness. However this is to abandon the individualist ethos and move towards a more communitarian one. Ramsay, *Liberalism*, p. 15.

34 John Maynard Keynes, quoted in Bramsted, *Western Liberalism*, pp. 705-6.

35 Ramsay, *Liberalism*, pp. 236-7.

36 Schaar, J H, 'Equality of opportunity and beyond', Pennock, J R and Chapman, J W, eds, *Equality: Nomos IX*, New York: Atherton Press, 1967, quoted in Ramsay, *Liberalism*, p. 93.

37 A classic text is MacIntyre, *After Virtue*.

38 Schumacher, *Small is Beautiful*, p. 124.

Chapter 10

1 Taylor, *Sources*, pp. 248-265.

2 Körner, *Kant*, especially pp. 137-147. Some use Kant's philosophy as a basis for a theory of rights. For example the legal philosopher H L A Hart defended natural rights on the basis that human are capable of choice. Hart, 'Are there any natural rights?', *Philosophical Review*, 1955, 64, quoted in Ramsay, *Liberalism*, p. 147.

3 E.g. Christine Korsgaard. Wainwright, *Morality*, p. 51.

4 Erdozain, *Soul*, p.220, quoting Keith Ansell-Pearson and Duncan Large, *The Nietzsche Reader*, Oxford: Blackwell. p. 372. Erdozain describes at length how nineteenth-century agnostics were torn between Christian moral standards and the Christian god threatening eternal Hell.

5 Rawls, *Justice*, p. 302.

6 'Justice as fairness: political not metaphysical', *Philosophy and Public Affairs*, 1985, 14, quoted by Ramsay, *Liberalism*, p. 230.

7 Gray, *Endgames*, p. 53. Similarly Ramsay responds that 'it is rather an odd defence of liberal principles of justice to say that they are liberal principles of justice; to say that people

conceived the way liberals conceive them would choose liberal principles; to say that a liberal theory of justice informed by liberal beliefs and values is one that liberals could accept' (Ramsay, *Liberalism*, p. 124).

8 A classic text is Jean-François Lyotard, *The Postmodern Condition: A Report on Knowledge*, Manchester University Press 1984. See also Milbank, John, *Theology and Social Theory: Beyond Secular Reason*, Oxford: Blackwells, 1990, pp. 330 and 346-7. A summary is in Vanhoozer, Kevin J, Ed, *The Cambridge Companion to Postmodern Theology*, Cambridge: CUP, 2003, pp. 8-16.

9 Plato, *Republic*, p. 65, §338.

10 Russell, *Devil*, p. 29.

11 A forerunner was behaviourism, whose best known proponent, B F Skinner, argued: 'In what we may call the pre-scientific view . . . a person's behaviour is at least to some extent his own achievement. He is free to deliberate, decide, and act, possibly in original ways, and he is to be given credit for his successes and blamed for his failures. In the scientific view . . . a person's behaviour is determined by a genetic endowment traceable to the evolutionary history of the species and by the environmental circumstances to which as an individual he has been exposed . . . the second view shows a marked advantage when we begin to do something about behaviour . . . The environment can be changed, and we are learning how to change it. *Beyond Freedom and Dignity*, Harmondsworth: Penguin, 1973, p. 101.

12 E O Wilson, *On Human Nature*, Cambridge, MA: Harvard UP, 1978, p. 167, quoted in Nitecki, *Evolutionary Ethics*, p. 117.

13 Alexander, 'The search for a general theory of behavior', *Biological Sciences* 1975: 20, p. 96, quoted in Rolston, *Genes*, pp. 256-7.

14 Ruse and Wilson, 'The evolution of ethics', *New Scientist*, 1985, 108, 1478 (17 October) , pp. 51-52.

15 Dawkins, *The Selfish Gene*, New York: Oxford UP, 1989, p. 4.

16 Michael Ghiselin, *The Economy of Nature and the Evolution of Sex*, Berkeley, CA: University of California Press, 1974, p. 247.

17 E O Wilson, 'Human decency is animal', *New York Times Magazine*, 12 Oct 1975, pp. 38-50, quoted in Rolston, *Genes*, p. 266.

18 E O Wilson, 'Human decency is animal', *New York Times Magazine*, 12 October 1975, p. 50.

19 Alexander, R, *The Biology of Moral Systems*, p. 40.

20 George C Williams, 'Huxley's evolution and ethics in sociobiological perspective', *Zygon* 1988, 23, p. 437.

21 *The Selfish Gene*, p. 3. Michael Ruse is an exception as he opts for moral scepticism: yes, morality is nothing more than practices evolved for survival. Ruse, 'Review of Peter Singer, *The Expanding Circle*', *Environmental Ethics* 1984, 6:91-94, p. 93.

A little earlier Skinner had argued much the same. His popular book *Beyond Freedom and Dignity* expresses the contradiction well. The concept of the mind is a fiction and we have no real freedom. To improve the lot of human life we should use his system of positive and negative reinforcers: 'In what we may call the pre-scientific view... a person's behaviour is at least to some extent his own achievement… In the scientific view... a person's behaviour is determined by a genetic endowment traceable to the evolutionary history of the species and by the environmental circumstances... the second view shows a marked advantage when we begin to do something about behaviour... The environment can be changed, and we are learning how to change it.' Skinner, *Beyond*, p. 101.

22 Rolston, *Genes*, p. 265.

23 Stevenson, *Ethics and Language*, pp. 21-26, 54-60.

24 MacIntyre, *After Virtue*, p. 24.

Chapter 11

1 Tolstoy, *Confession*, p. 27.

2 Tolstoy, *Confession*, p. 34.

3 Tolstoy, *Confession*, p. 30.

4 Nietzsche, *Power*, p. 327.

5 *The World as Will and Idea*, Vol. III, p. 383, quoted in Edwards, 'Meaning', p. 121.

6 Aldous Huxley, *Ends and Means: An Inquiry Into the Nature of Ideals and into the Methods Employed for their Realization*, London: Chatto and Windus, 1937, p. 273, quoted in Jaki, *Purpose*, p. 45.

7 Sartre, *Being*, p. 62.

8 Sartre, *Being*, p. 502.

9 Griffin summarises: 'Jean-Paul Sartre entitled one of his books *Nausea* to name the experience evoked in him by contemplating the meaninglessness of being. The absurdity of the universe was portrayed so effectively by Franz Kafka that the term *Kafkaesque* has become an adjective for the grotesquely absurd. The existentialists give what advice they can as to how to live a human life in an inhuman world. Paul Tillich, in his well-known book *The Courage to Be*, makes central to his philosophy the courage to affirm life in spite of its objective meaninglessness. Albert Camus, in *The Rebel*, advocates that we live a life of rebellion against the absurdity of the universe, even though there is no one in charge against whom to rebel.' Griffin, *God and Religion*, p. 17.

10 'The existentialist, on the contrary, thinks it very distressing that God does not exist, because all possibility of finding values in a heaven of ideas disappears along with Him; there can no longer be an *a priori* Good, since there is no infinite and perfect consciousness to think it. Nowhere is it written that the Good exists, that we must be honest, that we must not lie; because the fact is we are on a plane where there are only men. Dostoievsky said, "If God didn't exist, everything

would be possible"... Indeed, everything is permissible if God does not exist, and as a result man is forlorn.' Sartre, 'Emotions', p. 349.

11 Camus, 'Absurdity', pp. 70 & 72 respectively.
12 Nagel, *Mortal Questions*, p. 14.
13 Nagel, *Mortal Questions*, p. 15.
14 Nagel, *Mortal Questions*, p. 20.
15 Nagel, *Mortal Questions*, p. 20.
16 Nagel, *Mortal Questions*, pp. 20-21.
17 Nagel, *Mortal Questions*, p. 23.
18 Young, *Meaning*, p. 95.
19 Klemke, *Meaning*, contains contributions to this effect by a number of philosophers.
20 Taylor, 'Meaning', p. 141.
21 Taylor, 'Meaning', p. 143.
22 Taylor, 'Meaning', p. 144.
23 Taylor, 'Meaning', p. 146.
24 Taylor, 'Meaning', p. 146.
25 Taylor, 'Meaning', p. 148.
26 Taylor, 'Meaning', p. 150.
27 Edwards, 'Meaning', p. 128.
28 Nagel, *Mortal Questions*, p. 12.
29 Nagel, *Mortal Questions*, p. 12.
30 Nagel, *Mortal Questions*, pp. 16-17.
31 Nagel, *Mortal Questions*, p. 16.
32 Defenders of Edwards and Nagel may reply that, since we create our own values, the value of x and y are surd facts about human valuings: we do in fact value things in this kind of way. But this would be to abandon any attempt to offer a justification.
33 Tolstoy, *Confession*, p. 57.

Chapter 12

1 Markham, *Truth*, pp. 18-19.

2 Nisbet, *Progress*, p. 59.
3 Gray, *Straw Dogs*, p. 48.
4 Gray, *Straw Dogs*, p. 3.
5 Cottingham, *Meaning*, p. 71.
6 Cottingham, *Meaning*, p. 72.
7 Luke 10:27.
8 Modern Church Annual Conference at High Leigh, Hoddesdon, Herts, 12th July 2016.
9 Recent research on what religious people believe is summarised by Linda Woodhead in *Modern Believing*, 55:1, January 2014.
10 Hebblethwaite, *Ocean*, p. 42.

Chapter 13

1 Hick, *Evil*, p. 279. See also p 259.
2 Of course many religious believers define evil in ways other than harm done, like disobedience to a command in Scripture. Asking why God would allow those acts is a question internal to specific religious traditions, where there is a consensus on their scriptures. It can only be answered from within each tradition. The question addressed here is a more general one, making fewer presuppositions.
3 Some analysts refer to a third type of evil, metaphysical evil. Metaphysical evils are imperfections in the universe which are inevitable. For the purposes of this discussion they can be subsumed in natural evils.
4 There are Christians today who accept the theory of stages, but overwhelmingly the only reason is that they believe it to be essential Christian doctrine—and even they usually hold it in uneasy tension with the modern scientific account.
5 Augustine, *On Free Will*, 3,9,26, quoted by Hick, *Evil*, p. 93.
6 *Against the Heresies* 4.39.1.
7 *Proof of the Apostolic Preaching*, Chapter 12, cf. *Against the Heresies* 3.20.1.

8 *Against the Heresies* 4.38.3.
9 Like the Hebrew scriptures this tradition also appeals to divine punishment as an explanation for some evils. Hick, *Evil*, pp. 216, 221-223.
10 Hick, *Evil*, p. 174.
11 Hick, *Evil*, p. 238-9. As noted in Chapter 6 Augustine, following the logic of his position, had reluctantly reached the conclusion that God is, after all, responsible for evil. Schleiermacher accepted this conclusion but explained it as instrumental.
12 Hick, *Evil*, pp. 233-241.
13 Hick, Evil, p. 242.
14 Drummond, Henry, *The Ascent of Man*, London: H & S, 1894, pp. 436-437, quoted in Hick, *Evil*, p. 245.
15 Stark, *One True God*, p. 25, italics in original.
16 There are many such theogonies in Gnosticism. See Robinson, *Nag Hammadi*.
17 Hick, *Evil*, p. 19.
18 Russell, *Devil*, pp. 99-101.
19 This is best described in Plato's *Timaeus*.
20 Hick, *Evil*, pp. 160-172.
21 Quoted in Russell, *Devil*, p. 144.
22 Plotinus used two Greek terms, *ouk on* and *mē on*, which both tend to be translated into English as something like 'nothingness'. The first conveys absolute nothingness, the second the not yet realised potential to be a specific thing. It is the second one where the question of evil arises. Hick argued that, like many monists before and after him, Plotinus treated evil 'as passive when arguing that the universe contains no independent power of evil, but as active when addressing the human experience of evil.' Hick, *Evil*, p. 48.
23 Spinoza, *Ethics*, 4.64, quoted in Hick, *Evil*, pp. 28.
24 Russell, *Devil*, p. 101.

25 Adams, *Problem*, p. 70.

Chapter 14

1 Davis, *Encountering Evil*, p. 83.

2 *Summa Theologica* 1, q.42, a.2, quoted in Southgate, *Groaning*, p. 40.

3 Southgate and Robinson have recently distinguished three types of 'good-harm analysis'. The first, 'property-consequence', states that the existence of a good requires the possibility of harm. The second is 'developmental': a good goal can only develop through a process including the possibility of harm. The third is 'constitutive': the existence of a good is inherently and constitutively inseparable from the experience of harm. Southgate, *Groaning*, p. 41.

4 Hick, *Evil*, p. 293.

5 Puccetti, 'Loving', pp. 236-8. The quotation is from p. 236.

6 Hick, *Evil*, p. 363.

7 Hick in Davis, *Encountering Evil*, p. 49.

8 'Loving', p. 238.

9 Southgate, *Groaning*, p. 8.

10 http://academic.evergreen.edu/g/grossmaz/LEEPERFY/, accessed 14 December 2015.

11 Steffen, *World Changing*, Part 7, Chapter 4.

12 Juniper, *Harmony*, pp. 297-302.

13 http://academic.evergreen.edu/g/grossmaz/LEEPERFY/.

14 Jones, Patrice, in Best, *Igniting a Revolution*, Chapter 29.

15 Exodus 20:5.

16 Ezekiel 18.

17 Psalm 37:25-26: 'I have been young, and now am old, yet I have not seen the righteous forsaken or their children begging bread. They are ever giving liberally and lending, and their children become a blessing'.

18 There is no shortage of research attributing cancer levels to poor lifestyles and environment. One example is 'Substantial

contribution of extrinsic risk factors to cancer development', *Nature*, (2015) doi:10.1038/nature16166, available on http://www.nature.com/nature/journal/vaop/ncurrent/full/nature16166.html, accessed 17 December 2015.

19 David Seedhouse, *Health*; Vijay Kumar Yadavendu, 'Health', pp. 2784-2795.

20 Letter to Dr Gray May 1860, quoted in Helm, Paul, Ed, *Faith and Reason*, Oxford: OUP, 1999.

21 Southgate, *Groaning*, pp. 3-4. See also Hick, *Evil*, pp. 346-7.

22 Hick, *Evil*, p. 291. See also pp. 302-8.

23 Hick, *Evil*, p. 370.

24 Southgate, *Groaning*, p. 40.

25 Thus Hick asks: 'Would it not contradict God's love for the creatures made in His image if He caused them to pass out of existence whilst His purpose for them was still so largely unfulfilled?' *Evil*, p. 374.

26 Hick, *Evil*, p. 377.

27 Hick, *Evil*, pp. 383-4.

28 Puccetti, 'Loving', p. 240.

29 Puccetti, 'Loving', p. 241.

30 Taylor, *Secular*, pp. 232-233 and 388-389.

31 Evans, *Evil*, p. 29.

32 *Eichmann in Jerusalem: A Report on the Banality of Evil*, New York: Penguin, 1977.

33 Pp. 287-288, quoted in De La Torre, *Quest*, p. 44.

34 P. 276, quoted in De La Torre, *Quest*, p. 44.

35 We may get it wrong; those brought up in other cultures, or with different needs, may not feel as we do. This is a dangerous point: it is the basis for the rich person's argument that poor people are used to being poor so they may as well carry on in that state. Still, there is some truth in it.

Chapter 15

1 Zagzebski, *Motivation*, p. 315. See also pp. 185 and 218-220.

2 Zagzebski, *Motivation*, p. 196.

3 Zagzebski, *Motivation*, p. 317.

4 Zagzebski, *Motivation*, p. 185.

5 Zagzebski, *Motivation*, p. 220.

6 Mantzaridis, *Deification.*

7 A M Allchin, for example, noted its importance to Richard Hooker, Lancelot Andrewes and other Anglicans. Allchin, *Participation.*

8 *Summa Theologica* II.1, Q.94, a.2

9 *Tractatus Theologico-Politicus,* chap. 16, para. 2

10 Nitecki, *Evolutionary Ethics*, pp. 3-5.

11 One of Spencer's supporters, the American Graham Sumner, wrote in 1914: 'The struggle for existence is aimed against nature. It is from her niggardly hand that we have to wrest the satisfactions for our needs, but our fellow-men are our competitors for the meager supply. Competition, therefore, is a law of nature. Nature... grants her rewards to the fittest... If we do not like it... we can take from the better and give to the worse. We can deflect the penalties of those who have done ill and throw them on those who have done better... We shall favor the survival of the unfittest, and we shall accomplish this by destroying liberty. Let it be understood that we cannot go outside of this alternative; liberty, inequality, survival of the fittest; not-liberty, equality, survival of the unfittest. The former carries society forward and favors all its best members; the latter carries society downwards and favors all its worst members.' *The Challenge of Facts And Other Essays*, ed. A. S. Kelle. New Haven: Yale UP, 1914, p. 293, quoted in Nitecki, *Evolutionary Ethics*, p. 137.

12 Some have approved of evolution because of the element of 'group selection', where individuals act against their own interests for the sake of the group. The usual examples are

ants and bees, where the workers produce no offspring but benefit their kin. Peter Kropotkin and Julian Huxley argued that evolution sets a moral standard for us in this way. Most biologists today, however, believe group selection is only a very small part of natural selection. Thomas Huxley took a different view again. The 'evolution of society' was, he believed, opposed to the 'evolution of species'; the 'cosmic process' and the 'ethical process' were in mortal combat. Huxley, 'Romanes Lecture', published in Nitecki, *Evolutionary Ethics*, pp. 29-80.

13 Nitecki, *Evolutionary Ethics*, pp. 277-324.

14 Rolston, *Genes*, p. 233.

15 Daniel J Povinelli and Laurie R. Godfrey, 'The chimpanzee's mind: how noble in reason? How absent of ethics?' in Nitecki, *Evolutionary Ethics*, pp. 277-324.

16 *Iliad* 1:197ff & 19:86-90; Jaynes, *Origin*, pp. 72-73.

17 Williams, 'Can Beings', p. 234.

18 Nitecki, *Evolutionary Ethics*, p. 13.

19 Hynes, S, ed., *The Complete Poetical Works of Thomas Hardy*, Vol 1, Oxford: Clarendon, 1982, p. 333, quoted in Larrimore, *Evil*, p. 312.

20 Maslow, *Motivation and Personality*.

21 *Cianci, R and Gambrel, P A, 'Maslow's hierarchy of needs: Does it apply in a collectivist culture', Journal of Applied Management and Entrepreneurship, 8 (2), 2003, pp. 143–161.*

22 Mettinger, *Eden*, pp. 58-59. Hick does refer to this text (*Evil*, pp. 321-3) but does not develop it in the way I do here. I am grateful to John Barton for confirming its consistency with the Hebrew text.

23 Some have argued that it was never satisfactorily resolved.. See Lovejoy, *Chain*, pp. 82-90.

24 The idea that God is omnipotent but self-limiting is debated by theologians. See Byrne, 'Omnipotence', p. 154.

25 Some theologians argue that a satisfactory account must

include a better life after death. Hick believes his theodicy requires the faith that evil will eventually be overcome (*Evil*, p. 252). Here he disagrees with F R Tennant, whose theodicy is similar but who thinks that 'the continuance or the self-extinction of moral evil is irrelevant to theodicy' (*Philosophical Theology* 2, p. 197). I am inclined to agree with Tennant, and treat the freedom to choose between good and evil as worthwhile here and now. This is not to deny life after death, but to deny that it is necessary to defend God's justice.

26 Niebuhr, 'Self', p. 50.

27 Of course many atheist psychologists, philosophers and neuroscientists hold more moderate positions, but this is not to say that they can show how to derive these positions from their atheism.

Chapter 16

1 The idea that religious belief hinders scientific research dates from the late nineteenth century. It was the brainchild of Thomas Huxley and his disciples. Before then there was much disagreement about scientific theories, as there still is, but it did not divide religious believers from scientific researchers. Huxley was right that there were in his day people who rejected all scientific theories in the name of the Bible, but they were not typical.

2 *Against the Heresies* 4.39.1.

Bibliography

Adams, Marilyn M & Robert M, *The Problem of Evil*, Oxford: OUP, 1990.

Albertz, Rainer, *A History of Israelite Religion in the Old Testament Period Volume 1: From the Beginnings to the End of the Exile*, London: SCM, 1994.

Albertz, Rainer, *A History of Israelite Religion in the Old Testament Period Volume 2: From the Exile to the Maccabees*, London: SCM, 1994.

Albrektson, Bertil, *History and the Gods: An Essay on the Idea of Historical Events as Divine Manifestations in the Ancient Near East and in Israel*, Lund, Sweden: CWK Gleerup, 1967.

Allchin, A M, *Participation in God:* London: DLT, 1988.

Archbishop of Canterbury's Commission, on Urban Priority Areas, *Faith in the City: A Call for Action by Church & Nation*, London: Church House Publishing, 1985.

Arendt, Hannah, *Eichmann in Jerusalem: A Report on the Banality of Evil*, New York: Penguin, 1963.

Ariès, Philippe, *The Hour of our Death*, Harmondsworth: Allen Lane, 1981.

Assmann, Jan, 'Monotheism and Polytheism', Johnston, *Ancient Religions*.

Assmann, Jan, *Of God and Gods: Egypt, Israel, and the Rise of Monotheism*, London: University of Wisconsin Press, 2008.

Assmann, Jan, *The Price of Monotheism:* Stanford: Stanford University Press, 2010.

Athanassiadi, Polymnia, *Pagan Monotheism In Late Antiquity:* Oxford: Clarendon, 1999.

Attfield, R, *Creation, Evolution and Meaning:* Aldershot: Ashgate, 2006.

Atwell, James E, 'An Egyptian Source for Genesis 1', *Journal of Theological Studies* 51, Oct 2000.

Augustine, *City of God:* London: Penguin, 1984.

Aulén, Gustaf, *Christus Victor: An Historical Study of the Three Main Types of the Idea of the Atonement,* London: SPCK, 1950.

Baal, Jan van, *Symbols for Communication: An Introduction to the Anthropological Study of Religion,* Assen: Van Gorcum, 1971.

Baines, John, 'Egyptian Deities in Context: Multiplicity, Unity, and the Problem of Change', Porter, *One God.*

Barbour, Ian G, *Issues in Science and Religion,* London: SCM, 1966.

Barr, James, *The Concept of Biblical Theology: An Old Testament Perspective,* London: SCM, 1999.

Bartley III, W W, *Morality and Religion:* London: Macmillan, 1971.

Barton, John, *Understanding Old Testament Ethics,* London: Westminster John Knox Press, 2003.

Bauckham, R, *God Crucified: Monotheism and Christology in the New Testament,* Cambridge: Eerdmans, 1998.

Beiser, Frederick C, *The Sovereignty of Reason: The Defence of Rationality in the Early English Enlightenment,* Princeton: Princeton University Press, 1996.

Berlin, Isaiah, *Four Essays on Liberty:* Oxford: OUP, 1969.

Best, Steven, and Anthony J. Nocella, *Igniting a Revolution: Voices in Defense of the Earth,* Oakland, California: AK Press, 2006.

Blachowicz, James, 'Monotheism and the Spirituality of Reason', *Zygon* 37, June 2002.

Black, John, *The Dominion of Man: The Search for Ecological Responsibility,* Edinburgh: Edinburgh University Press, 1970.

Bonner, Hypatia Bradlaugh, *The Christian Hell:* London: Watts, 1913.

Bottéro, Jean, *Religion in Ancient Mesopotamia:* Chicago: University of Chicago Press, 2001.

Boyce, Mary, *Zoroastrians: Their Religious Beliefs and Practices,* London: RKP, 1985.

Bremmer, Jan, 'Atheism in Antiquity', Martin, *Atheism.*

Bremmer, Jan, *Greek Religion:* Oxford: 1994.

Brown, Peter, *Augustine of Hippo: A Biography,* London: Faber &

Faber, 1967.

Brown, Peter, *Religion and Society in the Age of St Augustine*, London: Faber & Faber, 1972.

Brown, Peter, *The Body and Society: Men, Women and Sexual Renunciation in Early Christianity*, London: Faber & Faber, 1989.

Brown, Peter, *The World of Late Antiquity:* London: Thames & Hudson, 1989.

Brown, William P, *The Ethos of the Cosmos: The Genesis of Moral Imagination in the Bible*, Grand Rapids, MI: Eerdmans, 1999.

Brueggemann, Walter, 'Response to J. Richard Middleton', *Harvard Theological Review* 87, 1994.

Brueggemann, Walter, *Israel's Praise: Doxology Against Idolatry and Ideology*, Philadelphia: Fortress, 1988.

Brueggemann, Walter, *The Message of the Psalms: A Theological Commentary*, Minneapolis: Fortress, 1984.

Brueggemann, W, *Theology of the Old Testament*, Minneapolis: Fortress, 1997.

Brunner, Emil, *The Mediator:* London: Lutterworth, 1934.

Buckley, Michael J, SJ, *At the Origins of Modern Atheism:* New Haven & London: Yale UP, 1987.

Bullock, Alan, et al, Eds, *The Fontana Dictionary of Modern Thought*, London: HarperCollins, 1988.

Bullough, Vern L, *Sexual Variance in Society and History:* London: John Wiley & Sons, 1976.

Burkert, Walter, *Creation of the Sacred: Tracks of Biology in Early Religions*, Cambridge, MA: Harvard University Press, 1996.

Burkert, Walter, *Greek Religion:* Cambridge MA: Harvard University Press, 1985.

Bury, John Bagnell, *The Idea of Progress: An Inquiry Into Its Growth and Origin*, New York: Dover Publications, 1960, first published 1932.

Byrne, Peter, 'Omnipotence, Feminism and God', *International Journal for the Philosophy of Religion*, 1995:37.

Byrne, Peter, *The Moral Interpretation of Religion:* Edinburgh: Edinburgh University Press, 1998.

Camus, Albert, 'The Absurdity of Human Existence', Klemke, *Meaning,* pp. 70-80.

Carmody, Denise Lardner, *The Oldest God: Archaic Religion Yesterday and Today,* Nashville: Abingdon, 1981.

Carroll, Robert P, *From Chaos to Covenant: Uses of Prophecy in the Book of Jeremiah,* London: SCM, 1996.

Chadwick, Owen, *From Bossuet to Newman:* Cambridge: Cambridge University Press, 1957.

Charlesworth, James H, *Jesus Within Judaism:* London: SPCK, 1990.

Clatworthy, Jonathan, *Liberal Faith in a Divided Church,* Ropley: O Books, 2008.

Clatworthy, J, *Making Sense of Faith in God: How belief makes science possible*, London: SPCK, 2012.

Clayton, Philip, and Steven Knapp, *The Predicament of Belief: Science, Philosophy, Faith,* Oxford: Oxford University Press, 2011.

Clifford, Richard J, *Creation Accounts in the Ancient Near East and in the Bible:* Washington DC: Catholic Biblical Association of America, 1994.

Collins, Adela Yarbro, *The Beginnings of the Gospel: Probings of Mark in Context,* Minneapolis: Fortress, 1992.

Collins, John J, *The Apocalyptic Imagination:* New York: Crossroad, 1984.

Cooper, David E, *Existentialism: A Reconstruction,* Oxford: Blackwell, 1990.

Coote, Robert B, and David Robert Ord, *In the Beginning: Creation and the Priestly History,* Minneapolis: Fortress, 1991.

Cottingham, John, *On the Meaning of Life*, London & New York: Routledge, 2003.

Cottingham, John, *Philosophy of Religion: Towards a More Humane Approach,* Cambridge: CUP, 2014.

Craig, Edward, General Editor, *Routledge Encyclopedia of Philosophy:* London & New York: Routledge, 1998.

Critchley, Simon, and William R Schroeder, *A Companion to Continental Philosophy*, Oxford: Blackwell, 1998.

Crossan, John Dominic, *The Birth of Christianity*, Edinburgh: T & T Clark, 1998.

Crossan, John Dominic, *The Historical Jesus: The Life of a Mediterranean Jewish Peasant*, San Francisco: HarperCollins, 1992.

Daly, Mary, *Beyond God the Father: Towards a Philosophy of Women's Liberation*, London: Women's Press, 1985.

Davis, Stephen T, Ed, *Encountering Evil: Live Options in Theodicy*, Edinburgh: T & T Clark, 1981.

Dawkins, Richard, *The God Delusion:* London: Transworld, 2006.

Day, Peggy L, *An Adversary in Heaven: Satan in the Hebrew Bible*, Atlanta, GA: Scholars Press, 1988.

De Haardt, Maaike, *Studies in Theology and Religion Volume 13: The Boundaries of Monotheism*, Boston: Brill, 2009.

De La Torre, Miguel A, and Albert Hernández, *The Quest for the Historical Satan:* Minneapolis: Alban, Feb 2011.

Delumeau, Jean, *Sin and Fear: The Emergence of a Western Guilt Culture 13th-18th Centuries*, New York: St Martin's Press, 1990.

Descartes, René, *Discourse on Method and The Meditations:* London: Penguin, 1968.

Dillistone, F W, *The Christian Understanding of Atonement:* Welwyn: Nisbet, 1968.

Drake, H A, 'Monotheism and violence', *Journal of Late Antiquity*, Volume 6, Issue 2, 2013.

Dunn, J D G, *Did the First Christians Worship Jesus?: The New Testament Evidence*, London: SPCK, 2010.

Dunn, John, et al, *The British Empiricists:* Oxford: OUP, 1992.

Dupré, Louis, *Religion and the Rise of Modern Culture*, Notre Dame: Univ Notre Dame Press, 2008.

Edwards, Paul, 'The Meaning and Value of Life', Klemke,

Meaning.

Eisenstadt, S, *Axial Age Civilizations:* New York: State University of New York, 1986.

Eliade, Mircea, *A History of Religious Ideas:* Chicago: University of Chicago Press, 1978.

Eliade, Mircea, *Patterns in Comparative Religion:* London & New York: Sheed & Ward, 1958.

Erdozain, Dominic, *The Soul of Doubt: The religious roots of unbelief from Luther to Marx,* Oxford: Oxford University Press, 2016.

Evans, G R, *Augustine on Evil:* Cambridge: Cambridge University Press, 1982.

Evans-Pritchard, E E, *Theories of Primitive Religion:* Oxford: OUP, 1965.

Feiveson, Harold A, Alexander Glaser, Zia Man and Frank N von Hippel, *Unmaking the Bomb: A Fissile Material Approach to Nuclear Disarmament and Nonproliferation,* London & Cambridge, MA: MIT Press, 2014.

Feliks, Yehuda, *Nature and Man in the Bible:* London: Soncino, 1981.

Finnis, John, *Natural Law and Natural Rights:* Oxford: OUP, 2011.

Fisher, Kathleen, 'The miracles of Mark 4:35-5:43: their meaning and function in the Gospel framework', *Biblical Theology Bulletin,* January 1981.

Fowden, Garth, *From Empire to Commonwealth: Consequences of Monotheism in Late Antiquity,* Princeton: Princeton UP, 1993.

Fox, Robin Lane, *Pagans And Christians:* London: Viking, Penguin, 1986.

Frevel, C, 'Beyond monotheism? Some remarks and questions on conceptualising "monotheism" in biblical studies', *Verbum et Ecclesia* 34(2), Art. #810, 2013.

Garr, W Randall, *In His Own Image and Likeness: Humanity, Divinity, and Monotheism*: Brill, 2003.

Geffré, C, J.-P Jossua and M. Lefébure, eds, *Monotheism:* Edinburgh: T & T Clark, 1985.

Geller, Stephen A, 'The God of the Covenant', Porter, *One God,* pp. 273-319.

George, Timothy, *The Theology of the Reformers,* Nashville, TN: Broadman, 1988.

Gerson, L P, *God and Greek Philosophy: Studies in the Early History of Natural Theology,* London: Routledge, 1994.

Gnuse, Robert Karl, *No Other Gods: Emergent Monotheism in Israel,* Sheffield: Sheffield Academic Press, 1997.

Goodman, Lenn E, *God of Abraham:* Oxford: Oxford University Press, 1996.

Goodman, Lenn E, 'Monotheism and Ethics', Langermann, *Abraham,* Pages 11-23.

Goodman, Martin, *Rome and Jerusalem: The Clash of Ancient Civilizations,* London: Penguin, 2007.

Gottwald, Norman K, *The Politics of Ancient Israel:* London: Westminister John Knox, 2001.

Gottwald, Norman, *The Bible and Liberation: Politics and Social Hermeneutics,* Maryknoll, NY: Orbis, 1993.

Graham, Elaine, *Between a Rock and a Hard Place: Public Theology in a Post-Secular Age,* London: SCM, 2013.

Grant, Robert, *Gods and the One God: Christian Theology in the Graeco-Roman World,* London: SPCK, 1986.

Gray, John, 'Enlightenment Humanism as a Relic of Christian Monotheism', Gifford, Paul et al, Eds, *2000 Years and Beyond: Faith, Identity and the 'Common Era',* London: Routledge, 2003.

Gray, John, *Endgames: Questions in late modern political thought,* Oxford: Blackwell, 1997.

Gray, John, *Liberalism:* Buckingham: Open University Press, 1995.

Gray, John, *Straw Dogs: Thoughts on Humans and Other Animals,* London: Granta, 2002.

Gray, John, *The Two Faces of Liberalism:* Cambridge: Polity, 2000.

Green, William Scott, 'Approaching distinctiveness: some preliminary considerations and data', Langermann, *Abraham.*

Griffin, David Ray, *God and Religion in the Postmodern World:*

Albany: State Univ of New York Press, 1989.

Gustafson, James M, *Theology and Ethics:* Oxford: Blackwell, 1981.

Hampson, Daphne, *After Christianity:* London: SCM, 1996.

Hampson, Daphne, *Theology and Feminism:* Oxford: Blackwell, 1990.

Hanfling, Oswald, *Essential Readings in Logical Positivism:* Oxford: Blackwell, 1981.

Hebblethwaite, Brian, *The Ocean of Truth: A Defence of Objective Theism,* Cambridge: Cambridge University Press, 1989.

Hedrick, Charles W, *Nag Hammadi, Gnosticism and Early Christianity:* MA: Hendrickson, 1986.

Helm, Paul, Ed, *Faith and Reason:* Oxford: OUP, 1999.

Helm, Paul, *Faith and Understanding:* Edinburgh: Edinburgh University Press, 1997.

Hengel, M, *Judaism and Hellenism:* London: SCM, 1974.

Hepburn, R W, 'Questions about the Meaning of Life', Klemke, *Meaning.*

Herodotus, Herodotus, *The Histories:* London: Penguin, 1966.

Heyward, Carter, *The Redemption of God: A Theology of Mutual Relation,* Washington DC: University Press of America, 1982.

Hick, John, *An Interpretation of Religion: Human Responses to the Transcendent,* Basingstoke: Macmillan, 1989.

Hick, John, *Evil And the God of Love,* London: Collins, 1966.

Hick, John, *God and the Universe of Faiths:* London: Fount, Collins, 1973.

Hobbes, Thomas, *Leviathan: Edited & abridged with an introduction by John Plamenatz,* London: Collins, 1983.

Honderich, Ted, *How Free Are You?:* Oxford: OUP, 1993.

Hume, David. (Eds: A. Wayne Colver & John Valdimir Price), *The Natural History of Religion & Dialogues Concerning Natural Religion,* Oxford: Clarendon, 1976.

Hunsinger, George, *How to Read Karl Barth: The Shape of his Theology,* Oxford: OUP, 1991.

Hunter, Michael, and Wootton, David, Eds, *Atheism from the*

Reformation to the Enlightenment, Oxford: Clarendon, 1992.

Hurtado, L W, 'First-Century Jewish Monotheism', *Journal for the Study of the New Testament*, 1998, Issue 71.

Hurtado, L, *Lord Jesus Christ:* Grand Rapids, MI: Eerdmans, 2003.

Hurtado, Larry W, *One God, One Lord: Early Christian Devotion and Ancient Jewish Monotheism,* London: SCM, 1988.

Hyman, Gavin, *Short History of Atheism*: I B Tauris, 2010.

Illich, Ivan, *Deschooling Society:* Middlesex: Penguin, 1971.

Jaki, Stanley L, *The Purpose of It All:* Edinburgh: Scottish Academic Press, 1990.

Janzen, Gerald, 'On the Moral Nature of God's Power: Yahweh and the Sea in Job and Deutero-Isaiah', *Catholic Biblical Quarterly* 56, 1994.

Janzen, Waldemar, *Old Testament Ethics: A Paradigmatic Approach,* Louisville, KY: Westminster/John Knox Press, 1994.

Jaynes, Julian, *The Origin of Consciousness in the Breakdown of the Bicameral Mind:* Harmondsworth: Penguin, 1982.

Jodock, Darrell, Ed, *Catholicism Contending with Modernity: Roman Catholic Modernism and Anti-Modernism in Historical Context,* Cambridge: CUP, 2000.

Johnston, Sarah Iles, Ed, *Ancient Religions: Beliefs and Rituals across the Mediterranean World,* Cambridge, MA: Harvard UP, 2004.

Jonas, Hans, *The Gnostic Religion:* London: Routledge, 2nd Edition 1992.

Joske, W D, 'Philosophy and the Meaning of Life', Klemke, *Meaning,* pp. 248-261.

Juniper, Tony, and the Prince of Wales, *Harmony:* London: Blue Door (HarperCollins), 2010.

Kee, A, *Nietzsche against the Crucified:* London: SCM, 1999.

Kee, Howard Clark, *Medicine, Miracle and Magic in New Testament Times,* Cambridge: CUP, 1986.

Kelly, Henry A, *Satan: A Biography,* Cambridge: CUP, 2006.

Kelly, J N D, *Early Christian Doctrines:* Edinburgh: R & R Clark,

1958, 1968

Kincaid, Harold, 'Positivism in the Social Sciences', Craig, *Encyclopedia.*

Kirkpatrick, Frank G, *A Moral Ontology for a Theistic Ethic: Gathering the Nations in Love and Justice,* Aldershot: Ashgate, 2003.

Klauck, H-J, *The Religious Context of Early Christianity: A Guide to Graeco-Roman Religions,* Edinburgh: T & T Clark, 2000.

Klein, Naomi, *This Changes Everything:* London: Penguin, 2014.

Klemke, E D, Ed, *The Meaning of Life,* New York & Oxford: OUP, 1981.

Klutz, Todd, *The Exorcism Stories in Luke-Acts: A Socio-Stylistic Reading,* Cambridge: Cambridge University Press, 2004.

Körner, S., *Kant:* London: Penguin, 1990 Edition.

Kors, Alan Charles, 'The atheism of D'Holbach and Naigeon', Hunter, *Atheism.*

Kraye, Jill, and Risto Saarinen, Eds, *Moral Philosophy on the Threshold of Modernity,* Dordrecht: Springer, 2005.

Lambert, W G, 'The Babylonian Background of Genesis', *Journal of Theological Studies* Volume XVI, Part 2, October 1965.

Lambert, WG, 'Destiny and Divine Intervention in Babylon and Israel, *Oudtestamentlische Studien* 17, 1972.

Lambert, WG, 'History and the Gods: A Review Article', *Orientalia* 39, 1970.

Lang, Bernhard, 'No God but Yahweh! The Origin and Character of Biblical Monotheism', Geffré, *Monotheism,* pp. 41-49.

Langermann, Y Tzvi, *Studies on the Children of Abraham Volume 2: Monotheism and Ethics*: Brill, 2011.

Larrimore, Mark, Ed, *The Problem of Evil: A Reader,* Oxford: Blackwells, 2001.

Lett, James William, *Science, Reason, and Anthropology: A Guide to Critical Thinking,* Oxford: Rowman & Little, 1997.

Lévy-Strauss, Claude, *The Savage Mind:* Oxford: OUP, 2004.

Lincoln, Bruce, 'Epilogue', Johnston, *Ancient Religions,* pp. 241-

251.

Lind, Millard C, 'Monotheism, Power, and Justice: A Study in Isaiah 40-55', *Catholic Biblical Quarterly* 46, 1984.

Lloyd, A B, Ed, *What is a God?: Studies in the Nature of Greek Divinity,* London: 1997.

Locke, John, *The Second Treatise of Civil Government:* Adelaide: University of Adelaide, 1764.

Lovejoy, Arthur O, *The Great Chain of Being: A Study of the History of an Idea,* New York: Harper & Row, 1960.

Lynch, Matthew J, 'Mapping monotheism: modes of monotheistic rhetoric in the Hebrew Bible', *Vetus Testamentum* 2014, Volume 64, Issue 1, pp. 47-68.

MacDonald, Nathan, 'Response to Patrick Madigan, 'The curse of monotheism', *Heythrop Journal* Volume 51, Issue 6, 2010.

MacIntyre, Alasdair, *After Virtue: A Study in Moral Theory,* London: Duckworth, 1981.

Mandelbaum, Maurice, *History, Man and Reason: A Study in Nineteenth Century Thought*, Baltimore: John Hopkins Press, 1971.

Mantzaridis, Georgios, *The Deification of Man:* New York: St Vladimir's Seminary Press, 1984.

Marino, Gordon, Ed, *Basic writings of existentialism,* New York: Modern Library, 2004.

Markham, Ian, *A Theology of Engagement,* Oxford: Blackwell, 2003.

Markham, Ian, *Against Atheism: Why Dawkins, Hitchens, and Harris are Fundamentally Wrong*, Chichester: Wiley-Blackwell, 2010.

Markham, Ian, *Truth & The Reality of God:* Edinburgh: T & T Clark, 1998.

Martin, Michael, Ed, *The Cambridge Companion to Atheism:* Cambridge: Cambridge University Press, 2007.

Maslow, Abraham, *Motivation and Personality:* London: Harper & Row, 1954.

Mays, James Luther, 'Justice: Perspectives from the Prophetic Tradition', *Interpretation* 37, 1983.

McDonald, JIH, *Biblical Interpretation and Christian Ethics:* Cambridge: Cambridge University Press, 1993.

McGrath, James F, *Only True God: Early Christian Monotheism in its Jewish Context,* Urbana: University of Illinois Press, 2009.

Meeks, Wayne, *The Origins of Christian Morality:* London: Yale University Press, 1993.

Merchant, Carolyn, *The Death of Nature: Women, Ecology and the Scientific Revolution,* San Francisco: HarperCollins, 1980.

Mettinger, Tryggve N D, *The Eden Narrative: A Literary and Religio-historical Study of Genesis 2-3,* Winona Lake, Indiana: Eisenbrauns, 2007.

Middleton, J R, 'Creation Founded in Love: A Rhetorical Reading of Genesis 1:1-2:3', *Society of Biblical Literature annual meeting* 19 November 1995.

Milbank, J, 'History of the One God', *Heythrop Journal,* October 1997, 38:4.

Milbank, John, *Theology and Social Theory: Beyond Secular Reason,* Oxford: Blackwells, 1990.

Minns, Denis, *Irenaeus:* London: Geoffrey Chapman, 1994.

Moberly, R C, *Atonement and Personality:* London: John Murray, 1917.

Momigliano, A, 'The Disadvantages of Monotheism for a Universal State', *Classical Philology,* October 1986, 81(4).

Moor, Johannes Cornelis de, *The Rise of Yahwism: The Roots of Israelite Monotheism,* Leuven: Leuwen UP, 1997.

Moule, C. F. D., *Man and Nature in the Old Testament:* Philadelphia: Facet, Fortress, 1967.

Muchembled, Robert, *A History of the Devil from the Middle Ages to the Present,* Cambridge: Polity, 2003.

Munnik, René, 'The Unity of God', De Haardt, *Studies,* pp. 106-128.

Murphy, Nancey, *On the Moral Nature of the Universe: Theology,*

Cosmology and Ethics, Minneapolis: Fortress, 1996.

Murray, Robert, *The Cosmic Covenant:* London: Sheed & Ward, 1992.

Nagel, Thomas, *Mortal Questions,* Cambridge: Cambridge University Press, 1979.

Nemet-Nejat, Karen Rhea, *Daily Life in Ancient Mesopotamia:* Westport, Conn., London: Greenwood Press, 1998.

Niebuhr, H Richard, *Radical Monotheism and Western Culture:* NY: Harper, 1970.

Niebuhr, Reinhold, 'The self and its search for ultimate meaning', Klemke, *Meaning,* pp. 41-52.

Nielsen, Kai, 'Linguistic Philosophy and "The Meaning of Life"', Klemke, *Meaning,* pp. 177-204.

Nietzsche, Friedrich, *The Will to Power,* New York: Random House, 1968.

Nietzsche, Friedrich, *Thus Spoke Zarathustra:* London: Penguin, 1987.

Nikiprowetzky, V, 'Ethical Monotheism', *Daedalus* 104, Issue 2, 1975.

Nisbet, Robert, *History of the Idea of Progress:* London: Heinemann, 1980.

Nitecki, Matthew H & Doris V, *Evolutionary Ethics,* Albany, NY: State University of New York Press, 1993.

Nongbri, Brent, *Before Religion: A history of a modern concept,* Yale: Yale University Press, 2013.

Northcott, Michael, *The Environment and Christian Ethics,* Cambridge: Cambridge University Press, 1996.

Nozick, Robert, *Anarchy, State and Utopia:* Oxford: Blackwell, 1974.

Oates, Joan, *Babylon:* London: Thames & Hudson, 1979.

O'Brien, Joan, and Wilfred Major, *In the Beginning: Creaton Myths from Ancient Mesopotamia, Israel and Greece,* Chicago: American Academy of Religion, 1982.

O'Hear, Anthony, *An Introduction to the Philosophy of Science:*

Oxford: Oxford University Press, 1991.
Olyan, Saul M, 'Is Isaiah 40-55 really monotheistic?', *Journal of Ancient Near Eastern Religions* Volume 12, Issue 2, September 2012, pp. 190-201.
Oord, Thomas Jay, *The Uncontrolling Love of God:* Downers Grove, IL: InterVarsity Press, 2015.
Otto, R, 'Moltmann and the Anti-Monotheism Movement', *International Journal of Systematic Theology,* November 2001, 3:3.
Outka, Gene, and John P Reeder, *Religion and Morality:* Garden City, NY: Anchor, 1973.
Packer, J I, *Knowing God:* London: H & S, 1973.
Pagels, Elaine, *Adam, Eve, and the Serpent:* London: Penguin, 1990.
Parpola, Simo, 'Monotheism in Ancient Assyria', Porter, *One God,* pp. 165-209.
Peterson, Michael L, Ed, *The Problem of Evil: Selected Readings,* Notre Dame, Indiana: University of Notre Dame Press, 1992.
Pickstock, C, *After Writing: On the Liturgical Consummation of Philosophy,* Oxford: Blackwell, 1998.
Placher, William C, *The Domestication of Transcendence: How Modern Thinking about God Went Wrong,* Louisville, KY: Westminster/John Knox Press, 1996.
Pongratz-Leisten, Beate, *Reconsidering the Concept of Revolutionary Monotheism:* Winona Lake, IN: Eisenbrauns, 2011.
Porter, Barbara Nevling, 'Monotheism in Ancient Assyria', Porter, *One God,* pp. 211-271.
Porter, Barbara Nevling, Ed, *One God or Many?: Concepts of Divinity in the Ancient World,* Chebeague, Maine: Casco Bay Assyriological Institute, 2000.
Puccetti, Roland, 'The Loving God: Some Observations on Hick's Theodicy', Peterson, *Evil,* pp. 231-246.
Raeburn, David, and Oliver Thomas, *The Agamemnon of Aeschylus:* Oxford: OUP, 2011.
Ramsay, Maureen, *What's Wrong with Liberalism?,* London:

Leicester University Press, 1997.

Rappaport, Roy Abraham, *Ritual and Religion in the Making of Humanity:* Cambridge: CUP, 1999.

Rashdall, Hastings, *The Idea of Atonement in Christian Theology:* London: Macmillan, 1919.

Rawls, John, *A Theory of Justice:* Oxford: Oxford University Press, 1972.

Reardon, Bernard M G, *Religious Thought in the Reformation:* London: Longman, 1995.

Rice, Hugh, *God and Goodness:* Oxford: Oxford University Press, 2000.

Richards, Jeffrey, *Sex, Dissidence and Damnation: Minority Groups in the Middle Ages,* London: Routledge, 1991.

Richardson, Alan, and John Bowden, ed, *A New Dictionary of Christian Theology:* London: SCM, 1983.

Ringgren, Helmer, *Israelite Religion:* London: SPCK, 1966.

Ringgren, Helmer, *Religions of the Ancient Near East:* London: SPCK, 1973.

Roberts, Alexander, and James Donaldson, Eds, *The Ante-Nicene Fathers Volume 1: The Apostolic Fathers - Justin Martyr - Irenaeus,* Edinburgh: T & T Clark, 1869.

Robinson, James M, *The Nag Hammadi Library: The Definitive New Translation of the Gnostic Scriptures, Complete in One Volume,* San Francisco: HarperCollins, 1990.

Rodd, Cyril, *Glimpses of a Strange Land: Studies in Old Testament Ethics,* Edinburgh: T & T Clark, 2001.

Rolston, Holmes, III, *Genes, Genesis and God: Values and Their Origins in Natural and Human History,* Cambridge: Cambridge University Press, 1999.

Römer, Thomas C, 'Yhwh, the Goddess and Evil: is 'monotheism' an adequate concept to describe the Hebrew Bible's discourses about the God of Israel?', *Verbum et Ecclesia,* 5 Sep 2013, 34(2).

Rousseau, John J, and Rami Arav, *Jesus and His World: An*

Archaeological and Cultural Dictionary, London: SCM, 1995.

Rudolph, Kurt, *Gnosis:* Edinburgh: T & T Clark, 1983.

Ruether, Rosemary Radford, *Sexism and God-Talk:* London: SCM, 1983.

Russell, J B, *Satan: The Early Christian Tradition,* Ithaca & London: Cornell University Press, 1981.

Russell, J B, *The Devil: Perceptions of Evil from Antiquity to Primitive Christianity,* Ithaca, NY: Cornell UP, 1977.

Saggs, H W F, *The Encounter with the Divine in Mesopotamia and Israel:* London: Athlone, 1978.

Saggs, HWF, *Civilization before Greece and Rome:* New Haven: Yale UP, 1989.

Sagi, A, and Statman, D, *Religion and Morality:* Amsterdam: Rodopi, 1995.

Sanders, EP, *Jesus And Judaism:* London: SCM, 1985.

Sartre, Jean-Paul, *Being and Nothingness: An essay on phenomenological ontology, Trans Hazel E Barnes,* London & New York: Routledge, 2003.

Sartre, Jean-Paul, 'Existentialism and Human Emotions', Marino, *Existentialism,* pp. 341-367.

Schumacher, E F, *Small is Beautiful,* London: Abacus, 1973.

Schwartz, Benjamin I, 'The Age of Transcendence', *Daedalus* 104, No. 2, 1975, pp. 1-7.

Schwartz, Regina M, *The Curse of Cain: The Violent Legacy of Monotheism,* Chicago: Univ Chicago Press, 1997.

Seedhouse, David, *Health: The Foundations for Achievement,* Chichester: Wiley, 2001.

Sheldrake, Rupert, *The Rebirth of Nature: The Greening of Science and God,* London: Rider, 1990.

Smith, B K, 'Monotheism and its Discontents: Religious Violence and the Bible', *Journal of the American Academy of Religion,* 1998 , 66:2.

Smith, Jonathan Z, *Drudgery Divine: On the Comparison of Early Christianities and the Religions of Late Antiquity,* London: School of Oriental and African Studies, 1990.

Smith, Mark S, *The Early History of God: Yahweh and the Other Deities in Ancient Israel,* San Fransisco: Harper & Row, 1990.

Smith, Mark S, *The Origins of Biblical Monotheism: Israel's Polytheistic Background and the Ugaritic Texts,* NY: Oxford University Press, 2001.

Smith, Mark S, *The Priestly Vision of Genesis 1:* Minneapolis: Fortress, 2010.

Smith, Morton, *Palestinian Parties and Politics That Shaped the Old Testament:* London: SCM, 1987.

Smith, Wilfred Cantwell, *The Meaning and End of Religion,* London: SPCK, 1962.

Southgate, Christopher, *The Groaning of Creation: God, Evolution and the Problem of Evil,* Louisville, Kentucky: Westminster John Knox Press, 2008.

Stark, R, *For the Glory of God: How Monotheism led to Reformations, Science, Witch-Hunts, and the End of Slavery,* Princeton: Princeton University Press, 2003.

Stark, R, *One True God: Historical Consequences of Monotheism,* Princeton: Princeton University Press, 2001.

Steffen, Alex, Ed, *World Changing: A User's Guide for the 21st Century,* New York: Abrams, 2008.

Stevenson, Charles L, *Ethics and Language,* New Haven: Yale University Press, 1944.

Stott, John, *The Cross of Christ:* Leicester: IVP, 1986.

Stout, Jeffrey, *The Flight from Authority: Religion, Morality and the Quest for Autonomy,* Notre Dame: Univ Notre Dame Press, 1981.

Stoyanov, Yuri, *The Other God: Dualist Religions from Antiquity to the Cathar Heresy,* New Haven & London: Yale University Press, 2000.

Taylor, Charles, *A Secular Age,* Harvard: Harvard University Press, 2007.

Taylor, Charles, *Sources of the Self: The Making of the Modern*

Identity, Cambridge: Cambridge University Press, 1989.
Taylor, Richard, 'The Meaning of Life', Klemke, *Meaning,* pp. 141-150.
Tennant, F R, *Philosophical Theology: Volume 2: The World The Soul and God,* Cambridge: Cambridge University Press, 1930.
Theissen, G, *Biblical Faith: An Evolutionary Approach,* Philadelphia: Fortress, 1985.
Theissen, Gerd, *The Miracle Stories of the Early Christian Church:* Edinburgh: T & T Clark, 1983.
Tolstoy, 'My Confession', Klemke, *Meaning,* pp. 9-19.
Toulmin, Stephen, *Cosmopolis: The Hidden Agenda of Modernity,* Chicago: University of Chicago Press, 1990.
Trigg, R, *Reality at Risk:* Brighton: Harvester, 1980.
Turner, Alice, *The History of Hell:* New York & London: Harcourt Brace & Co, 1993.
Twelftree, GH, *Jesus the Exorcist: A Contribution to the Study of the Historical Jesus,* Tubingen: Mohr, 1993.
Twelftree, Graham H, *Christ Triumphant: Exorcism Then and Now,* London: H & S, 1985.
Twelftree, Graham H, *In the Name of Jesus: Exorcism Among Early Christians,* Grand Rapids, Mich: Baker Academic, 2007.
Uffenheimer, B, 'Myth and Reality in Ancient Israel', Eisenstadt, *Axial Age Civilizations,* pp. 135-168.
Van De Mieroop, Marc, *A History of the Ancient Near East,* Oxford: Blackwell, 2004.
Van Riel, Gerd, *Plato's Gods:* Farnham: Ashgate, July 2013.
Van Wolde, Ellen, *Stories of the Beginning: Genesis 1-11 and Other Creation Stories,* London: SCM, 1996.
Vanhoozer, Kevin J, Ed, *The Cambridge Companion to Postmodern Theology,* Cambridge: Cambridge University Press, 2003.
Varkemaa, Jussi, 'Justification through Being: Conrad Summenhart on Natural Rights', Kraye, *Threshold,* pp. 181-193.
Vermes, Geza, *Jesus and the World of Judaism:* London: SCM, 1983.
Vermes, Geza, *Jesus the Jew:* London: SCM, 1983.

Versnel, H S, 'Thrice One: Three Greek Experiments in Oneness', Porter, *One God,* pp. 79-163.

Versnel, H S, *Coping with the Gods: Wayward Readings in Greek Theology,* Leiden & Boston: Brill, 2011.

Versnel, H S, *Inconsistencies in Greek and Roman Religion 1. Ter Unus:* Leiden: 1990.

Veyne, Paul, Ed, *A History of Private Life: From Pagan Rome to Byzantium,* Harvard: Harvard University Press, 1987.

Vidal, Gore, *Selected Essays of Gore Vidal:* New York: Doubleday, 2008.

Voak, Nigel, *Richard Hooker and Reformed Theology: A Study of Reason, Will, and Grace,* Oxford: OUP, 2003.

Vos, Nienke, and Willemien Otten, Eds, *Demons and the Devil in Ancient and Medieval Christianity:* Leiden: Brill, 2012.

Wainwright, William J, *Religion and Morality:* Aldershot: Ashgate, 2005.

Walker, Nigel, *Sentencing in a Rational Society:* Harmondsworth: Penguin, 1972.

Ward, Keith, *God, Chance & Necessity:* Oxford: OneWorld, 1996.

Ward, Keith, *In Defence of the Soul:* Oxford: OneWorld, 1992.

Weil, Eric, *What is a breakthrough in history?* Daedalus 104, no. 2, 1975, pp. 21-36.

Welch, Sharon D, *A Feminist Ethic of Risk:* Minneapolis: Fortress, 1990.

Westermann, Claus, *Creation:* London: SPCK, 1974.

Whiteley, D. E. H., *The Theology of St. Paul:* Oxford: Blackwell, 1972.

Wilkinson, Richard, and Kate Pickett, *The Spirit Level: Why Greater Equality Makes Societies Stronger,* London: Bloomsbury, 2010.

Williams, Patricia, 'Can beings whose ethics evolved be ethical beings?', Nitecki, *Evolutionary Ethics,* pp. 233-239.

Wootton, David, 'New histories of atheism', Hunter, *Atheism,* pp. 13-53.

Wright, NT, and Marcus Borg, *The Meaning of Jesus:* London: SPCK, 1999.

Yadavendu, Vijay Kumar, 'Social construction of health', *Economic and Political Weekly*, Volume. 36, No. 29, 21 July 2001.

Young, Frances, 'Insight or Incoherence? The Greek Fathers on God and Evil', *Journal of Ecclesiastical History* Vol 24, April 1973, pp. 113-126.

Young, Julian, *The Death of God and the Meaning of Life*, London & New York: Routledge, 2003.

Zagzebski, Linda Trinkaus, *Divine Motivation Theory:* Cambridge: Cambridge University Press, 2004.

CHRISTIAN
ALTERNATIVE

CHRISTIAN ALTERNATIVE

THE NEW OPEN SPACES

Throughout the two thousand years of Christian tradition there have been, and still are, groups and individuals that exist in the margins and upon the edge of faith. But in Christianity's contrapuntal history it has often been these outcasts and pioneers that have forged contemporary orthodoxy out of former radicalism as belief evolves to engage with and encompass the ever-changing social and scientific realities. Real faith lies not in the comfortable certainties of the Orthodox, but somewhere in a half-glimpsed hinterland on the dirt track to Emmaus, where the Death of God meets the Resurrection, where the supernatural Christ meets the historical Jesus, and where the revolution liberates both the oppressed and the oppressors.

Welcome to Christian Alternative... a space at the edge where the light shines through.

If you have enjoyed this book, why not tell other readers by posting a review on your preferred book site.

Recent bestsellers from Christian Alternative are:

Bread Not Stones
The Autobiography of An Eventful Life
Una Kroll
The spiritual autobiography of a truly remarkable woman and a history of the struggle for ordination in the Church of England.
Paperback: 978-1-78279-804-0 ebook: 978-1-78279-805-7

The Quaker Way
A Rediscovery
Rex Ambler
Although fairly well known, Quakerism is not well understood. The purpose of this book is to explain how Quakerism works as a spiritual practice.
Paperback: 978-1-78099-657-8 ebook: 978-1-78099-658-5

Blue Sky God
The Evolution of Science and Christianity
Don MacGregor
Quantum consciousness, morphic fields and blue-sky thinking about God and Jesus the Christ.
Paperback: 978-1-84694-937-1 ebook: 978-1-84694-938-8

Celtic Wheel of the Year
Tess Ward
An original and inspiring selection of prayers combining Christian and Celtic Pagan traditions, and interweaving their calendars into a single pattern of prayer for every morning and night of the year.
Paperback: 978-1-90504-795-6

Christian Atheist

Belonging without Believing

Brian Mountford

Christian Atheists don't believe in God but miss him: especially the transcendent beauty of his music, language, ethics, and community.

Paperback: 978-1-84694-439-0 ebook: 978-1-84694-929-6

Compassion Or Apocalypse?

A Comprehensible Guide to the Thoughts of René Girard

James Warren

How René Girard changes the way we think about God and the Bible, and its relevance for our apocalypse-threatened world.

Paperback: 978-1-78279-073-0 ebook: 978-1-78279-072-3

Diary Of A Gay Priest

The Tightrope Walker

Rev. Dr. Malcolm Johnson

Full of anecdotes and amusing stories, but the Church is still a dangerous place for a gay priest.

Paperback: 978-1-78279-002-0 ebook: 978-1-78099-999-9

Do You Need God?

Exploring Different Paths to Spirituality Even For Atheists

Rory J.Q. Barnes

An unbiased guide to the building blocks of spiritual belief.

Paperback: 978-1-78279-380-9 ebook: 978-1-78279-379-3

The Gay Gospels

Good News for Lesbian, Gay, Bisexual, and Transgendered People

Keith Sharpe

This book refutes the idea that the Bible is homophobic and makes visible the gay lives and validated homoerotic experience to be found in it.

Paperback: 978-1-84694-548-9 ebook: 978-1-78099-063-7

The Illusion of "Truth"

The Real Jesus Behind the Grand Myth

Thomas Nehrer

Nehrer, uniquely aware of Reality's integrated flow, elucidates Jesus' penetrating, often mystifying insights – exposing widespread religious, scholarly and skeptical fallacy.

Paperback: 978-1-78279-548-3 ebook: 978-1-78279-551-3

Do We Need God to be Good?

An Anthropologist Considers the Evidence

C.R. Hallpike

What anthropology shows us about the delusions of New Atheism and Humanism.

Paperback: 978-1-78535-217-1 ebook: 978-1-78535-218-8

Fingerprints of Fire, Footprints of Peace

A Spiritual Manifesto from a Jesus Perspective

Noel Moules

Christian spirituality with attitude. Fourteen provocative pictures, from Radical Mystic to Messianic Anarchist, that explore identity, destiny, values and activism.

Paperback: 978-1-84694-612-7 ebook: 978-1-78099-903-6

Readers of ebooks can buy or view any of these bestsellers by clicking on the live link in the title. Most titles are published in paperback and as an ebook. Paperbacks are available in traditional bookshops. Both print and ebook formats are available online.

Find more titles and sign up to our readers' newsletter at
http://www.johnhuntpublishing.com/christianity
Follow us on Facebook at
https://www.facebook.com/ChristianAlternative